THE
MOTIVATED
COLLEGE
GRADUATE

A JOB SEARCH BOOK FOR
RECENT COLLEGE GRADUATES

BRIAN E. HOWARD, JD, CCMC, CJSS, CPRW

CERTIFIED CAREER MANAGEMENT COACH
CERTIFIED JOB SEARCH STRATEGIST
CERTIFIED PROFESSIONAL RESUME WRITER

Virginia

Published in the United States by WriteLife Publishing
(An imprint of Boutique of Quality Books Publishing Company)
www.writelife.com

Printed in the United States of America

978-1-60808-209-4 (p)
978-1-60808-210-0 (e)

Library of Congress Control Number: 2018967992

Book design by Robin Krauss, bookformatters.com
Cover design by Ellis Dixon, ellisdixon.com
First editor: Caleb Guard
Second editor: Michelle Booth

LinkedIn, the LinkedIn logo, the IN logo and InMail are registered trademarks of LinkedIn Corporation and its affiliates in the United States and / or other countries. Screenshots contained in this book are used for informational and educational purposes.

The Certified Career Management Coach (CCMC) and the Certified Job Search Strategist (CJSS) designations are sanctioned by The Academies, as approved by the International Coach Foundation (ICF).

The Certified Professional Resume Writer (CPRW) designation is sanctioned by the Professional Association of Resume Writers.

Other Books by Brian E. Howard

The *Motivated* Job Search
The *Motivated* Networker
Over 50 and *Motivated!*
The *Motivated* Job Search Workbook
Motivated Resumes & LinkedIn Profiles

Message from the Author

Graduating from college is an achievement that will be with you for your entire life. It has been estimated that in a world of seven billion people, only 6.7 percent have a college degree.[1] That's elite company. I congratulate you for achieving something truly special!

As completed chapters in your life close, new ones open. You are about to begin a new chapter in your life: becoming a responsible, financially self-sustaining adult. The path to that goal starts by getting a job. Not the kinds of jobs you may have had before, but rather a professional-level career job . . . the kind that requires a college degree.

Securing your first professional-level job will require a job search. This is a process that most college graduates are wholly unprepared for. Gone are the days of walking into a business, asking for and filling out an application for an hourly job. A job search in the professional world is an entirely different process. This book will teach you how to do it and in ways that will make you stand out in the eyes of potential employers. You will have a competitive advantage!

I know for a fact that the process I teach in this book works! At its core, it is the same process I promote to tenured professionals who have read my other job search books as they have secured new jobs . . . thousands of them.

More importantly (and perhaps more persuasively), the process in this book was used by my college-aged children to get internships, summer jobs, and their first professional-level jobs. You could say they were the "beta test" (I prefer guinea pigs), in testing the process for recent college graduates. Both of my college-aged kids used the techniques in this book to get summer jobs (with large corporations), internships, and their first career-level job. The benefit you have is the process has been refined with additional insight from experts who focus on helping recent college graduates find professional-level jobs. You will benefit from their knowledge as you read through the book.

It is my hope that the contents of this book put you on a career path where you can benefit most from your academic achievement . . . a college degree!

To your success!

Brian E. Howard

---

[1] Lancaster, Julie. "Who in the World Holds a College Degree," *College America*, October 9, 2011, https://www.collegeamerica.edu/blog/who-in-the-world-holds-a-college-degree.

Table of Contents

Introduction

Don't bunt. Aim out of the ballpark.
Aim for the company of immortals.
— David Ogilvy[2]

Welcome to the Real World

You are about to embark on a job search. To be successful, you must grasp some very important concepts about the real world. By understanding these elementary concepts, you will have a distinct advantage over your peers who may not fully appreciate these realities.

The Business World

First, a company exists to make a profit. Companies make a profit by selling their products or services for more than the costs to produce those products or services. A company will cease to exist if it is not profitable.

Second, a job within a company must either make or save money for the company. If it does not, it will be eliminated. As a college graduate job seeker, you must present your skills in a way to make or save the company money and contribute to the profitability

[2] "David Ogilvy Quotable Quote," *Goodreads*, http://www.goodreads.com/quotes/262108-don-t-bunt-aim-out-of-the-ballpark-aim-for-the (accessed May 28, 2015).

of the company. If there is no perceived value in hiring you, you will not receive a job offer. Thereafter, your performance on the job must provide value beyond the cost of your employment.

The Non-Commercial Professional World

Careers in non-commercial fields have similar realities and value evaluations. As a recent college graduate, you must present your skills and background to further the mission of the organization (governmental agency, public entity, non-profit and so on). Once hired, your job performance must meet or exceed expectations or you are at risk of losing your job.

These are real-world realities. Too many college graduates fail to understand, let alone truly appreciate, these realities. They believe that every company or organization is nothing but an entity that can afford to give them a job. Clearly understand this concept: All companies must be profitable to survive. All entities in other fields must meet their mission to continue to exist. And, all employers are sensitive to the productivity of their employees. If your productivity (the value you bring as an employee) falls below the cost of having you, or you fail to meet the minimum standards of performance, you will be fired. Sound harsh? Welcome to the real world.

However, understanding these realities can work to your advantage during your job search. Why? When you understand these real-world realities, you can present yourself to employers by speaking their language. You will be able to sell your abilities in a way that a hiring executive will see value in hiring you. It's a matter of appealing to the mentality of the hiring executive who can offer you a job. Much of this book is about teaching you how to present yourself in a way that displays your value.

Let's talk about another reality. Do the "best" qualified college graduates always get the best jobs? No, they don't. Let me explain: To get a career-level job as a recent college graduate, you must certainly be qualified for the open positions in your field of endeavor. However, with increasing frequency, the college graduates that get the better jobs are those that execute a better job search. In other words, you can out-flank your peers with higher GPA's and perhaps better experience when you execute a more effective job search.

Realize that employers value initiative, perseverance, work ethic, effort, and a host of other professional characteristics (to be discussed further in the pages that follow). When you execute an efficient, self-motivated job search, you put those professional character traits on display, with your qualifications. You will do better than you think against your competition and perhaps get more job offers by effectively executing a job search better than they do.

How to Use This Book

This job search book is written for the motivated college graduate who wants a proven methodology on how to effectively conduct a job search in today's competitive marketplace.

As you read this book, have a highlighter and a pen available. Study the book and highlight concepts you want to remember. Write in the margins. Fold the page corners. Use a notepad to write down thoughts and to-do's as they occur to you. Then, after your job search is underway, review this book to stay motivated and on track. Be careful! There are several things during a job search that can cross the line from being productive to just doing busy-work disguised as productivity. Ask yourself: Am I being productive with my time and effort, or am I just doing busy-work, thinking that I am being productive? You'll know the answer.

Pay particular attention to the stars ★ throughout the book. These useful, powerful job search topics or techniques will differentiate you from other recent college graduates and shorten your job search.

Remember that a successful job search is about presenting yourself in a professional manner, engaging in conversations with those that can help and hire you, providing hiring executives and talent acquisition professionals in interviews with your college record, examples of your skills, accomplishments, and character traits. When you do, you heighten your chances of landing job offers for opportunities you want.

Meet Your Coaches and Resume Writers

The following professional career coaches and resume writers will be providing you with additional advice and insight throughout the book. They were selectively chosen based on their experience and professional credentials.

The career coaches and resume writers have graciously donated their time and their work. They did not receive any compensation to be included in this book.

If you believe it would be beneficial to your job search to have a professional career coach, you are encouraged to reach out to these coaches. They are experienced in coaching recent college graduates with their job search.

Additionally, if you choose to have your resume professionally written, please consider contacting the resume writers in this book whose work appeals to you or perhaps located closest to you. Each resume writer has provided samples of their work (see Chapter 18).

Understand that resume writing is an art form. It takes time and focused concentration. What you may see in the samples may not completely align with the instructional section of this book. However, each sample resume was written with a specific job, strategy, or goal in mind. You have the wonderful advantage of having the education of the instructional part of this book with their insight and the resume samples to blend and create your own unique resume. Or, you may decide that a professionally prepared resume is the right way to go.

Bryan Lubic, M.A., J.D., CCMC, CJSS

(650) 427-9265
bryanlubic@gmail.com
linkedin.com/in/bryanlubic

Bryan Lubic is a strengths-based career and professional development practitioner with a background in the leadership and administration of career services in higher education. He earned certifications as a Certified Career Management Coach (CCMC) and Certified Job Search Specialist (CJSS) and has completed advanced training in helping people identify, connect, and communicate their amazing value to potential employers easily and effectively.

Cheryl Minnick , M.Ed., Ed.D, CCMC, NCRW
University of Montana – Academic Enrichment

(406) 243-4614
cminnick@mso.umt.edu

Passionate, lively and engaging, Dr. Cheryl Minnick is career counselor/internship coordinator at the University of Montana with nearly thirty years' experience in higher education, twenty of those in the area of career counseling. She holds both a masters and doctorate with specialization in career counseling. Trained by top industry experts, she is one of less than fifty Nationally Certified Resume Writers in the country. Cheryl is a guest instructor with Career Thought Leaders, a think tank for the now, new, and next in careers; teaches webinars for the Career Academy; and sits on the NRWA Certification Board for resume writing certification. Over a three-year period, she partnered with the Montana Department of Labor to train employment professionals statewide on best practices in resume creation, cover letter writing, and applicant tracking systems.

Cheryl is a certified Academies Career Management Coach whose career advice has been featured on AOLJobs, Voice America radio, CareerSparx and Resume Writer's Digest; who has published career development research in the Journal of Academic Administration in Higher Education and The New Accountant; and who's resumes and cover letters are published in books including, *Motivated Resumes & LinkedIn Profiles, Modernize Your Resume: Get Noticed – Get Hired, Designing the Perfect Resume, How to Pop your Resume, Gallery of Best Cover Letters, The Twitter Job Search Guide* and *101 Job Seeking Tips for Recent College Grads*. If not on campus working with students, she can be found helping mid-level to senior-managers through her boutique career consulting business, The Paper Trail. Cheryl has successfully helped hundreds of students and professionals successfully navigate careers and achieve professional success.

Ellen Steverson, NCRW, GCDF, CEIC

(843) 832-4567
ellen@startingblockcs.com
www.linkedin.com/in/ellensteverson

Ellen Steverson is the President and Founder of StartingBlock Career Services (SBCS) LLC, a career management firm specializing in career advancement services. SBCS offers customized writing and coaching services specifically designed to meet clients' needs. Working collaboratively with clients, Ms. Steverson writes resumes, cover letters, bios, LinkedIn profiles, and other career documents. Her coaching helps clients articulate their value, ace interviews, and generate offers. From personalized, targeted resumes to coaching services, Ms. Steverson tailors her approach and services to help clients move to their next great opportunity faster.

Ellen Steverson is a Nationally Certified Resume Writer, 1 of only 55 nationwide, and has over ten years of experience helping clients worldwide. She is a Global Career Development Facilitator and a Certified Employment Interview Consultant. After graduating with a Bachelor's degree in Business, Ellen had a successful sales career and then moved into executive recruiting. As a former executive recruiter, Ms. Steverson understands the hiring process from the perspective of both the hiring manager and the job seeker. She combines her sales and recruiting expertise to help position clients for job offers and promotions. Her clients expect quality products, and she delivers. SBCS has grown through loyal customers who return for updates and send referrals.

Ms. Steverson's unique client approach and passion for educating clients empower people to understand and communicate their value and talent to hiring managers with confidence. From college grads to executives, in a broad range of industries, she provides the tools, information, and documents needed so clients can take charge of their careers.

**Jered Lish, M.S., Gallup-Certified Strengths Coach, GCDF
Associate Director of Career Education**

(970) 491-5126
Jered.Lish@colostate.edu

Currently, Jered Lish serves as the Associate Director of Career Education at the Colorado State University, Career Center. Previously, Jered worked at UC San Diego overseeing the pre-med/pre-health advising program and has a passion for developing compassionate and patient-centered future health professionals. Jered additionally helps students with establishing tangible and actionable steps towards their personal and professional career goals and finds his work with college students to be fulfilling and rewarding. On the side, Jered is a music composer and writes strings arrangements for a variety of television commercials and local bands. He additionally enjoys using his certifications as a Gallup Strengths Coach and MBTI instructor to consult organizations and companies on how best to inspire and optimize performance using a strengths-based approach to employee motivation.

Juliet Murphy, MBA

(714) 642-3777
www.julietmurphy.com

Juliet Murphy, MBA and MA – Career Development, is the President of a career management company, Juliet Murphy Career Development (JMCD), delivering career solutions to young adults, executives and corporations. Her specialties include millennial career development, with Juliet having a strong background in working with new college graduates. Her website is: *www.julietmurphy.com*

**Lorraine Beaman, MA, ACRW, CARW,
NCRW, CEIC, MCD**

(866) 966-2665
Lorraine@interview2work.com
www.interview2work.com
www.linkedin.com/in/lorrainebeaman/
www.facebook.com/interview2work/
Twitter: @interview2work
Instagram: Interview2work

Interview2Work grew out of a passion to bring the most innovative job search strategies to college graduates working "survival" jobs because they were not successful securing jobs in their fields. During her thirty years of experience working with college students and serving as the director of career services for a regional business college, Ms. Beaman discovered it is not a lack of knowledge of their fields that cause new graduates to be underemployed, rather a lack of job search skills.

After multiple successful job placements among new college graduates, Ms. Beaman expanded Interview2Work's services to include coaching on salary negotiation and how to effectively transition into a new job. Through these services, many of her clients have received starting salaries higher than they imagined and gained the skills necessary to successfully navigate their first days on the job.

Ms. Beaman holds several certifications including the prestigious AWRA, CARW, and NCRW in resume writing. She is a Certified Employment Interview Consultant and AAUW Salary Negotiation Facilitator. She also holds certificates in Negotiation and Leadership from Harvard University, job search applications of social networking, and strategies for those dealing with employment barriers. She is a member of Career Directors International, National Resume Writers Association, and Career Thought Leaders.

Ms. Beaman holds a Master's degree from California State University, Chico, and a Bachelor's degree from the University of California, Berkeley.

Mary Jo King, NCRW
Alliance Resume and Writing Service

(262) 681-5682
MJ@alliancewritingservice.com

Mary Jo has written more than 5,000 resumes for college graduates, mid-career professionals, STEM careers, and executive clientele. Her work at Alliance Resume and Writing Service is characterized by in-depth personal consultations and ongoing client support. As a former hiring authority, she is also able to offer insight to employer recruiting perspectives.

Her thirty-year career in professional writing began in 1982 as the Denver franchise owner of a national resume writing company. In her first year with the company, she was recruited to serve—ultimately for six years—as Regional Director of a five-state region with twenty-three offices.

After leaving Professional Resume Service, she enjoyed a consulting and media career working with business owners to enhance operations and develop marketing solutions. In 2010, she returned to her own resume writing practice, where she create resumes, cover letters, LinkedIn profiles, biographies, performance profiles, and other marketing tools.

Mary joined the National Resume Writers' Association in 2011, where she earned the prestigious Nationally Certified Resume Writer (NCRW) credential. She is currently in her sixth year of board service for this nonprofit organization.

As the name of her company suggests, Mary likes to build long-term partnerships. You are the expert in your field, and she is the expert in hers. Together, she creates your compelling value proposition. Your satisfaction is both paramount and guaranteed.

Paula Christensen, CPRW, CJSS, CCMC
Strategic Career Coaches

(920) 264-0806
strategiccareercoaches.com
paula@strategiccareercoaches.com
www.linkedin.com/in/paulachristensen1

As a Certified Professional Resume Writer, Interview Coach, Career Coach, and Certified Job Search Strategist, Paula's expertise is helping job seekers land jobs they love. What makes Paula different? She cares about their successes. Paula loved her corporate recruiting job but was sometimes frustrated because she knew with a bit of fine-tuning, new graduates could be more successful. Her main strength is connecting with people to help identify their differentiators, thereby making them more marketable. She loves her job and can't imagine doing anything else.

Whether you are ready for help landing that first internship or job after graduation, Paula is here to assist with resume writing, interview preparation, and developing job search strategies.

Paula's background is in Corporate Recruiting and Human Services. She is excited to help people find jobs. As a former Human Resource Pro-fessional, she knows what companies are looking for in applicants. After interviewing thousands of candidates over the course of a decade, she's learned what makes job seekers stand out.

Tina Kashlak Nicolai, PHR, CPBA, CARW
Resume Writer's Ink

(407) 578-1697
tina@resumewritersink.com
www.resumewritersink.com
www.linkedin.com/in/tinakashlaknicolai
www.facebook.com/resumewritersink
Twitter: @tinanicolai

Resume Writers' Ink was founded in 2010 by Tina Kashlak Nicolai. She offers her clients a strategic, trifecta approach by combining her unique background weaving together pragmatic client results with creative marketing.

Tina's trifecta approach comes from having a tenured career:
- Hiring leader for several Fortune 100 companies (including Disney World)
- Full cycle recruiter (20+ years and currently working in talent acquisition)
- Journalist and Marketing expertise

Tina holds two degrees from Duquesne University in Pittsburgh, PA; BA Journalism and BA Media Communications. Additionally, she holds the following certifications:
- Certified Behavioral Coach, CPBA
- Lominger/Korn Ferry Certification
- Certified Advanced Resume Writer, CARW
- PHR SHRM

Additionally, Tina is sought out on an ongoing basis by leading industry career journalists and media where she contributes best practices, tips, and advice in major media streams, including, Business Insider Careers, Forbes Careers, International radio groups, and Monster Careers. She's been featured in numerous book publications as well as sought out for keynote speaking and career motivation talks.

PART I

Preparation and Messaging

Chapter 1

Things to Know About Your Job Search as a Recent College Graduate

In the end, what we regret most are the chances we never took.

—Frasier Crane[3]

Job Search Methods

There are four generally accepted job search methods for recent college graduates that generate the most job leads:

1. On-Campus Career Fairs
2. Networking (through various means and sources)
3. Direct - Proactively Marketing Your Collegiate Credentials to Employers
4. Job Boards and Online Job Applications

All four methods could lead you to your next career position. However, some are more effective than others.

---

3 "Goodnight, Seattle: Part 2." *Frasier*. 13 May 2004 by NBC. Directed by David Lee and written by Christopher Lloyd and Joe Keenan.

On-Campus Career Fairs

The on-campus career fair is one of the time-efficient job search strategies available to you. Career fairs are convenient and allow you to interact with a number of employers in a reasonably short period of time. For the employers, there is already a general interest in meeting you and your peers, otherwise the employer would not be attending.

Networking

Networking is an effective job search method. It is estimated that 60 to 80 percent of all jobs are found through some form of networking.[4] However, networking as a recent college graduate presents some challenges because most graduates do not have a developed network of professional connections to tap into. Nonetheless, there are ways to successfully use networking as a recent college graduate.

Direct - Proactively Marketing Your Collegiate Credentials to Employers

This is a method where you approach an employer directly regardless of whether there is a known job opening. It can be very effective when properly executed. This requires preparation and effort, and it will differentiate you from the vast majority of other recent college graduates.

Job Boards and Online Job Applications

This method tends to be the least effective and the statistics are not promising. It's been referenced that for every online posting there are 118 applicants.[5] The odds of you getting a job from an online job posting are less than one percent.

Should you even bother to apply to jobs posted online? Yes, though selectively. If you find a posted job opening that you are clearly qualified for, attempt to identify the actual hiring executive. Contact that person directly using the techniques described in this book (from the Direct approach referenced above). If that is unsuccessful, then apply for the position online.

If you know the specific industries you are interested in, follow specialized job boards used by employers in those industries. This can increase your chances of success.

But most importantly, control your expectation of success when applying for jobs posted online (job boards) and do not rely upon it as your main job search method.

This method will not be specifically discussed in the book except by occasional reference.

---

4 LinkedIn, "Using LinkedIn to Find a Job"; Beatty, "The Math Behind the Networking Claim"; Rothberg, "80% of Job Openings."

5 Smith, Jacquelyn. "7 Things You Probably Didn't Know About Your Job Search." *Forbes.* April 17, 2013. http://www.forbes.com/sites/jacquelynsmith/2013/04/17/7-things-you-probably-didnt-know-about-your-job-search/#71fe2c6e64e6 (accessed February 12, 2016).

What the Coaches Say:

In your experience, what are the most effective job search methods for recent college graduates? (E.g. On-campus career fairs, networking, job boards, etc.)

Regardless of career level, new college graduate or chief executive officer, a recent survey reveals 85% of ALL jobs are filled via networking (*LinkedIn Recruiting & Hiring, 2/29/16*). College students can network at campus career fairs, yes, but their best strategy is to identify, nurture and grow their "Circle of Champions," friends, family, colleagues and peers within their network. Then, add Prospects, 2nd and 3rd level connections and Activators, 1st connections, in targeted companies to their network. Other ways to build a Circle of Champions are to join industry associations as a student member, network at community events, and connect and interact with alumni via LinkedIn. Use the Circle of Champions to ask for introductions to 2nd or 3rd level connections or to people in their Circle.

Dr. Cheryl Minnick, NCRW, CCMC, CHJMC, CAA

I recommend all students attend job fairs to start talking to a broad range of potential employers. They should have a great introduction about themselves (elevator pitch) and have a plan prior to attending since many colleges post which employers will be there in advance. I also recommend students join associations in their career field, as many will have reduced membership fees or none for college students. For example a student wanting to be in Human Resources should join the Society for Human Resources Management (SHRM). Networking is always critical. New grads, like all people, should be networking their inner and outer circle.

Ellen Steverson, NCRW, GCDF, CEIC

Your Job Search Arsenal: Considerations, Tools, and Tactics

The following is a reasonably comprehensive, though not necessarily an exhaustive list of considerations, tools, and tactics for a college graduate job search. The checklist is designed as a visual reminder of the tools and tactics at your disposal. Use it as a checklist as you prepare for your search as well as action items as you proceed. Read the chapters in this book for in-depth information.

It's recommended that you review this list every once in a while as a reminder of what you should be doing or can be doing to advance your job search.

Item	Comments	Check off
Cleanse all social media sites	All inappropiriate pictures and comments must be deleted.	○
Emotions - positive attitude	Stay away from negative throughts / feelings. Keep a positive attitude.	○
Resume	It is imperative to have an impactful resume.	○
LinkedIn profile	Like a resume, an optimized LinkedIn profile is imperative to your job search.	○
Business cards	Select the one(s) you will use in your search: • Traditional • Networking • Resume • Infographic	○
Keywords	Know the keywords that apply to you especially for your LinkedIn profile and resume.	○
Job Alerts	Get a flow of job openings by setting up job alerts.	○
Master job description	Doing this helps you think like the hiring executive.	○
Accomplishments	Know what differentiates you.	○
Transferrable skills and professional qualities	Those skills and qualities that make you truly unique and are often sought after by employers.	○
Success stories	Pre-write three. Helps in interviews and answering behavior based questions.	○
Personal branding	Those words and statements that announce to the market who you are and what you offer.	○
Elevator speech	Who you are, accomplishments, start a conversation, scripted and practiced.	○
Cover letter	Write a template. Then modify. Use as a marketing email.	○
List target employers	Create a list. Add new employers when they are discovered.	○

Item	Comments	Check off
Short-list of networking contacts	People you can reach out to about your job search.	○
Networking	A high percentage of all jobs are found through some form of networking.	○
Ice breaker questions	Prepared in advance of on-campus career fairs, networking events. Having them reduces anxiety in conversations.	○
Proactively marketing your collegiate credentials by phone • Script marketing call • Voicemail script • Responses to objections • Script for handling the gatekeeper	This approach is the most direct method for getting interviews and job leads.	○
Proactively marketing your collegiate credentials by email	This approach can be easier to execute but follow up calls must be made.	○
Drip marketing	Used to stay in touch with a hiring executive with new information.	○
Last ditch effort email	Last email contact to a hiring executive that is not responding.	○
Interviewing • Scripted answers to common questions • Research	A lot of information about interviewing in the book. Prepare for common or anticipated questions. Do research before every interview.	○
References	Wisely chosen and listed. Unsolicited third party affirmation technique.	○
Direct U.S. mail contact to hiring executives	Traditional approach. Can be useful for hard-to-reach hiring executives or as a last ditch effort.	○
Career fairs	Useful for some college job seekers.	○
Emotion - rejections	Disappointments will happen. Continue to move forward. Don't get stuck!	○
Effort	Stay busy!	○
Avoid busy-work	Focus on those tasks that truly advance your search.	○

★ Clean Up All Social Media Before Starting a Job Search

Take this fact very seriously: Around 33 percent of employers have rejected candidates based on information discovered on social media.[6] This is significant! Consider the ramifications—you put in years of effort, focus, and perseverance towards your college degree. You got good grades and worked as a summer intern. But a potential employer rejects you (and you may not even know it) for unprofessional or inappropriate information on your social media sites. All of your time and effort is blown. And, there's no recovery once it happens.

Today, it is imperative that you clean up all of your social media sites *before* you start a job search. It is recommended that the cleansing process begins a few months in advance of actual job search activities. This allows for plenty of time for deleted information to cleanse itself out of cyber-space. Then, after you have cleansed your social media sites, wait awhile and again, before engaging in active job search activities, double check all social media for inappropriate information. Re-cleanse as necessary.

Part of this cleansing process includes getting "tagged" into inappropriate conversations. You may need to inform your friends or block them from tagging you if necessary. If you have a pseudo (secondary) account under another name, perhaps it is time to close and delete it. Ask yourself, is it worth the risk of discovery to get passed over for a job, or even possibly fired? The answer is obvious.

Cleaning up your social media sites is not hard, but you must be thorough. Start by running a Google search on your name. Delete all inappropriate photos and written content wherever you find it. Consider tightening your privacy settings as necessary after all inappropriate photos and content have been removed. Run a search for yourself in each and every social media site which you have an account. Cleanse everything everywhere you find it! There are now services that will scan and scrub your social media for harmful posts. Check into www.repnup.com and www.scrubber.social.

Begin professionalizing your social media sites. Post new photos that represent you in a positive light. All new content should also have a positive spin or be professionally appropriate.

Your college life is evolving into your professional career life. Along with that, you must evolve your social media life to support your professional career life.

---

6 Herman, Lily. "How to Clean Up Your Social Media During the Job Search." *The Muse*. https://www.themuse.com/advice/how-to-clean-up-your-social-media-during-the-job-search. (Accessed May 22, 2017).

What Employers Look for and Discover on Social Media

It is undeniable that social media will play a role in your job search. The significance of that role depends largely on how much you use social media. But employers also use social media.

To help you better understand the role of social media in your job search, CareerBuilder. com conducts a yearly survey that asks hiring managers and human resource professionals if, how, and why they incorporate social media into their hiring process.

The results from a recent survey found that out of the 2,300 hiring managers and human resource professionals 70 percent of employers use social networks to screen potential job candidates (this trend has consistently grown over the years).[7] That means more and more companies browse your social media profiles to evaluate your character and personality. What they find about you will influence their hiring decision.

In the survey, employers that chose not to pursue a job applicant after researching social media sites indicated the following reasons:

- Job seeker posted inappropriate pictures, videos or information   39 percent
- Found evidence of job seeker's use of alcohol or drugs   38 percent
- Job seeker made negative remarks about previous employer or fellow employee   30 percent
- Discriminatory comments made about race, gender, religion, etc.   32 percent[8]
- Poor communication skills   27 percent
- Lied about qualifications   27 percent
- Linked to criminal behavior   26 percent
- Shared confidential information from a previous employer   23 percent
- Screen name or handle was inappropriate or unprofessional   22 percent
- Lied about an absence   17 percent

However, over 44 percent of hiring executives discovered information that improved a job seeker's candidacy, including:

---

7 Nauen, Rachel, "Number of Employers Using Social Media to Screen Candidates at All-Time High, Finds Latest CareerBuilder Study." *CareerBuilder*, June 15, 2017, http://press.careerbuilder.com/2017-06-15-Number-of-Employers-Using-Social-Media-to-Screen-Candidates-at-All-Time-High-Finds-Latest-CareerBuilder-Study.

8 Ibid

- Job seeker's background matched qualifications of position   38 percent
- A professional image   36 percent
- Creativity   35 percent
- Communication   37 percent[9]

According to the research, employers utilize social media to gain additional insight into your behavior and personality outside the interview. They use all tools available to help ensure a good hire.

What the Coaches Say:

What is your advice about cleaning up social media sites before starting a job search?

Once, in an appointment with a student, I was talking about the importance of googling their own name in preparation for job searching in order to ensure all outward facing social media was in alignment with the image they wanted to portray professionally. The student shared, "I haven't checked that in a long time, let's see what my name generates." I agreed and we googled their name. In the process of searching the search engine, a YouTube video popped up of the student, and he immediately turned red in the face. He then proceeded to tell me not to click on the icon, and I, of course, laughed with the student because it was a case and point of the importance of knowing what exists out there, and to "clean up" anything that could be deemed questionable by a future employer. Long story short, I encourage students and recent graduates to reflect on how they desire to present themselves professionally through social media, and remembering whatever they put out to social media is a representation of their values, identities, belief systems, and that ultimately, they don't get to control how a person interprets what they see. It is better to be conservative and "clean up" their social media in order to present a polished and professional, outward facing image.

Jered Lish M.S., Gallup-Certified Strengths Coach, GCDF

---

9 Ibid

Before beginning a job search, conduct a 30-day social media cleanse. Check your social media privacy settings; add a vanity URL to LinkedIn, as well as an updated professional headshot and an un-polarizing picture to Facebook; confirm your contact data is correct. Pull or delete any political rants, unbecoming photos and content shares. Next, google yourself—potential employers do and they learn more about us through our social media which leads to judgment and application rejections. Identify and build a brand, market and manage that brand via your professional behavior, headshot, character, integrity, appearance, tweets and posts.

Dr. Cheryl Minnick, NCRW, CCMC, CHJMC, CAA

How Important is Your GPA When Searching for a Job?

The short answer: It depends.

A strong GPA (3.5 and above on a 4.0 scale) is clearly an advantage when searching for your first career-focused job. If you have achieved this level of academic success, congratulations! Your hard work has paid off. You're in a good spot!

The importance of your GPA in your job search depends largely on your field of interest. Desirable employers in the fields of accounting, engineering, finance, science, technology, among others tend to use grade point average as a screening tool to limit the size of the overall candidate pool for sought-after positions. A high grade point average can qualify you for an interview with these selective employers, but it does not guarantee you a job. There are many other factors that come into play in securing employment beyond your GPA. (Much of this book is dedicated to those "other factors" to a successful job search.)

What the Coaches Say:

What is your opinion regarding the importance of a G.P.A. and its influence on a graduate's job search?

Some employers recruit students based on G.P.A. Most understand that what you learned and how well you work with others is a better predictor of job success. If you are not in the top 10% of your class, be prepared to explain your G.P.A. Did working to pay for college impact the time you had to study? Did you choose challenging classes or a major where top grades were harder to earn? Do you excel in your field but not on tests? Explain why the mitigating factor will make you a better employee, and how you learned to work harder and smarter and focus on goals rather than on grades.

Lorraine Beaman, MA, ACRW, CARW, NCRW, CEIC, MCD

Depending on the job a graduate is pursuing, a high GPA may be a requirement. For example, some highly competitive roles or employers may require a higher GPA to use as a screening process to reduce the list of potential candidates to consider for any position. Because a new graduate does not have a lot of experience, companies will rely on their performance in college as a gauge of how the candidate will perform on their job and how they will approach their work. In general, many companies will target a GPA of at least 3.0. However, the key is to understand that the GPA is used more as a filter than as a rule. If a candidate has a GPA that is less than 3.0, it does not necessarily mean that a company will not consider them; it just means that they should have some other qualities that will let them stand out and be competitive to the employer so they will still be a contender.

Juliet Murphy, MBA, MA

For many employers, the first item of interest is the actual completion of the degree, followed by GPA and other factors. Completion of the degree is a demonstration of perseverance, work ethic, focus, dedication, and delayed gratification. All are sought-after qualities that employers look for in new hires. The thing to remember is employers are looking for skills that will translate into making or saving the company money or achieving organizational mission goals. A GPA is a factor but not an accurate way to measure for those abilities. Having soft skills like communication abilities, problem solving abilities, creative thinking, as well as previous experience through internships or working through school can be more valuable to an employer than a GPA.

According to *The Chronicle of Higher Education* and *American Public Media's Marketplace*, relevant work experience is more important than academic GPA to many employers:

> "Employers place more weight on experience, particularly internships and employment during school vs. academic credentials including GPA and college major when evaluating a recent graduate for employment."[10]

This reasoning makes sense. If a college graduate has a successful track record performing the tasks (or some of them) required in a position, it is a clear predictor of success regardless of academic GPA.

When it comes to your job search, your academic record will be a factor. However, it is not everything. Your job search success will likely turn on three additional things beyond your academic record: First is your ability to demonstrate value to an employer by referencing your previous work or internship experience. Then, proof of character traits and soft skills such as work ethic and honesty. Finally, the hiring decision will be influenced by cultural fit. That is, the subjective determination by an employer that you will blend into the company's culture.

So how important is your GPA? It matters to qualify you with some companies in some industries for an interview. Beyond that, depending upon the employer, it can matter less. This can be good news for those with less than a stellar GPA. Work experience, character traits, and cultural fit tend to influence the hiring decision beyond the GPA.

---

10 "The Role of Higher Education in Career Development: Employer Perceptions." *The Chronicle of Higher Education.* December 2012. http://www.chronicle.com/items/biz/pdf/Employers%20Survey.pdf.

What the Coaches Say:

What are your thoughts regarding the importance of a G.P.A. and the overall success of a college graduate's career?

Research has consistently shown there is not a direct correlation between college G.P.A. and career success. College coursework provides the basic knowledge for entering a profession; it is hard work, commitment to continuous learning, and drive that are the key to professional success.

Lorraine Beaman, MA, ACRW, CARW, NCRW, CEIC, MCD

I think students should try to earn the highest grades possible. However, life happens and for those who have a lower GPA and still finish, they can still go on to earn just as much as someone with a high GPA, as long as they have the internal drive, work ethic, and abilities to advance.

Ellen Steverson, NCRW, GCDF, CEIC

GPA matters during college, on internship, graduate school, professional school (medical, pharmacy, etc.) and first job applications, but after that nobody asks—they prefer to judge you on your accomplishments in the boardroom not the classroom. Success itself is subjective—a stellar GPA could indicate success, but the act of graduating college could be success to a single mother, or graduating college without debt to a military veteran. We often correlate success with financial gain, but perhaps success is living the life you want, having a strong loving family, doing the thing you want to do, or being proud of yourself. If this is true, then GPA is far less important than visionary career and life planning.

Dr. Cheryl Minnick, NCRW, CCMC, CHJMC, CAA

How Important to Your Career is Your First Job after College?

Your first job *is* important.

Your first job after college is important because it is your starting point. It should be a professional-level position, meaning a position that requires a college degree as a qualification for the position.

Do what you can to find a position that fits your general interests and skill, realizing that your first job will not be glamorous. Anticipate junior level titles like trainee, associate, analysts, project assistant, and the like. As best as you can, try to get a job with an employer that has a good business reputation.

As you evaluate first-job opportunities, get a sense whether you will be given opportunities to do new and different things over the course of time. Try to avoid a job that is strictly mundane functions. You want to learn and grow professionally as much as the position will allow.

Your first job is important as your starting point and sets you up for the next job, which sets you up for the next, and so on. (See, "What You Want to Achieve in Your First Job" later in this book.)

Your first job is *not* that important.

Your first job is where you start. However, it will have reasonably little effect on how your career will end up over the course of the next forty to fifty years. As a professional, you will meet people and you will network. Business and job opportunities will come your way. These opportunities could take your career in directions you never imagined. Or, you will choose to explore new opportunities. It will be a journey!

As time passes, the importance of your first job will fade as your interests change, your jobs change, and life progresses.

What the Coaches Say:

How important is the first job out of college?

Your first job is the first step on a career path that can lead to years of fulfilling work or a series of forgettable jobs. Spend time determining your career goals before accepting your first job. Choose an organization in which you can take pride and where you will have the opportunity to develop new skills and take on interesting projects. It is not impossible to change the direction of your career or jobs; but starting off in the right direction will save you a lot of work and anxiety.

Lorraine Beaman, MA, ACRW, CARW, NCRW, CEIC, MCD

I would say the first job out of college isn't as important as your first boss out of college. I encourage recent graduates to not only search for a job around interest areas, values and strengths but to also be diligent in seeking a supervisor who can serve as a facilitator of professional growth in your first position post college. This is particularly important for the post college job seeker to find a boss who can serve as a mentor and facilitator of their growth. With this being said, while interviewing for any position, I encourage my recent graduates to be inquisitive around the work values of the supervisor, along with learn their philosophy of professional development. Any insights gained in those areas can be an indicator of what their first job will mean for them, and it can make all the difference in how they grow and thrive in their first position.

Jered Lish M.S., Gallup-Certified Strengths Coach, GCDF

People can put a lot of emphasis on the first job. However, having worked with students from high school through college, I can say it takes some people longer than others to determine the correct career path. So even if the first job is one you hate, it's better to discover that and move on to something better than to feel paralyzed by fear of making the wrong choice so they delay working. We live in an era where career paths are allowed to change, so I recommend they learn from every job, what they like and what they don't, keep developing skills, and then continue to advance forward accordingly!

Ellen Steverson, NCRW, GCDF, CEIC

What Employers are Looking For When Hiring New College Graduates

This is a difficult topic because the answers can vary widely from industry to industry and employer to employer. The contents for this topic are based on research of the topic, interviews with college placement professionals, and talent acquisition professionals.

The first thing employers are looking for is the most obvious—completion of a college degree. That achievement alone gets you to the starting line of a career and qualifies you for many career-focused positions.

Experience and applicable skills[11] are often cited by employers when interviewing college graduates. This is why internships can be so important. Summer jobs, especially those that are relevant to the position being pursued, also have significant influence with an employer. (There is much more on how to capitalize upon internships and job experience in your job search later in the book.)

Your major and GPA are varying factors depending upon the industry, employers, and position being pursued. For some employers, your major and GPA can be very important and a gateway into your career endeavors (Accounting, engineering, medicine, and many others). Or, they could be of far less concern. There are millions of college graduates who have successful careers in areas completely unrelated to their college major. It depends.

Soft skills and professional characteristics are far more significant in a successful job search than most college graduates appreciate.[12]

This is understandable since your primary focus in college was academic achievement.

---

11 Lorenz, Mary.,"New study shows job seekers what hiring managers really want." *CareerBuilder*. May 17, 2016. http://www.careerbuilder.com/advice/new-study-shows-job-seekers-what-hiring-managers-really-want (Accessed August 27, 2017). (77% of employers are looking for candidates with the skills that match what they need.)

12 Ibid., (63% of employers are looking for the right soft skills.)

This is where employers look for examples of leadership ability, communication skills (verbal, written, listening), analytical or problem solving abilities. Closely related are professional character traits such as a strong work ethic, honesty, and integrity. Employers value soft skills and professional character traits.

Often overlooked by many college graduates is an employer's need, spoken or unspoken, for someone with business acumen or organizational vision. This is your understanding of the bigger picture. It is your understanding that to succeed an employer must generate revenue from its customers or clients. The business enterprise must be profitable. In the non-commercial world, it is your understanding of the organization's mission. It is the understanding that your performance in the position you are pursuing must contribute to the success of the company or organization (very likely achieved in conjunction with your co-workers).

Knowing what an employer looks for in a college graduate is important. You will have insight and a distinct competitive advantage against others who have not thought this through.

What the Coaches Say:

In your experience, what are employers looking for when hiring a recent college graduate?

Today's workplace is constantly changing. However, certain skills are basic requirements that will never change. It is important to have excellent communication and writing skills. This is particularly important in a world of texting and emoji's where communication is carried out using symbols and "made-up" abbreviations.

Employers are also looking for initiative and creativity. They are looking for someone who is eager to learn and is not afraid to share their thoughts and opinions to add value. New college graduates must also be able to work as a team as well as independently. They must be self-directed and be able to work with little supervision. This is especially important in today's workplace where work is conducted from any location at any time and not necessarily from the corporate office.

Below are some of the key skills needed to succeed in the 21st century workplace according to Hanover Research:

- Collaboration and teamwork
- Creativity and imagination
- Problem solving
- Global and cultural awareness
- Leadership
- Oral and written communication skills
- Technology literacy

- Innovation
- Critical thinking
- Flexibility and adaptability
- Information literacy
- Civic literacy and citizenship
- Social responsibility and ethics
- Initiative

Juliet Murpny, MBA, MA

From my experience employers report looking for innovative, team oriented, strong communicators, and solutions based thinkers, who can thrive in the complexities of the unknowns and the unexplored. In short, companies want to hire creative, smart, fun, engaging, critically thinking, hard-working graduates who also have a high emotional intelligence. Now how does a recent graduate articulate all of that to them? I was speaking with a recruiter from Google and was asking them if they could give any piece of advice to students pursing software engineering positions at their company, what they would recommend. I was surprised to learn they will often score a resume higher if they saw tutoring in a recent graduate's documents. This insight was particularly interesting to me because it validated the importance of soft skills such as communication and coaching, and it was apparent as a value of Google to find good critical thinkers who have great soft skills.

I was speaking with a CEO out in San Diego who owns a staffing company, and he shared he often scored resumes higher if he saw a student was an athlete. His company has a high performing sales team and he attributes the recruitment of athletes being tied to them being team oriented, competitive, and disciplined, and those are attributes he seeks when hiring recent graduates. With these two examples in mind, employers seek out candidates who they theorize will be strong contributors to their teams, and it's through

> impressive experiences, competencies gained and soft skills demonstrated, do most candidates advance when those attributes are presented.
>
> Jered Lish M.S., Gallup-Certified Strengths Coach, GCDF

Who Hires New College Graduates?

You graduated from college and soon learn that many of the positions that appeal to you require previous experience. It's a conundrum. How can you get hired for jobs that require experience but you can't get experience unless you get hired?

Fortunately, there are a lot of employers that hire recent college graduates! Check out collegegrad.com (specifically, collegegrad.com/topemployers). There you will find an extensive list of employers that hire entry level employees. Below is an example of a recent list:

Employer Name	Hires
Enterprise Rent-A-Car	9500
EY	5000
Hertz	4500
The Progressive Corporation	4200
PxC	3900
KPMG LLP	3300
Deloitte	3000
Federal Bureau of Investigation	2900
Avis Budget Group	2500
Bank of America	2500
U.S. Customs and Border Protection	2200
Vanguard	1850
General Electric	1600
Amazon.com	1500
Epic	1500
Intel	1500
National Security Agency	1500
The PNC Finanical Sercies Group	1500
Chevron	1400
Sodexo	1400

Pursue companies that may be in your industry of interest, but don't be too restrictive. Open your mind to new avenues. For example, the first company on the above list is Enterprise-Rent-A-Car®. You may not want to pursue a career in the rental car business—that's fine. However, did you know that many of the employers listed above are "recruiting sources" for other employers once you have one to three years of successful experience working in the real world? It's true! Just because you start with a company in an industry right out of school doesn't mean that you have to pursue that career track long term. The key is to get experience in the real world that can qualify you for the next better opportunity.

Of course, there are exceptions. If you want to pursue a career in engineering, you need to land in an engineering firm or something related to engineering. The same would hold true for accounting and other industries. The point remains the same: The key to launching a career is getting a job in the real or commercial world, create a track record of success, and gain experience. From there you can springboard to new and better opportunities. Where you start will not determine where you end up fifty years from now when you choose to close out your professional career. But, the point is to get a good start.

Common Job Search Mistakes of Recent College Graduates

On average, it takes recent college graduates about six months to land their first career-level position.[13] That timeline can be longer if you make job search mistakes. Below are some of the common job search mistakes graduates make that can lengthen a job search.
Not Contacting Your Career Placement Center.
This next statement is written in the tone of a parent:

"Walk your butt over to the Career Placement Office and introduce yourself!"

That office and the people in it are there to help you. Let them! Most, if not all, of their services are free or of little cost. Use them. There are a wide range of services the Career Placement Office can provide. Some provide more than others. Some Career Placement Offices are better than others. The only way to know how much help there is for you is to talk to these people and learn. Regardless, having another resource to help in your job search doesn't hurt.

---

13 "Manage Your Career," *Experience*, https://www.experience.com/alumnus/article?article_id=article_ 1247505066959&channel_id=career_management&source_page=additional_articles.

Waiting to start job search.

The longer you put off starting your job search, the longer it will take to land your first career-level position. Ideally, begin to prepare for your job search one to two semesters before graduation. The key is not to wait. Start putting together the tools for your search now if you haven't already. You want to avoid starting your search until after all the graduation parties are over. If you wait, you could miss out on good opportunities that may lead to even better jobs. Read the job search checklist and get moving.

Failure to clean up all social media accounts.

Get into all of your social media accounts and clean them up. Read the topic, *Clean Up All Social Media Before Starting a Job Search* for more detailed information.

Not having a job search plan.

When you follow the guidance in this book, you have a job search plan! Not only do you have a plan, you have instruction on how to execute that plan. All that's needed now is your effort. Put the plan in action and you are on your way!

Not fully utilizing LinkedIn.

LinkedIn is clearly the dominant career social website in the world. To fully leverage its power requires an optimized LinkedIn profile. Read the topic on LinkedIn and optimize your profile. Activate the Open Candidates Feature and signal employers and talent acquisition professionals that you are looking for a job. Doing both of these (optimizing your profile and activating the Open Candidate Feature) makes you discoverable so employers can *contact you* about jobs!

A boring resume.

Too many recent college graduates have "boring college biographies" rather than impactful resumes that intrigue and sell potential. A resume is a marketing piece—it's advertising! How it presents you on paper creates an impression in the mind of the reader. Read the Impactful Resumes topic and your resume will not be boring but will stand out amongst your peers.

Over-reliance on posted job openings.

It's a digital age and you will explore job boards and job websites for opportunities. The job search mistake, however, is relying on these posted job openings as your only source for job leads. Applying for a job online does not work as well as you might believe. In fact, it is inefficient due to the sheer volume of potential applicants. A far more effective approach is the strategies promoted in this book—a proactive, self-motivated job search where you take yourself to the market rather than reacting to what the job market advertises.

What the Coaches Say:

In your experience, what are the common job search mistakes that recent college graduates make?

The most common mistakes I see are:
- Not having a clear picture of their employment goal.
- Waiting until after graduation to start a job search.
- Assuming their college career center will find them a job.
- Not understanding the job search process.
- Not asking for help.

Lorraine Beaman, MA, ACRW, CARW, NCRW, CEIC, MCD

A Gap Year and Your Job Search

A "gap year" is that period of time after college when you take a break before entering your career (or graduate school). There are a number of advantages and career hazards to a gap year. The purpose of this section is to discuss the job search ramifications of a gap year.

From a job market point of view, it is generally acceptable to most employers to have taken a gap year so long as your time was spent with a purpose. For example, teaching school in impoverished areas in Latin America, AmeriCorps, or any one of hundreds of worthy causes or endeavors.

Your time off does not necessarily need to be spent on high noble purposes—spending a year traveling the world exposing yourself to different cultures and lifestyles, for example.

In many cases, the gap year experience can enhance your candidacy with some employers. Some view these experiences as "maturing events" that make you a better employee.

What the Coaches Say:

What is your advice to college graduates who have taken a gap year after graduation?

Be able to explain why the gap year experience makes you a more competitive candidate. Most graduates taking a gap year work on projects, build relationships, and achieve goals that demonstrate the soft skills employers are seeking. Whether you spend your year doing home repair or traveling around Europe, you can show how you developed and executed a plan and talk about the people you networked with during the process.

Lorraine Beaman, MA, ACRW, CARW, NCRW, CEIC, MCD

I think it's acceptable for some students. However, it can really make it much more difficult and can appear the student is just lazy. So unless they are doing something very productive during the gap year, like traveling, learning to be a global citizen, or volunteering, most students cannot afford the luxury of a gap year.

Ellen Steverson, NCRW, GCDF, CEIC

Enjoy the year but spend it in a meaningful way: live at home to save money for first/last month rent and a U-Haul, pay down debt, volunteer and network in your area of career interest, explore careers by job shadowing, take career assessments, conducting online and in-person research for graduate or professional schools, teach English abroad, tour the world, take online certification courses to build skills, maybe unwind and relax, but have a strategy, goal and a benchmark for success. Don't waste the year.

Dr. Cheryl Minnick, NCRW, CCMC, CHJMC, CAA

I think GAP years are awesome if the time is spent wisely. GAP years can serve as a pivotal time of reflection, a time of growth, and a time of exploration. I've had students who have struggled with a variety of mental health disorders go and take a GAP year in order to heal their minds, and learn how to navigate the challenges they were facing in a productive and healthy way. The intentionality of their time spent in self growth multiplied exponentially for them because they returned to their career goals focused, empowered, and no longer were at risk from life burn out. It was truly a gift to see the growth they experienced in that year, and it was time well invested. If a recent graduate can, in their GAP year, identify ways they can continually and intentionally grow whether in an experience capacity or a skills capacity, GAP years can absolutely be beneficial.

Jered Lish M.S., Gallup-Certified Strengths Coach, GCDF

What does not play so well with employers is when you take a gap year to "find yourself," you move home, and proceed to do nothing. Or, worse yet, when you take a gap year, get a job tending bar, only to wake up when you're thirty and you've had six bartending jobs in the last eight years. Launching your professional level career now will be difficult, if not insurmountable.

If you pursue a gap year, do so with a well-thought purpose in mind. You must be able to tell a potential employer a "story" of what you did, why you did it, what you learned, and (this is the important part) how the experience benefits the employer with you as a better employee because of the gap year experience.

What the Coaches Say:

Is a gap year the death-knell of securing a professional-level job?

Students should have a plan before they just take a year off since that gap will influence a hiring manager's decision to interview/hire or not. They may have to look much longer and network more to land a job after the gap. However, it shouldn't be the death-kneel of securing a job and they should have a plan to communicate the value and what they learned over the year while aligning it to career goals or the target job.

Ellen Steverson, NCRW, GCDF, CEIC

Absolutely not. A GAP year from my perspective if done right, can yield even more professional and personal opportunities. In short, a GAP year serves as an opportunity to continue to self-reflect on values, goals, and aspirations in life, and that process of self-reflection helps with life focus and deliberation of next steps in a person's career.

I once counseled a dermatology resident at a medical school I worked at who had an incredibly impressive background. He graduated Johns Hopkins at the age of 19, graduated medical school at the age of 23, and landed a top residency in California for dermatology by the age of 24. After speaking with him about his impressive journey, this talented young physician did share that his only regret so far in life was not taking a GAP year post undergrad. His reasoning was a GAP year would have enabled him to pursue life curiosities he was thinking about outside of medicine, and given the formative years he was in, he jokingly reflected on how he might have turned out had the real world been his teacher at the age of 19 instead of medical school. He's happy and grateful for where he is at now, proud of the things he accomplished, and in retrospect admires the power a GAP year can have in a person's life.

Jered Lish M.S., Gallup-Certified Strengths Coach, GCDF

Dealing with a Criminal Record

You did something you should not have been doing, got caught, and now you have a criminal record. Most employers will perform a background check, so ignoring your record and hoping it will not affect your job search is not a good strategy. Fortunately, there are steps you can take that can minimize your mistake from significantly harming your job search and your future career.

Sealing or Expunging Your Record. Contact your attorney and see if your criminal record can be sealed or expunged. Generally speaking, when a record is sealed your conviction remains on your record but only law enforcement and the district attorney's office can see it. The general public cannot see it and this includes employers. If your record is expunged, the conviction is removed from your record as if it never even happened.

Virtually all states allow a prior criminal record to be sealed or expunged depending on the offense and the offender. The younger you were at the time of the offense is helpful. It allows your attorney to argue that your criminal behavior was the foolishness of your youth. If your offense was "victimless," your attorney can argue that you are not a danger to the community. Offering the completion of a college degree, good G.P.A., college activities, and no additional criminal offenses are all helpful to persuade the court that you deserve a second chance with a clean record.

If you pursue this strategy, contact your attorney right away. These types of proceedings can take several months.

Broaden Your Target Company List. Your criminal record (if it is not sealed or expunged) can, and likely will, affect whether certain companies can hire you. Since your pool of employers will be smaller, you need to expand the number of potential employers and open your mind to fields of endeavor you may not have considered or even know about. Identify companies and industries where you believe your conviction could be of less concern.

Focus your job search efforts towards smaller to mid-sized companies. These employers may be more understanding or forgiving of your past.

Be Honest. Do not hide your criminal record from employers. Be honest and forthright about your past. You will be in a far better position and be viewed more favorably by putting the topic on the table and explaining the events. Honesty is a valued character trait. Being straightforward with the employer about the existence of your criminal record shows you are honest and many employers will tell you that they appreciate the honesty. On the other hand, if you try to hide your criminal record and you are discovered, which will happen sooner or later, you risk being viewed (this is intended to sound harsh) as an "educated convict" and a risky hire. The message here is do the right thing and be honest.

You must emphasize to the employer that you take full responsibility for your actions, and that you were foolish (or wrong). Then, most importantly, state that you have learned from your mistake, that you never again want to be mired up in the criminal justice system, and the employer will not need to worry about anything like that happening again. Then, turn the interview towards the positive aspects for hiring you, such as your college activities, summer jobs, positive traits like work ethics and so on.

Having a criminal record as a recent college graduate does not end your career before it starts. It can make things more difficult to initially get started, but it is not insurmountable. Take heart, there are good employers who will be forgiving and will hire you.

What the Coaches Say:

What is your advice for college graduates who have a criminal record?

It is better to tell employers you have a criminal record than have them find out when they do a background check. The good news is many employers understand that humans make mistakes; it is what they do about it that matters. There are employers who pride themselves on giving people a second chance. When you respond to questions about your background, take responsibility for what you did and share what you learned from the experience that will make you a better employee.

Lorraine Beaman, MA, ACRW, CARW, NCRW, CEIC, MCD

Depending on the depth and severity of the criminal record, there are definitely ways in which opportunities can be generated. This topic can be incredibly complex and every individual's situation is different. In general, it can be advantageous for the recent graduate to target locations that may not be as popular and desirable for job placement; for instance, in smaller cities, colder cities, and more rural communities. Essentially the strategy

I'm recommending is the "go where the employers are who will hire you" approach, and this can be an effective job search strategy as long as the recent graduate isn't overly picky or bound to a particular geographical location.

Jered Lish M.S., Gallup-Certified Strengths Coach, GCDF

The Psychology of Persuasion and Your Job Search

Before we dive into the steps and techniques for conducting a college graduate job search, it's beneficial to talk briefly about the psychology of persuasion.

What follows are some very important concepts woven throughout the rest of this book. Knowing them will help you maximize your job-search success because they combine so effectively with the self-motivated approach.

According to Robert Cialdini, a leader in the field of psychology and persuasion, there are six principles that persuade others to think and act as they do:

1. Scarcity
2. Authority
3. Liking (and Personal Chemistry)
4. Social Proof
5. Commitment and Consistency
6. Reciprocity/Reciprocation[14]

Let's discuss each principle and how it affects your job search.

Scarcity

If a recent college graduate is viewed to be unique or special, he or she is seen as valuable.[15] How do you capitalize upon the persuasion principle of scarcity? Answer: Differentiation. Much of this book is about creating differentiation (separation) between you and other

14 Cialdini, Robert. *Influence: Science and Practice,* 4th ed. Needham Heights, MA: Allyn & Bacon, 2001, quoted in Kurtzberg and Naquin, Essentials, chapter 5, p. 94–101.

15 Cialdini, Robert. *Influence.* p. 204–205, and chapter 7, "Scarcity: The Rule of the Few," quoted in Kurtzberg and Naquin, *Essentials*, p. 94–101.

college graduate job seekers. During the course of the interviewing process, seemingly small and isolated thoughts of differentiation compound upon themselves in the mind of the hiring executive, such as if he/she dresses well, displays desirable character traits, has internship experience, a good GPA, interviews well, and so on. All of this affects your perceived value and motivates the hiring executive to continue the interviewing process with you, hopefully ending in an employment offer.

The more unique you can justifiably portray yourself, the more you are using the persuasion principle of scarcity.

Authority

Most people respond to and respect authority, whether it is a title, position, professional designation, experience, or station in life.[16] A good example of creating intangible authority is appropriate interview attire: A starched white shirt or stylish blouse, pressed suit, polished hard-soled shoes, the pen you use, or even the watch you wear can all project professional authority that others may react to favorably. This applies to a recent college graduate as well as a tenured professional.

Any job search technique or information that triggers professional respect with the hiring executive is using the persuasion principle of authority.

Liking (and Personal Chemistry)

Sixty percent of most hires are based on personal chemistry.[17] In other words, hiring executives are persuaded to hire job seekers they personally like. Getting others to like you is often based on similarity or common interests. We tend to like other people similar to ourselves.[18]

There are several ways to lay the foundation for similarity and personal chemistry. Here are a few ideas:

1. Common personal interests.

2. Attending a common college or university.

---

16 Cialdini, *Influence,* p. 180–185, and chapter 9, "Authority: Directed Deference," quoted in Kurtzberg and Naquin, *Essentials,* p. 94–101.

17 DiResta, Diane. Interview by Christina Canters, "Episode 29—How to Blitz Your Job Interview—Secrets of Executive Speech Coach Diane Diresta." *DesignDrawSpeak*. Podcast audio, June 12, 2014. http://designdrawspeak.com/029/ (accessed June 19, 2015).

18 Byrne, Donn Erwin. *The Attraction Paradigm*. New York: Academic Press, 1971. Quoted in Kurtzberg and Naquin, *Essentials,* p. 35.

3. Giving the hiring executive a sincere compliment.

4. Name dropping (identifying common friends or a professional colleague that the hiring executive feels good about).

Any job search technique that creates a positive impression on the hiring executive based on association or personal chemistry is using the persuasion principle of liking (and personal chemistry).

Social Proof

What others say about you is more persuasive than what you say about yourself. That's the power of social proof.

Psychologically, social proof is more influential and persuasive when decisions are shrouded in uncertainty. A hiring executive may be thinking: Which of these college graduates is better qualified? Who would fit in best? What about compensation? This is why recommendations, references, or any form of affirmation from a trusted source can impact the hiring decision.

Any job search technique that contains a recommendation or positive affirmation of you as a qualified college graduate (and as a person) is using the persuasion principle of social proof.

Consistency and Commitment

People desire a reputation of upholding their own commitment and generally do not like to go back on their word.[19] It's that simple.

An example of this principle in action is when you close an interview by asking if you will be proceeding in the process. If the hiring executive indicates that you will, it will be more difficult to retreat from that answer due to the persuasion principle of consistency and commitment.

Any job search technique that tends to bind a hiring executive to a self-imposed course of action is using the persuasion principle of consistency and commitment.

Reciprocation

There is a strong psychological motivation to return favors and not to feel indebted to

---

19 Cialdini, *Influence*, p. 53, and chapter 3, "Commitment and Consistency: Hobgoblins of the Mind," quoted in Kurtzberg and Naquin, *Essentials*, p. 94–101.

others. People feel the compulsion to repay another. This can be especially true if the item (of whatever nature) was given for free.[20]

An example of using this persuasion technique in a job search is offering to help the hiring executive in some way. This will not be easy given your limited experience, but be on the lookout for those opportunities should they present themselves. To be most effective, the gesture should be done with the expectation of receiving nothing in return, but with the awareness that the psychology of reciprocity is present.

Any job search technique that endears you to a hiring executive by doing something for him or her (especially for free) is using the persuasion principle of reciprocity.

By raising your awareness to these persuasion principles, you will be on the alert for opportunities to capitalize upon them when opportunities present themselves. You can use the psychology to advance your candidacy.

Now that you have a basic understanding of the principles of persuasion, you understand the reasons for (and persuasive power of) many of the job search techniques presented throughout this book—the same techniques used by many others, to their success. Occasional reference is made to these persuasion principles to help your job search be more effective.

★ Getting Off to a Successful Start

Beyond "I need to write my resume," many college graduates don't know what to do or in what order to do things to get started in their job search. It can easily become overwhelming. In this topic we will list, then briefly discuss, the A-1 priorities to successfully launch your job search and reduce any feelings of anxiety:

1. **Get organized.** You will need to make lists—of companies, people, and "to-do" lists. Think through how you will keep track of everything. Create a system that works for you. Relying on your memory or sticky-notes in a shotgun fashion is a recipe for disaster. In the thick of your job search, you won't be able to keep track of what you're doing without a system. Excel spreadsheets are highly recommended for creating lists of companies and people. Only create columns for the information you will really need (name of contact, company, company website, email address, phone number, date contacted). Don't get carried away recording non-useful information. There are commercial services that can help you stay organized in your job search.

---

20 Cialdini, *Influence*, p. 144, 161, and chapter 5, "Liking: The Friendly Thief," quoted in Kurtzberg and Naquin, *Essentials*, p. 94–101.

Check out JibberJobber (www.jibberjobber.com) and Career*Shift* (www.careershift. com). Microsoft Outlook's calendar feature can also help. You can record tasks to be done, schedule follow-up calls, and so on.

2. **Create or update your resume.** Read the Impactful Resumes section, and either prepare one yourself, or seek professional services (which will free your time for other job search activities, but it will incur a cost). Having your resume professionally done could be a good investment. The end product will likely look better than those who do it themselves. Refer to (and perhaps contact) the resume writers who have provided sample resumes later in the book.

3. **Create or update your LinkedIn profile and expand your network.** Consult the LinkedIn section in this book and optimize your LinkedIn profile. Make sure your resume and LinkedIn profile are in sync with each other (especially the names of former employers, internships and dates). After you look over the Networking chapter, expand your network by adding new connections through LinkedIn (it's not as hard as you may think). These connections have to be the right kind of high-value connections (explained later) that will advance your job search.

4. **Identify your keywords.** What words apply to you? Start simple. What character traits apply to you? What industries do you want to work in? What technical knowledge do you have? These concepts and others will form the messaging behind who you are and how you present yourself to the job market. They will be used in your resume, LinkedIn profile, personal branding, and elevator speech among others. There will be much more on keywords as you progress through the book.

5. **Create job alerts.** Use websites like Indeed.com and SimplyHired.com. You can choose to be alerted about titles, locations, specific companies, and so on. Set up job alerts on LinkedIn too. Companies (and recruiters) post jobs on LinkedIn and you can receive notifications when they do. Are there any industry-specific or niche job boards you could search? Get a sense of the job market, and start the flow of information on opportunities coming to you about jobs you are looking for. If a position pops up, and you're interested, **do not** apply for it through the website! Research the likely hiring executive(s) and contact them directly first.

6. **Create a short list of target employers you would be interested in working for.** It may be only two, five, or ten companies to start with. Add to the list as you discover new companies. But the point here is to start the list that gets you thinking. Now,

look up the companies on LinkedIn. Follow them by setting up alerts to receive news, press releases, and job postings. Google Alerts may also be used. If you have Twitter, follow the companies. This starts the flow of information from these companies (and others you'll add), including jobs and industry trends, which will benefit your job search. Add this information to your Excel spreadsheets to create a complete picture of each company before moving ahead, to eliminate needless backtracking for additional research.

7. **Create a short list of networking contacts.** This one is like the list of companies from the last step. Make a list of friends, family, and all professional-level contacts you have. This includes all contacts that your parents may have, including financial planners, bankers, dentists, and the list goes on. As you think of people, add to the list. This list likely will not exceed ten to fifteen names to begin with (although it could be more). After you make out the list, **do not** contact them! You are not ready (even though you may think you are). Regardless of the level of the relationships, don't blow it by not being properly prepared. Be patient. Read the Professional Networking section, and do things right the first time.

These seven action items establish the foundation for your job search. Once you have these in place, other action items will naturally follow. Having the right starting point gets you off to a good start.

Chapter 2

Essential Job Search Topics and Tools

Job Skills, Professional Qualities, and Character Traits

Start by doing what's necessary, then what's possible,
and suddenly you are doing the impossible.

— St. Francis of Assisi[21]

Job skills come in two forms. First are the technical skills (expertise or ability). If you have a degree in engineering, you know engineering things. With a degree in education, you have knowledge about teaching, and so on. We will refer to these skills as your "hard skills."

The second type of job skills used in most professional level positions is "soft." They are in addition to your technical education and experience. Here is a list of some sought-after soft job skills (not listed in any order of preference):

- **Communication Skills** (writing, listening, and speaking)—This is the most frequently mentioned skill employers desire.[22]

---

21 "Doing What's Necessary. What's Possible, and What Seems to be Impossible." *The Recovery Ranch.* http://www.recoveryranch.com/articles/necessary-possible-impossible/ (accessed May 27, 2015).

22 Hansen, Randall S., PhD, and Katharine Hansen, PhD. "What Do Employers *Really* Want? Top Skills and Values Employers Seek from Job-Seekers." *Quintessential Careers.* http://www.quintcareers.com/job_skills_values.html (accessed May 27, 2015).

- **Analytical Ability** (problem solving)—This is your ability to view a situation, identify issues, evaluate relevant information, and implement a plan.

- **Time Management** (prioritizing)—This is your ability to prioritize and devote the appropriate amount of time to a task.

- **Innovation** (out-of-the-box thinking)—This involves harnessing creativity and reasoning skills.

- **Collaboration** (teamwork)—This means working with others toward a shared goal.

- **Management** (people leadership)—This is your ability to gain buy-in or respect from a team, lead by defining goals and methods, and manage and guide a group toward shared goals or production targets.

- **Customer Focus** (customer service)—This is your understanding that your employer must please and serve customers to be successful.

- **Business Understanding** (business acumen)—This is your ability to understand business realities and the influences in the market and how they affect your employer.[23]

Closely aligned with the concept of soft job skills are **Professional Qualities or Character Traits**. Here is a list of professional qualities and traits sought after by employers:

- **Honesty**—This is the foundation of every employment relationship. An employer must be able to trust you and respect you as a professional for the employment relationship to last and flourish.[24]

- **Positive Attitude**—Make no mistake—this is a big deal. Employers gravitate toward

23 Hansen, Randall S., PhD, and Katharine Hansen, PhD. "What Do Employers *Really* Want? Top Skills and Values Employers Seek from Job-Seekers." *Quintessential Careers.* http://www.quintcareers.com/job_skills_values.html (accessed May 27, 2015).

24 Hansen and Hansen, "What Do Employers *Really* Want?"

people who show enthusiasm, energy, and a positive outlook.[25] As you will read later in this book, displaying a positive attitude will give you a competitive advantage in interviews and is a career management strategy. A positive attitude is *that* important.

- **Interpersonal Relationships**—Employers want employees that can get along with other co-workers. They avoid those that "rock the boat" and do not fit the culture.

- **Work Ethic**—Employers seek employees that put forth their best efforts at all times. They seek out employees that are motivated, internally driven, and stick to it. They want employees who are persistent and passionate about their jobs.[26]

- **Dependable**—Employers seek out employees who will show up on time. They want to rest assured you will "be there" for the company.

- **Willingness to Learn**—This is your intellectual flexibility and curiosity. Always be willing to learn about new technology and improve your skills (and discover new ones). Markets change. Business changes. Your industry changes. You must be open and pursue opportunities to learn and change.[27] Doing so increases your value and marketability as a professional. **Even though you are a recent college graduate, never stop learning and growing.**

These skills are the "bigger" ones. Employers also look for these professional skills and qualities: Accountability, accuracy, ambition, assertiveness, autonomy, competitive, consensus-building, decision-making, enthusiasm, goal-oriented, initiative, motivation, organization, presentation skills, quality management/improvement, tactfulness, and ability to work under pressure, among many others.

Once you have identified your job skills (through your education and experience), soft skills, and professional qualities (character traits), there are several things you can do with this valuable information. Your skills and qualities could be

- A component of your personal branding message.

- Woven into the summary section of your resume and LinkedIn profile.

---

25 Victoria Andrew. "The Power of a Positive Attitude." *Kavaliro*. Kavaliro Employment Agency. May 23, 2013, http://www.kavaliro.com/the-power-of-a-positive-attitude. See also, "Jobvite Recruiter Nation Report 2016," http://www.jobvite.com/wp-content/uploads/2016/09/RecruiterNation2016.pdf. (78% of recruiters cite enthusiasm as most likely to influence a hiring decision).

26 Hansen and Hansen, "What Do Employers *Really* Want?"

27 Ibid.

- Mentioned in various sections of your resume.
- Used to write success stories based on your internships and summer jobs.
- Included in cover letters and emails.
- Included as a part of your elevator speech.
- Used in networking conversations.
- Used in interviews.

★ The key to using these skills in your job search is to translate those skills and your unique professional qualities as valuable and match them to solve an employer's need. Provide success stories of the skills and qualities in action (more on Success Stories in a minute). Providing this connection makes it easy for the employer to see your value The connection speaks their language.

Soft skills and professional qualities cut across industry lines. For example, an employer will always value an employee with a strong work ethic whether they are an accountant or a zookeeper.

What the Coaches Say:

From your experience, how frequently do employers ask about or explore soft skills with recent college graduates?

More and more employers are reporting that the candidates they interview lack the soft skills required for the job they are trying to fill. Without the ability to communicate effectively, work well in a team, and embrace a company's culture, employers know new employees will not be successful. I feel most college graduates have used the soft skills—employers are seeking—during their academic career. Graduates have a hard time translating their academic experience into terms prospective employers understand and employers do not know the questions to ask to start a conversation about job-related soft skills.

Lorraine Beaman, MA, ACRW, CARW, NCRW, CEIC, MCD

Soft skills are inquired about both explicitly and implicitly with recent college graduates. An implicit inquire of soft skills could be in the form of how a company examines a resume and cover letter. If an innovative company like Disney writes in their job description, "we're seeking a really dynamic, people-driven, and innovative person for X position," and if the tone of the documents from the recent graduate writes from, is bland, direct, and lacks luster, Disney may assume that person doesn't have the communication or personality needed for the role. Explicit examples when interviewing may be in the form of questions such as what role the recent graduate like to play on a team, or how they manage conflict, or tell me about a time you failed on a project or what feedback would a previous supervisor share with us from your performance evaluation? Those types of questions are not only frequent, but a way for an employer to learn the level of soft skill development and competence a recent graduate has. It's imperative, graduates have an understanding of how to articulate both implicitly and explicitly through their marketing documents and in person, they have the soft skills they seek in a future employee.

Jered Lish M.S., Gallup-Certified Strengths Coach, GCDF

Understanding the Employer's Mindset

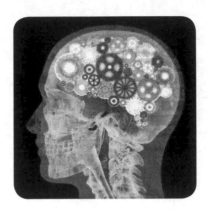

There isn't a ruler, a yard stick or a measuring tape in the entire world long enough to compute the strength and capabilities inside you.

— Paul Meyer[28]

The Business World

There are a variety of motivations that prompt an employer in the commercial market to hire. However, the true essence underlying each motivation comes down to two reasons: to make or save the company money. We briefly touched on this topic when we discussed the "real world."

The sole reason a job exists in a company is to contribute to the profitability of the company. The level of your performance in your job must add value. Depending upon the job, you can help an employer's bottom line in two ways:

1. **Making the company money (Generating new revenue)**—You can achieve this from being a part of a team that works on sales, client retention, product development, and so on. You help the company make money by being a part of a group that focuses its effort towards generating new revenue and helps keep the revenue the company already has.

2. **Saving the company money (Productivity improvements)**—This is achieved by contributing to a team that focuses its efforts on increasing productivity, increasing

28 "Unleashing Your Genius," *Quotes from the Masters,* http://finsecurity.com/finsecurity/quotes/qm121.html.

or creating operational efficiency, saving time, making others' jobs easier (more efficient or effective), and so on.

There are many ways to generate revenue or save money for a company. Revealing them to an employer establishes or increases your value (Your ROI – Return on Investment). Here is a short list to get you thinking:

- Think about your duties and responsibilities from your internships and summer jobs and how they have value to the employer.

- Identify your professional qualities and character traits, how you used them, and the resulting value provided during your internship and summer jobs.

- Involvement in duties and responsibilities that saves time, efficiency, and streamlines workflow.

- Improve company image and branding—interaction with the public or consumers.

- Expand business/sales through existing accounts.

- Enhance competitiveness through best practices, innovation, and so on.

- Improve client or customer experience, customer satisfaction.

- Improve company culture, morale, and employee retention.

The Non-Commercial Professional World

As previously mentioned, there are several motivations that cause an employer to hire. In the non-commercial professional world, the driving motivation is the continued achievement of the organization's mission—its purpose for existing. This is often found by reading the organization's mission statement. As a recent college graduate, the presentation of your education and skills must correlate and advance the organization towards its stated purpose.

Due to the number and breadth of these career fields, it is difficult to list specific items like those listed in the business world. However, there is a logical way to approach the situation. Start by reading and understanding the organization's mission. With that in mind, try to identify reasonably specific results, professional behaviors, and character traits that would advance the purpose of the organization through the position you are pursuing. Then, list all education, experience, activities, and character traits that would be valuable towards the achievement of the mission or purpose.

This process requires some conceptual and abstract thinking. However, by taking the time of thinking through this intellectual exercise, you will begin to think like the employer (of these non-commercial organizations) and understand how you can sell yourself towards fulfilling the organization's mission.

Employers who hire recent graduates are looking for any substantive value you can bring. They know you will not have made an invention or discovery that is going to revolutionize their industry. However, by understanding their mentality then selling your education, internships, summer jobs, campus activities, and athletics, you give them a justification to hire you.

Knowing What an Employer Wants in an Open Position

An employer's purpose when hiring is to make the company profitable or advance an organization's mission. There is a way to gain additional insight into an employer's mind and determine what he or she is looking for in the position (or position types), but you'll need to do a little research, as follows:

1. **Gather Job Postings.** Go online and collect some well-written job postings for the kind of entry-level jobs you would be interested in. Websites such as www.indeed.com and www.simplyhired.com are rich resources.

2. **Create Your Own Master Job Description.** Create a document. Call it your "Master Job Description" (or anything else creative you want, i.e., "My First Job").

   a. **Title**. Start with titles. What words do employers use? These titles will likely reflect jobs you target when you search. The key is to use these same words—or very similar—on your resume, LinkedIn profile, cover letters, elevator speech, and so on.

   b. **Skills, Duties, and Responsibilities.** Examine the job postings for skills, duties, and responsibilities that are common or frequently mentioned. Identify these skills and note how often they are used.

   c. **Match.** Tie these skills sought by employers to your experience, professional qualities, and character traits. Using the keywords from the skills and titles in your written communications (including your resume) raises your chances are of getting noticed, because you make yourself directly relevant to an open job position.

Once it's done, familiarize yourself with your Master Job Description. Think about it. What would you look for to fill this position if you were the hiring executive? Be objective. Pause . . .

Congratulations—you are thinking like an employer!

Now that you're thinking like an employer, **relate** or **match** how your education, experience from internships and summer jobs, campus activities, professional qualities and character traits would have value to an employer while keeping your Master Job Description in mind. This is a crucial step, because you'll be tying an executive's hiring needs to your own experience, education, professional qualities and character traits.

As you proceed, remember these insights as you create other communication tools (resume, LinkedIn profile, cover letters, emails, and so on).

Matching Experience and "Word Clouds"

There is a very clever way to help match your experience with what an employer is looking for in a position(s). "Word clouds" are images made out of large words interspersed with smaller ones (you may have seen them). Some websites that create word clouds include www.wordle.net, www.tagcrowd.com, and www.worditout.com. Here's how you use this concept to your advantage:

Copy a job description electronically, go to one of these sites, and paste the job description into the space provided. Give it a second and *voila*, you have a word cloud. Pay particular attention to the larger words. Those are the words that are mentioned most frequently or deemed more important by the website's programming. Write down these larger words, and make sure they appear on your resume, LinkedIn profile, and other communications. For example, let's say you see terms like "customer experience" or "client success" in the word cloud. Therefore, you want to use that terminology to match the language employers are using (at least for that employer). Using the same words as the employer is "speaking their language" when you communicate with them.

This technique works especially well when you have an actual job description on a position you are interested in.

★ Accomplishments

You were designed for accomplishment, engineered for success,
and endowed with the seeds of greatness.

—Zig Ziglar[29]

An essential part of your job search preparation will be creating your accomplishment history. This will be a list of your most significant experiences and successes from work, internships, academics, volunteer projects, extracurricular activities, community engagement, and so on. Accomplishments are honors and achievements that prove that you exceeded average performance in academics, athletics, employment, internships, or undergraduate research. Gather documentation that will support your accomplishments. This would include all job and internship performance reviews, letters/emails of appreciation, letters of recommendation, awards, scholarships, committee appointments, and anything else from your work or collegiate experiences that are or would support an accomplishment. Once you begin documenting your accomplishment history, you may find you have more accomplishments than you think. These accomplishments, whether one or twenty-one, might be what differentiate you from others.

Accomplishments are important to your job search. It has been said that qualifications (education) often get you an interview, but accomplishments can get you the job.[30]

29 Brainy Quote, https://www.brainyquote.com/quotes/zig_ziglar_724588?src=t_accomplishment (Accessed April 18, 2018)

30 Bozorgi, Bob. "Qualifications Will Get You an Interview, But They Won't Get You Hired." *The Undercover Recruiter.* http://theundercoverrecruiter.com/qualifications-will-get-interview-wont-get-hired/ (accessed May 29, 2015).

Accomplishments:

- Demonstrate your ability to contribute to the productivity and/or profitability of the employer

- Emphasize past achievements and successes by using quantifiable and measurable information

- Indicate that past successes are a predictor of future performance

- Highlight the value, benefits, and contributions that you bring to the organization

- Showcase your transferable skills, professional character traits, and experience

Accomplishments also include digital technology proficiencies whether they are in Microsoft Office Suite, Excel VLook-up, IF Function, and Pivot Tables, Google Drive, or in an industry-specific platform or software program, such as a CRM (customer relationship management program) or POS (point-of-sale) system. Your accomplishments in this area might also include project management, data analysis, programming, social media, and technical writing.

The most impressive accomplishments have measurable improvements and results from an organization's perspective. How did you contribute to the organization's success? Or, how did your actions lead to a beneficial result?[31] The specific value of your accomplishments should be readily apparent to a talent acquisition professional.

---

31 See also, Safani, "Tell a Story."

What the Coaches Say:

What is your advice to a recent college graduate about the value and use of accomplishments in a job search?

When college grads think about accomplishments they need to think about how they participated in clubs or activities on campus. Did they take on leadership roles and what were the results? Did they contribute to raising funds for a charity? If yes . . . how much, was it more than others, what percentage to the total amount raise did you raise?

Having metrics (numbers) on a resume really makes for a stronger resume and better networking conversations. Numbers allows the reader to understand how you contributed or what you did. So if you made phone calls to alumni to raise funds don't just put that on the resume. Instead put something like: Generated donations by proactively calling 70+ alumni during phone-a-thon resulting in $2,540 worth of pledges.

Someone making 70+ calls was working hard then adding a dollar amounts for how much you raised shows you delivered results. (Results are what all employers are looking for.)

Think about accomplishments in all different areas: academic projects, on-campus work, volunteering, sports, clubs, research, and off-campus work. Keep the accomplishments relevant to your target job, if possible.

Ellen Steverson, NCRW, GCDF, CEIC

One of the goals prospective employers use interviews for is to ascertain how hard you will work. Your accomplishments help prove that you have gone above and beyond. Recruiters and hiring managers know that the best predictor of **future** performance is **past** performance. Many new graduates make the mistake of *only* listing job duties – or in other words, what *every* person who has held that role has done. It's your job to show evidence of how you have gone above and beyond – accomplishments are a tool for you to demonstrate this. Including facts and figures to support your work will also help. Recruiters and hiring managers appreciate achievements supported by hard data.

An example in action:

Before:

Responsible for sales to end users via website. SEO main sales tool.

After:

#1 Summer Intern Sales Associate – outperforming closest associate by 44%. Exceeded outbound calling expectations by 60%.

The first example reads like a job description. Being responsible for sales to end users is the job duty of *every* sales representative. The second example gives scope, how this individual compares to both other sales reps and to goal expectations.

Paula Christensen, CPRW, CCMC, CJSS

★ **Success Stories**

*There is no passion to be found playing small—in settling for a life
that is less than the one you are capable of living.*

— Nelson Mandela[32]

A success story is a description of an event that provides evidence to the hiring executive regarding the use of your education, skills, abilities, competencies, qualities, and motivation to succeed at the job for which you are interviewing. In a business context, success stories are case studies supporting your professional value proposition (what you're good at).

Writing success stories can be fun and challenging at the same time. Think about school projects, challenges and problems you encountered during your internships and summer jobs. Think in terms of what you did to identify, prevent, and solve a problem. Or, what you did to achieve a goal. What did you do? How did you do it? What was the positive result of your efforts?

It's highly recommended to compose several success stories as a part of your job search. By writing them down and reviewing them, you will be able to more easily remember them, have ready responses to interview questions (especially for behavior-based interviews), and use them in written communication. These success stories will differentiate you from other college graduates, support your brand, and display your qualifications.

32 Nsehe, Mfonobong. "19 Inspirational Quotes From Nelson Mandela." *Forbes.com*. December 6, 2013. http://www.forbes.com/sites/mfonobongnsehe/2013/12/06/20-inspirational-quotes-from-nelson-mandela/ (accessed May 27, 2015).

When writing a success story, there is a simple formula that seems to work:

C. Challenge (Situation, Task)

A. Action

R. Result[33]

Describe the challenge you faced, task you were assigned, or a goal you wanted to achieve. This could include an unexpected situation you faced. Describe what you did, or the plan of action you took, and the positive result. Try to quantify the results with numbers or percentages whenever possible. This could be tough to do as an intern or with your summer job, but if you can it will increase the impact of your story. If you received (or can get) a positive recommendation from a supervisor based on what you did or the results of the project, that will work well, too. The recommendation acts as proof of a job well done.

When you write your success stories, do so with different skills and competencies in mind (transferable job skills, professional qualities, and character traits). For example, stories that reflect true technical ability, analytical thinking, communication skills, work ethic, leadership, and so on, including complementary combinations of skills and competencies within a single story.

When preparing for interviews, read the job description (if you have one) and think about what the employer is looking for (in terms of hard skills, soft skills, and professional qualities). Then create some success stories that align with what you believe will be asked of you in the interview.

Preparing success stories is powerful because most college graduates will not do this kind of preparation. You can clearly differentiate yourself by having well-prepared success stories.

It will give you a competitive advantage in your job search. You will be viewed as better qualified and prepared.

---

33 Safani Barbara. "Tell a Story Interviewers Can't Forget." *TheLadders*. http://www.theladders.com/career-advice/tell-story-interviewers-cant-forget (accessed May 29, 2015).

What the Coaches Say:

What is your advice to recent college graduates about writing success stories when preparing for a job search?

This method is incredibly helpful especially when brainstorming potential answers for behavioral based interview questions. I'll often have students and recent graduates map out multiple examples of how their strengths have helped them successfully navigate a challenge they were facing. I'll utilize the S.T.A.R method [functionally identical to the C.A.R. method previously mentioned] of interviewing (situation, task, action and result) and have them write out how their contributions led to a positive outcome using that framework. The more experiences a recent graduate reflects on, the more stories they'll have to share in an interview. Nothing worse than using the same story over and over in an interview, so my goal when helping students to write their success story is to think of many diverse stories as possible. Writing down success stories is a fantastic way to prepare and land a great interview.

Jered Lish M.S., Gallup-Certified Strengths Coach, GCDF

Review several job descriptions for the type of position you are seeking. Highlight all of the job requirements and preferred skills/experience. Circle the ones you have. Now create stories that show your effectively using each of these skills or telling about your experience. Structure the stories so it is easy for the interviewer to understand the situation, the challenges you faced, the actions you took, and the outcome.

Lorraine Beaman, MA, ACRW, CARW, NCRW, CEIC, MCD

★ Personal Branding

*Always remember: a brand is the most valuable piece of real estate
in the world; a corner of someone's mind.*

— John Hegarty[34]

The idea of creating a "brand" for yourself as a recent college graduate likely sounds very odd. How can you have a brand before you even have your first job? Actually, doing so is not as difficult as it may sound and it will significantly differentiate you from other college graduate job seekers.

A personal brand announces your distinct talents and what you represent to the marketplace. The process of branding is discovering who you are, what you are, what your unique abilities are, and communicating them through various mediums as a part of your job search.

There are numerous benefits of creating an impactful brand:

1. You differentiate yourself from other recent college graduates who are also looking for a job, and gain a huge advantage.

2. You create the initial impression the employer has of you.

3. You can more quickly convey your value to the employer.

4. You can more easily match your skills and value to the employer's needs.

5. You can better determine which opportunities to pursue.

---

34 "10 Ways You're Building a Fantastic Brand." *Design Aglow*. February 3, 2015. http://designaglow.com/blogs/design-aglow/16728432-10-ways-youre-building-a-fantastic-brand (accessed May 28, 2015).

The drawback of not having a brand is simple: You become a commodity—you're just another college grad looking for a job. Perhaps worse, employers will determine for themselves what they want to see in you. They will cast you in a light based on their own conclusions, which may not be the message you want to communicate.[35]

Perhaps the biggest benefit of creating a personal brand as a recent college graduate is the self-awareness of your unique skills, experience, education, qualities, and traits and the recognition of how they all work together to create messaging for who you are. You will project the value of your abilities more clearly, resulting in a job that's a good match for your skillset, professional qualities, and character traits. Branding can also help you set your sights on what you want your future career to be.

The branding process requires introspection and thoughtful reflection. In some cases, thinking through your branding can be both an emotional and an enlightening event.

Think of it this way: As a college graduate job seeker, your goal is to connect with employers both intellectually (you can do the job) and emotionally (you're a good fit). Having a well-crafted, personal brand helps on both levels. You must be perceived as the right candidate and through branding, you are better able to align yourself to an open job position.

Create a succinct brand. Think of it, in analogous terms, as a tagline or a theme that will be at the foundation of your job search.

To help determine your brand, ask yourself some questions:

1. What am I good at?

2. What are the academic or job achievements I am most proud of?

3. What qualities and character traits do I have?

4. What have I been recognized for?

5. What is my reputation with others (friends, supervisors)?

6. What have been my strong points in past jobs or internships?

7. What differentiates me from others with the same job or internship?

8. What qualities do I have that I can promote?

The answers to these questions and the thoughts they provoke are essential to forming your brand. Now, synthesize the answers and thoughts into single words or short phrases that capture the concept of your responses. Here are some examples:

---

35 Ibid.

Recent College Graduate Offering a Strong Work Ethic and Sales Achievements from Summer Jobs / Two Internships

College Graduate with Double Major, Marketing and Advertising / Internship with New York Marketing Firm of Travis and Hudlin

Client-focused College Graduate with Customer Service Experience in a Call Center of a Fortune 500 Corporation / Strong Job Performance Reviews.

When you come to this book's resume and LinkedIn chapters, you will see a few examples of branding in action.

Branding Is Important

Creating a brand is important and a clear differentiator. Reasonably few recent college graduates will know the importance of creating a brand or take the time to do it. Take the necessary time to reflect on this. The purpose of branding is to get you known for the value you offer, get you in the door, and differentiate you from other college graduate job seekers.

What the Coaches Say:

Is it possible to create a professional brand as a recent college graduate? Please explain.

Absolutely! A student is creating a brand throughout college whether they know it or not. They are marketing themselves and showcasing their aspirations, attributes, value-proposition, and identity everyday both on and off campus. To build a brand, a student should identify personal strengths and ROI to share that with campus peers/professors and potential employers, then move them forward. To do that, they can join clubs, join professional associations as a student member, be a teacher's assistant in a subject area, complete internships and apprenticeships, and volunteer to elevate their brand.

Dr. Cheryl Minnick, NCRW, CCMC, CHJMC, CAA

You bet! I encourage students to use such tools as Portfolium.com, build their own website, or find a platform that's industry specific to highlight moments of brilliance in their collegiate or life experience. Visual branding is one of the easiest ways to leave a great impression on a future employer. Any good professional branding of oneself should leave the viewer wanting more and it should stimulate curiosity around how placement of your talents could be specifically utilized within their organization.

I worked with a sophomore international student from China who built a website for herself that highlighted the impressive accomplishments she had achieved both in high school and in her first year of college. She had a career dream to work at one of the top four accounting firms in the world and she had specific goals and strategies identified on what she needed to do to make them happen. She applied for an internship at Deloitte (one of the big four accounting firms in the world) and they were so impressed with how articulate she was both in writing, her marketing documents and her digital presence, they hired her as an intern at the end of her first year of undergrad. After completing the internship at the end of her sophomore year, Deloitte offered her full-time employment and she's one of the only students I've ever coached to have a professional, full-time job offer with two years left of school to complete. Her success I believe to be as a result of her incredible work ethic, being goal-oriented, and she ultimately developed a brand around her competence, skill sets and innovation that Deloitte saw into the future and thought, "we cannot lose her to another company." Talk about the power of a professional brand!

Jered Lish M.S., Gallup-Certified Strengths Coach, GCDF

★ Elevator Speech

The only people who don't need elevator pitches are elevator salesmen.
— Jarod Kintz[36]

By definition, an elevator speech is "the 30-second speech that summarizes who you are, what you [can] do, and why you'd be a perfect candidate."[37] In essence, it is your job search commercial.

The purpose of your elevator speech is to grab the listener's attention, quickly provide relevant information, and *initiate conversation*. A crisply delivered elevator speech is a differentiator from other college graduate job seekers. While others may struggle and stumble, you will be able to concisely inform the listener about your professional value proposition, your own brand.

Take some time and develop a handful of variations for different situations, including all forms of networking, interviews, association and industry conferences, job fairs and strictly social gatherings.

---

36 "Jarod Kintz Quotable Quote." *Goodreads.* http://www.goodreads.com/quotes/1234580-the-only-people-who-don-t-need-elevator-pitches-are-elevator (accessed May 28, 2015).

37 Collamer, Nancy. "The Perfect Elevator Pitch To Land A Job." Forbes. February 4, 2013. http://www.forbes.com/sites/nextavenue/2013/02/04/the-perfect-elevator-pitch-to-land-a-job/ (accessed May 28, 2015).

Here are some tips on crafting your elevator speech (a couple of examples can be found at the end of this chapter):

1. **Know your target audience.** This single factor will give your speech the most impact. If you are speaking with a HR talent acquisition professional, you may choose to promote your education and character traits followed by summer experiences. If you are speaking with the actual hiring executive, you may choose to promote your experiences with summer jobs and internships (realizing that the hiring executive is looking for previous experience and shorter start up time). The key is to promote what you have in your background and education that will most impress the person you are speaking to.

2. **Know what your value proposition is.** This is where your branding comes into full play. Identify as precisely as possible what you offer and what benefits you bring to an employer.

3. **Write down ideas about what you want to possibly say.** Give yourself some time to ponder the ideas and concepts you may include—it isn't necessary to start drafting the speech immediately, but begin with notes reminding you of your bottom-line message. The objective is to gather concepts and ideas first, so be careful not to edit yourself. Refer back to the concepts you used to form your brand.

4. **Write your speech.** Now that you have ideas and concepts about yourself to promote, begin drafting your speech's initial version. Here are some steps to guide you.

    a. Identify yourself.

    b. Statement regarding your value proposition as a professional.

    c. Accomplishment or proof statement that supports your value proposition as a professional.

    d. Call to action in the form of a subtle invitation (a question perhaps) to have a conversation.

5. **Tailor the speech to them, not you.** As a rule, people are tuned into WIIFM (What's In It For Me?). So, review what you have written to ensure your message addresses *their* potential needs.

Instead of, "I am a recent college graduate looking for my first job. I'm open to most anything," you could say, "I am a recent college graduate with a double major in marketing and advertising. I have two summer internships with two marketing and advertising firms. I'm looking for my first professional level job with a marketing firm where my education and experience can have the most impact." Hear how much more impactful that is—and how much more effective the branding is?

6. **Practice, practice, practice.** Read your speech aloud. Then tinker with the words. The goal is to have a speech that sounds authentic and confident. Now, memorize the speech and rehearse it. Consider practicing in front of a mirror or recording it on your smartphone. This could feel odd, but with practice, your delivery will be conversational (one of the keys to making it effective). Smiling while saying the words will increase the impact of the speech.

When you are ready, try the speech out on some of your friends. Make eye contact, smile, and deliver your message with confidence. Afterward, ask them what they think. If their response doesn't line up with what you want from your speech, the speech still needs work.

7. **Prepare a few variations.** You'll want to have a different variation of your speech for an HR talent acquisition professional at a career fair or conference than for a personal friend of your parents at a social gathering. Much of this will happen naturally as you speak with people (as long as you remember your talking points).

You can create shorter and longer versions with your computer's word-count function. It's generally accepted that you can comfortably say about 150 words in sixty seconds.[38]

Remember, the purpose of an elevator speech is to quickly inform the listener of your value proposition as a professional and begin a conversation. Putting these tips into action is the real trick. Check out these websites that contain scores of elevator speeches (not all are designed for job seekers) for a variety of industries: www.improvandy.com and www.yourelevatorpitch.net.

---

38 Walters, *Secrets of Successful Speakers*, p. 59.

Examples

"My name is Justin Bryant and I recently graduated with a marketing degree from State University. I have work experience in marketing having interned with the marketing and advertising firm of Price and Osborn where I have recommendations from the managing partner for my job performance. I also have leadership skills having been the president of my fraternity, Sigma Phi Theta. I am conducting my first job search for my first professional level position. I'm looking for an opportunity with either an independent advertising firm or the marketing department of a larger corporation. Could you tell me more about your organization?"

Or, "Do you have any advice on what you see in the jobs market in this arena?" Or, any other question that can create a conversation. Here is another example:

"My name is Emily Jordan and I recently graduated from Private University with a degree in Education. For my classroom teaching semester, I chose to teach in a rural public school. I was successful in dealing with behaviorally challenged students from non-traditional family arrangements. I am strategically patient but know when to be stern. I'm looking for my first entry-level teaching position. Have you by chance ever hired a teacher who graduated from Private University?"

What the Coaches Say:

What is your advice for recent college graduates in creating an "elevator speech"?

Your "elevator speech" is the self-introduction you will use more frequently than any of your other job search marketing tools. It is the answer to the statement, "Tell me about yourself," the way you will greet recruiters at career fairs, introduce yourself to prospective employers, and it is the information people will share when they are networking on your behalf. Also known as the "30-second me," the elevator speech needs to be carefully crafted, practiced, and shared. It should include your name, your field of study, your most outstanding job-related qualifications (up to 3), and a quick story that highlights your experience.

Lorraine Beaman, MA, ACRW, CARW, NCRW, CEIC, MCD

Elevator speeches might be one of the most important things to develop, practice, and have prepared at all times. As far as developing your pitch, remember it should always lead to conversation. Lead with areas of passion, things that excite you, things your proud of. Identify things that are memorable. You want the person who just heard your pitch to remember you so share something interesting about yourself.

I once asked a colleague how she got into career counseling and she shared "because I was a bartender and was giving career advice regularly. I thought I should get paid for it." She later said that integrating "from bartender to career coach" tended be an interesting hook for most people so she's always used that in pitches for when people are getting to know her and her story. In short, have fun developing your pitch, be creative, be memorable, and share it with the world!

Jered Lish M.S., Gallup-Certified Strengths Coach, GCDF

Business Cards

High expectations are the key to everything.

— Sam Walton[39]

Having business cards during a job search is a differentiator for a recent college graduate. Having a business card projects you as a professional (even though you are a recent college graduate). Circumstances will present themselves where providing a business card can create a positive first impression whereas providing a resume is awkward or inappropriate.[40]

There are four different approaches to the standard three-and-a-half-inch by two-inch business card for a job search: traditional business cards, networking business cards, resume business cards, and infographic business cards.

A solid case can be made for getting two sets of cards to use in different settings. For example, traditional for truly social events, and a networking or resume card for job networking events.

Here are examples for each kind of job-search business card:

39 Bergdahl, Michael. *What I Learned From Sam Walton: How to Compete and Thrive in a Wal-Mart World.* Hoboken, New Jersey: John Wiley & Sons, 2004. p. 39.

40 Ayres, Leslie. "Why You Need a Resume Business Card." *Notes from the Job Search Guru: A Career Advice Blog.* March 16, 2009. http://www.thejobsearchguru.com/notesfrom/why-you-need-a-resume-business-card/ (accessed November 4, 2015).

Traditional Business Cards

This business card is simple in design. It contains only your name, city of residence, street address (optional), telephone number(s), email address, and LinkedIn profile address. It is used for contact information-exchange purposes.

Bob Johnson

Blue Springs, MO
(816) 987-6543 (C)
(816) 123-4567 (H)

Bob.johnson1340@gmail.com
www.linkedin.com/in/bobjohnson

Networking Business Cards

Networking business cards contain the same key contact information as a traditional card, except this variety also has a concise statement regarding your career focus and unique value proposition or brand.[41] Remember to keep the messaging consistent among your networking card, resume, elevator speech, LinkedIn profile, and so on. There is some room for variation, but the theme of these job-seeking tools must align.

Recent College Graduate Offering a Strong
Work Ethic and Sales Achievements from
Summer Jobs / Two Internships

Bob Johnson

Blue Springs, MO
(816) 987-6543 (C)
(816) 123-4567 (H)

Bob.johnson1340@gmail.com
www.linkedin.com/in/bobjohnson

---

41 Hansen, Randall S., PhD. "Networking Business Cards: An Essential Job-Search Tool for Job-Seekers, Career Changers, and College Students When a Resume Just Won't Do." *Quintessential Careers.* http://www.quintcareers.com/networking-business-cards/ (accessed November 4, 2015).

Resume Business Cards

A resume business card takes the networking card one step further. Here you can put key educational qualifications and accomplishments on the back. This next point is optional, but leave a little white space at the bottom of the back of the card, allowing the recipient room to jot a note about you. Hopefully the note will read, "Need to call."[42]

Recent College Graduate Offering a Strong Work Ethic and Sales Achievements from Summer Jobs / Two Internships **Bob Johnson** Blue Springs, MO Bob.johnson1340@gmail.com (816) 987-6543 (C) www.linkedin.com/in/bobjohnson (816) 123-4567 (H)	**Qualifications Summary** • Double major in Marketing and Advertising - GPA 3.2 • Division I Athlete - Baseball • Summer Internship
Front	*Back*

It's fine to mix and match the concepts from any of the three types. For example, you may determine that it would be best that the front of the card has a traditional look. But on the back you may choose to put a branding statement and a couple of college achievements. That's fine. Exercise your best judgment.

Business cards can be printed at most office supply stores and are reasonably inexpensive for a few hundred cards. In addition, many online companies produce business cards inexpensively. And if you're technology savvy, you can print your cards using special paper and a template that is already loaded on most computers.

When creating your job-search business cards, keep the design simple. Use traditional fonts and conservative, business-appropriate color schemes. If you are pursuing jobs in advertising, media marketing, or other creative fields, you have more latitude with design and use of colors. Since you have put your time, effort, and money into creating your business cards, consider purchasing a business-card holder to keep your cards clean and crisp. Providing a tattered business card defeats a great first impression.

---

42 Ayres, "Resume Business Card."

Infographic Business Cards

An infographic business card is a very unique concept. It is not a "business card" in the traditional sense. Instead, it is more of a "networking handbill." In concept, an infographic business card is a colorful, high-resolution document containing impactful and persuasive college background information and accomplishments presented through creative designs.

Conceptually, an infographic business card is larger than the standard three-and-a-half-inch by two-inch business card. Although there is no hard-and-fast rule, a four-by-six-inch card is a good starting point.

The infographic business card is ideal for networking events, career fairs, especially for association gatherings and conventions. Printed on business-card-grade paper, with colorful graphics, it is a clear differentiator. If it's not too large, it can still easily slip into the inside jacket pocket or portfolio of a networking contact or hiring executive.

If this infographic card idea appeals to you, it is highly recommended that you use the services of a professional with experience creating infographic resumes, as this experience translates directly to infographic cards. Or you can check out Piktochart (www.piktochart.com) if you want to try your hand at creating your own infographic document. There are advantages and disadvantages that need to be carefully considered before you pursue this job-search tactic (Refer to the topic on Infographic Resumes).

What the Coaches Say:

Would you recommend that recent college graduates get business cards as a part of their job search? If so, please explain.

Business cards are a great way to make sure someone has your contact information. I recommend new graduates create business cards with their name, their career/employment goal, phone number, LinkedIn address, and email address. If you have a branding statement, putting it on the bottom of the card helps send the message of why you would be a good candidate. Consider listing three reasons you would be a top candidate on the back of the card; these could be your degree, internships, or work experience.

Lorraine Beaman, MA, ACRW, CARW, NCRW, CEIC, MCD

Sure. A professional business card is the simplest, most pocket-friendly networking tool you have. That, and your winning smile, firm handshake, good eye-contact, and listening skill!

Mary Jo King, NCRW

Chapter 3

Impactful Resumes

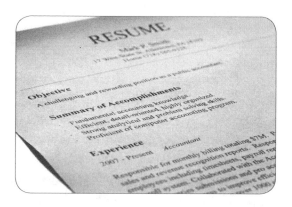

Great works are performed, not by strength, but by perseverance.

— Prince Imlac, character from Samuel Johnson's *Rasselas*[43]

What a Resume Is Not

You are not writing an autobiography! Some college graduates put too much information on a resume. It's easy to let that happen. You start writing and packing the document full of information going back to junior high school and before you know it, you have a resume that is a blizzard of words with useless information. Talent acquisition professionals as well as hiring executives refuse to read resumes like that. They get discarded. A resume must be an informative marketing piece—easy on the eyes and the right amount of white space.

So, What is a Resume?

A resume is a unique form of written communication designed to quickly gain the attention of the HR talent acquisition professional or hiring executive, inform them about you, sell

---

43 "Quotes on Perseverance." *The Samuel Johnson Sound Bite Page.* http://www.samueljohnson.com/persever. html; "Rasselas: A Word of Caution." *The Samuel Johnson Sound Bite Page.* http://www.samueljohnson.com/rasselas.html (accessed June 2, 2015).

you as a qualified candidate, and differentiate you from other college graduate job seekers. You have complete control of the appearance and content, and should feel comfortable about how it represents you, but (as previously stated) it is not your autobiography—it's a marketing brochure. The sooner you grasp that concept the more impactful your resume will become.

What the Coaches Say:

What is your definition of a resume?

Resume is from the French "resumer" meaning "to sum up." Therefore, a resume is a summary, a story, a personal marketing document summarized for and tailored to an audience. It is not an autobiography, nor should it be randomly written. A resume is a tool to help an audience make a decision about your education, experience, talents and strengths whether to offer a scholarship, job, admission to professional school or make an introduction as a presenter.

Dr. Cheryl Minnick, NCRW, CCMC, CHJMC, CAA

A resume is a strategic financial document that markets your best skills, experiences, and accomplishments to show value to an employer. It is a financial document as it will impact salary and negotiations.

Ellen Steverson, NCRW, GCDF, CEIC

★ Time is of the Essence

Most talent acquisition professionals spend between five and twenty seconds when first looking at a resume. So assume your resume will not have much time to make a positive impression. If you're perceived as valuable to the company, you're in! If not, you're out! An employer must be able to quickly determine your potential value to the organization. This is another reason to use the word cloud technique so key words and phrases appear on your resume and "speak" to the HR talent acquisition professional or hiring executive.

How can you make the most of those precious seconds? Showcase your most impactful qualifications, education, activities, and accomplishments in the top half of the first page of your resume. Grab their attention quickly. The title of your resume, branding words/ phrases/statement, and the first few sentences of your summary create the biggest impact. By then, time's up! If these grab the interest of the employer, you get the next few seconds and perhaps more. This is why titling, branding, and a well-formatted resume are so important.

What the Coaches Say:

Studies have repeatedly shown that employers spend between five to twenty seconds when first looking at a resume. What can be done to capitalize on such a brief period of time?

Take the first page of your resume and fold it in half. Your best information should be above the fold. Put most of your writing effort into this critical area. Stay away from buzzwords and worn out phrases like motivated, track record, and goal oriented. These words are meaningless to HR professionals because they are so overused.

Instead, create branding statements that showcase your differentiators and are loaded with industry keywords. Consider adding a core strengths/ skills/competencies area populated with keywords that help your resume stand out when viewed by a real person and an applicant tracking system

(ATS). Your goal is to have the top half of your first page engage the HR professional/Hiring Manager so they will take the time to continue reading.

Paula Christensen, CPRW, CCMC, CJSS

Communicate the most relevant qualifications and achievements first in a short summary. Create a clean, appealing format that is easy to navigate. Use white space and bullets to draw the human scanner's eye to important content and accomplishments. (Tip: Don't bullet every line. It renders all bullets useless.)

Mary Jo King, NCRW

Most of us believe recruiters spend 5-10 minutes reviewing a resume, and at least 20 minutes on ours! The truth: recruiters spend about 6 seconds on all resumes before they make the initial "fit/no fit" decision. This means it is important to present information in a well-thought out, strategic and prioritized way.

Dr. Cheryl Minnick, NCRW, CCMC, CHJMC, CAA

Your Resume Is Your Marketing Brochure

Your elevator speech is your commercial. Your success stories are your case studies. Your resume is your marketing brochure.

Your resume is frequently the first formal presentation of your collegiate credentials to an employer. Take the time to write an impactful resume (or have one professionally prepared for you). In order for your resume to provide that positive first impression, make sure that it contains the following:

- **A clean, professional appearance.** Develop a document that is easy on the eyes, with plenty of white space, and plain, simple language. Also be sure that the use of font size, bold print, lines, headings, spacing, bullet points, and so on, are used sparingly and consistently throughout. Any graphics and shading must be readable. Your resume must have a "wow" factor.

- **A title.** A title announces the qualifications to follow in the resume's body.

- **Branding words or a branding statement**. Either of these will help present your value proposition. Often, a title and a branding statement can be combined.

- **Accurate contact information.** Review to ensure your contact information is up-to-date.

- **A concise summary.** This should highlight your education, activities, internships, background and give information to support your professional value proposition (your potential).

- **Character traits**. List those qualities and character traits that make you unique.

- **Activities and achievements**. State what separates you from the pack.

- **Honest background representation.** It is estimated that "more than 80 percent of resumes contain some stretch of the truth."[44] Be honest about your education, activities, background and achievements. If an embellishment is discovered, you will lose your opportunity for the position not to mention lose your integrity and credibility.

It is perfectly acceptable, and encouraged, to write a generic form of your resume. From this generic resume, you can modify it for specific opportunities that you pursue. Just remember what form of your resume you use with specific employers!

What the Coaches Say:

Should a resume be written or revised for each position a college graduate job seeker pursues? Please explain.

Tailoring your resume for each position is the single best way to differentiate. Recruiters report job seekers continue to be lazy when making revisions. Candidates are not taking the time to update their resumes for each job.

---

44 Bucknell Career Development Center. "Creating an Effective Resume." Bucknell University. http://www.bucknell.edu/documents/CDC/Creating_An_Effective_Resume.pdf (accessed February 19, 2016).

Spending 20-30 minutes to tailor your resume for a specific role shows initiative and will help you pass applicant tracking system (ATS) requirements. Assemble keywords from job descriptions, previous work experience, volunteer and educational skills, and your personality characteristics. Add these keywords to your resume's core skills/strengths/competencies section. Also, include them in your professional summary and add/change bullet points to emphasize these keywords.

Jobscan.co is a useful tool for evaluating your resume against job postings. Copy and paste the job posting in one box and your resume in the other box. Jobscan.co calculates where your resume comes up short and makes suggestions for hard and soft skill keywords to incorporate.

Paula Christensen, CPRW, CCMC, CJSS

I recommend creating a lengthy, comprehensive resume that can be quickly edited for each job. Your resume needs to send the message "I am perfect for this job" not "Here is a lot of information about me; if you read it all, you will be able to find the information you need to decide if you should invite me in for an interview."

Lorraine Beaman, MA, ACRW, CARW, NCRW, CEIC, MCD

Use of Keywords

Keywords are specific words or phrases that reflect your education, experiences, abilities, and are frequently buzzwords, or terms-of-art used by the employer or in the industry you are pursuing. Your resume must contain keywords to get the employer's attention and communicate that you are qualified for a particular position. Keywords can include the following:

- Position titles you are interested in or qualified for
- Education (school name, degrees, GPA)
- Character traits, qualities
- Professional designation you may be pursuing

- Skills, knowledge, competencies
- Industry terms-of-art (and abbreviations)
- Licenses, certifications (if any, even if partially complete)
- Location (state, city)
- Software and technologies you're familiar with

You are likely familiar with many of the keywords of your industry of interest (terms-of-art), your abilities, and characteristics. Make sure they appear prominently on your resume.

When pursuing a particular opening, use the word cloud technique to capture keywords used by that employer. Strategically placing those words on your resume is using the "language of the employer," which is persuasive, and enhances your candidacy for the position.

What the Coaches Say:

The use of keywords is important on a resume. What would you consider are the more important kinds of information that leads to keywords?

Keywords can be found in the Requirements, Preferred Requirements and Education sections of a job posting. If one analyzes the job posting, keywords can be identified, and sometimes will appear in multiple forms multiple times in multiple areas, including the job description section itself. I suggest students take the job description apart—put hard skills in a column, soft skills in another, and active verbs (manage, coordinate) in another. We put tally-marks next to each skill that is stated more than once and count. If "audit" is repeated four times in an accounting job posting, we know there will be a bunch of auditing going on, so we speak to that in the resume. If a job is analyzed in this way, it is easier for a student to digest, understand and identify keywords. Keywords can sometimes be found in the LinkedIn profile of a person currently in the role, or who had the role in the past, as well as in job postings for similar jobs.

Dr. Cheryl Minnick, NCRW, CCMC, CHJMC, CAA

> The best keyword clues come from job posts. These are the nouns that reflect skills and abilities, like communication, leadership, supervision, customer service, training, project management, business analysis, financial statements, budget, B2B sales, cost control, etc.
>
> Other important keywords are those common to the industry or position at hand, but not necessarily listed in the job post. These "hidden" keywords affect scoring, nevertheless. The theory is that candidates who have the right qualifications will naturally include these keywords in their copy, making it difficult for unqualified candidates to "fake it" by mining keywords from the job post.
>
> Mary Jo King, NCRW

Resume Formats

The three fundamental variations are: Chronological, Functional, and Showcase.

- The **Chronological** format is the most traditionally used resume format. For a college graduate, education normally comes first, followed by work experience and internships. This is a common format frequently used by tenured professionals with consistent work experience in one field or position type.[45]

- The **Functional** format is a format you will not use as a recent college graduate. However, it is worth knowing how it works. A Functional Resume emphasizes skills and qualifications to strategically sell experience that may align to the needs of the employer. A job seeker's experience is divided into a skill-based section that demonstrates qualifications, training, education, and specific accomplishments, and a reverse chronological listing of employment including company name, title, and dates (toward the end of the resume).

- The **Showcase** resume is a growing trend that has developed over the last several years and combines the best features of the Chronological and Functional formats. It can work well for college graduates! The concept is to showcase your best selling points—education, activities, qualifications, internships, knowledge,

---

45 Yate, Martin. *Knock 'em Dead 2017: The Ultimate Job Search Guide.* New York: Adams Media, 2017. p. 45–46.

and achievements—immediately on the top half of the resume. Work experience is then listed in reverse chronological order just like a traditional chronological resume.

There is an additional kind of resume called an Infographic resume. It is a colorful, high-resolution document that visually presents your education, background, internships and accomplishments by using graphics, pie charts, bar graphs, and timelines in creative ways. More about an Infographic resume at the end of this chapter.

Parts of a Resume

Aside from the Infographic resume, there are essential components of a resume:

Identification/Contact Information

This section appears at the top of your resume and includes your name, address (optional), telephone numbers (home and/or cell phone), and email address. Including your LinkedIn profile address is optional. A new trend is omitting your residential address. This is acceptable, but still include city and state. You may choose to include your college address as well as your permanent address.

No photos should appear on your resume (unless it is required in your industry). If they want to know what you look like they can check out your LinkedIn profile.

Email Addresses

Your email address must be professional and current. Do not use an inappropriate college email address e.g. bombed24/7@xyz.com. There are several professional formats you can use:

- Jsmith1234@xyz.com

- john.smith@xyz.com

- smithj@xyz.com

- johnsmith@xyz.com

If you need to, add your lucky number, area code, ZIP code, or other number prior to the @ symbol. Be absolutely sure the address is professional.

Title

Differentiate yourself by titling your resume. It announces what the resume is going to describe so the reader doesn't have to scan the entire resume to determine your background. Be reasonably specific with your title. For example, "Accounting Graduate with a 3.7 GPA," or "College Graduate with a Degree in Industrial Engineering."

The title should align with your LinkedIn profile, networking or resume business card, and at least share a theme similar to your elevator speech.

What the Coaches Say:

Is it important to have a title on a resume? Why or why not?

Having a resume title is essential for three reasons:

1. Adding a title helps with identification and tracking within the hiring company. In a smaller company where they don't do a lot of hiring, identification may not be an issue. In a larger company, your information may be distributed to several HR associates and hiring managers. Adding a title makes it clear what position you are applying for.

2. Adding a title helps with applicant tracking system (ATS) recognition. It's another chance to help you identify with the exact position you are applying for. Having the exact keyword on your resume is especially important for new graduates who may never have held the role they are targeting. It's a bit covert; you're adding the role even though you haven't held that job – the computer doesn't know the difference.

3. Seeing the exact job title on your resume can provoke a subliminal response from readers. A hiring manager sees Targeted Role: Human Resource Assistant front and center on your resume and they think "Hey! I'm looking for a Human Resource Assistant!"

Paula Christensen, CPRW, CCMC, CJSS

When resumes arrive, especially at large companies, they are sorted according to the job being applied for. The title makes it very clear the job you are seeking and assures your resume is processed correctly. The title sends a message to the reader: As you read this resume, you will learn why I am qualified to be "job title." Job title helps readers focus on what they will be reading.

Lorraine Beaman, MA, ACRW, CARW, NCRW, CEIC, MCD

Branding Statement

Adding a branding statement can set your resume apart from others. It should appear under or be combined with your resume's title. Her's an example:

Accounting Graduate with a 3.7 GPA / Two Internships
Proven ability to solve problems through application of accounting principles

What the Coaches Say:

In your opinion, is it important to have a brand (either a branding statement or branding words) on a college graduate resume? Please briefly explain.

Branding words are a powerful addition to resumes. I have clients fill out an extensive questionnaire to help formulate their personal brand. Sample personal brand questions:

When were you complimented by a supervisor, co-worker, or customer?

When did you go above and beyond the call of duty?

If you had to pick one word to describe yourself professionally, what would it be?

What are three descriptive adjectives that help describe you?

What is a favorite quote of yours?

Incorporate your responses to these questions into your headlines, professional summaries, job experience summaries, and LinkedIn profiles.

Paula Christensen, CPRW, CCMC, CJSS

Yes. The branding statement is an abbreviated way to differentiate one candidate from other competitors. Everyone has a brand, even if only a philosophy that has yet to be practiced. Some college graduates are already workplace veterans with a transferrable brand—about customer service excellence, reliability, passion, or attention to detail.

Mary Jo King, NCRW

Objective Statement

An Objective Statement has fallen out of favor over the last several years. The traditional Objective Statement has been used to inform the employer of what *you* want. However, an employer is far more interested in what you can do or offer that is of value to the company (regardless of what you want). They are differing points of view.

As a recent college graduate, you can still use an Objective Statement if you choose, but it needs to be focused on the needs of the employer. Here's an example:

> To secure an entry-level accounting position using my education and internship experience to benefit a reputable accounting firm.

If you choose to use an Objective Statement, avoid such nebulous and potentially self-serving phrases as:

- "Opportunity for advancement" or "Advance my career"
- "Challenging opportunity"
- "Professional growth"

> ### *What the Coaches Say:*
>
> **What is your opinion regarding the use of an Objective Statement?**
>
> ———
>
> Forget it. Objective statements all read the same to humans, and consume valuable document real estate with largely meaningless trivia. Professional resume writers are trained not to use them anymore. We write headlines, instead.
>
> Mary Jo King, NCRW
>
> ———
>
> Don't use objective statements unless you want to identify yourself as old-school and outdated. The purpose of a resume is not to identify what you want but to instead highlight how you are perfect for what the employer wants. Think like a recruiter, why do they care that your objective is to seek an entry level marketing position with opportunities for growth? Instead, they want to know how you will solve a problem, help grow their bottom line, and make their processes more efficient.
>
> Paula Christensen, CPRW, CCMC, CJSS
>
> ———
>
> Use a branding statement rather than an Objective Statement. Traditional Objective Statements tell what you want from a job; a branding statement says what you bring to the job. Employers want to know what you can do for them, not what they can do for you.
>
> Lorraine Beaman, MA, ACRW, CARW, NCRW, CEIC, MCD

Summary

The summary brings together your education and experience into a concise paragraph. When well-written, your summary section can differentiate you from other recent college graduates.

The summary could contain some of the following information: reference to internships and summer jobs, level of responsibility, skills and responsibilities, potential contributions (as seen from the employer's perspective), and strengths, accomplishments, and character traits. It emphasizes key information detailed in the body of the resume.

A simple three-part formula to help you create the foundation for an impactful summary is:

1. A statement regarding the function or title you are pursuing.

2. A statement identifying your education, abilities and qualifications (Accomplishments can be included here as well).

3. A statement regarding your transferrable job skills and/or character traits.

For example:

Position you are pursuing: Entry-level Accountant

Statement regarding function or title: A detail-oriented college graduate with a 3.7 GPA in Accounting.

Statement regarding technical ability or qualifications: Proven ability from summer internships in financial forecasting and analysis, audit, and reconciliation.

Statement regarding transferrable job skills/professional qualities: Conscientious, self-motivated, and service-oriented professional who enjoys solving problems through the application of accounting principles.

Complete Summary:

A detail-oriented college graduate with a 3.7 GPA in Accounting. Proven ability from summer internships in financial forecasting and analysis, audit, and reconciliation. Conscientious, self-motivated, and service-oriented professional who enjoys solving problems through the application of accounting principles.

From this foundation, you can expand your summary. But, an effective summary section should be concise and to the point. By using the three-part formula you will be crafting a solid, impactful summary.

A summary section can have several different names, including:

• Description

• Summary

- Qualifications
- Profile
- Summary of Qualifications

What the Coaches Say:

As a resume writer for college graduates, do you use a summary section? If so, what do you want to say or achieve?

I use a summary more often than not, simply because most graduates have more to offer than a degree. This approach creates a "combination" format, using both functional and chronological components to tell the story.

The summary should convey all primary qualifications, potentially including degree, workplace achievements, certifications, licenses, and language skills. It might contain transferable skills from previous experience, and soft skills that will be useful in the target role, e.g. communications, teamwork, decision-making, and problem solving.

When effectively written, the summary helps the human reader make a quick determination that the candidate belongs in the "qualified" category for deeper review. You get 5 seconds to earn 5 minutes.

Mary Jo King, NCRW

Most often I will include a 3-5 line career summary of the student's skills and experience for the job written specifically for the job or industry, nothing added randomly or without strategy. Sometimes, it is in a short 3-5 sentence paragraph, sometimes written as two one-line career statements, and sometimes placed into a 2-column table with 2 short 1-2 line paragraphs in the left column and a list of keyword skills in the column to the right. Depends upon the student, industry and job target.

Dr. Cheryl Minnick, NCRW, CCMC, CHJMC, CAA

Showcase Section(s)

If you elect to use a showcase-style resume, the next section (or two, depending upon your circumstances) can be your showcase section. Although you have a lot of discretion on titling and content, the key to this section is to make it substantive and succinctly impactful. Use lists and bullet points to make the information in these sections easier to read.

In a recent study, it was found that 39% of employers want to see examples of work the candidate has done.[46] If this should apply to you (like an online portfolio, for example), add a URL or web address on your resume.

These are possible topics and titles for showcase sections:

• Achievement summaries

• Internships

• Volunteering

• Languages (Foreign or IT)

• Recommendations

• On Campus Activities

• Awards

Education

The Education section will appear on the top half of the first page and is the first substantive presentation of your collegiate credentials. If your credentials are strong, your education section could function as a "showcase" section.

Use logical formatting in presenting the information, including name of your college or University, date of graduation, degree, major, and possibly G.P.A. (more on that in a moment). Abbreviations for your degree are fine: B.S., B.A., MBA, and so on. Obviously, high academic designations such as Cum Laude, Summa Cum Laude, and Magna Cum Laude are listed (and will always be on your resume for your entire career). List scholarships, college athletics, and notable activities (social fraternities and sororities, professional collegiate groups, and so on).

As a general rule, your G.P.A. should be put on your resume if it is 3.0 or above. In addition, if your G.P.A. in your major is above 3.0, list it separately. To some employers, your academic performance in your major is more important than your over-all G.P.A.

If your G.P.A. is below 3.0, the best strategy is to leave it off your resume.

---

46 Lorenz, Mary. "New study shows job seekers what hiring managers really want." *CareerBuilder. May 17, 2016.* http://www.careerbuilder.com/advice/new-study-shows-job-seekers-what-hiring-managers-really-want (Accessed August 27, 2017).

What the Coaches Say:

Do you have any unique techniques in writing the education section?

In addition to the pertinent information about where you went to school, major, and G.P.A., you may choose to include a sentence about relevant coursework. Example:

Relevant Coursework: Design for Manufacturing & Assembly, Energy Systems Design, Thermodynamics, Engineering Mathematics V: Vector Calculus.

Only list your courses that could be important keywords for positions you are targeting. If you graduated with a Communications degree and you are pursuing Social Media Marketing positions, only list courses that are relevant for that position like Social Media Strategies, Digital Communications, Mass Media Advertising, and Business and Media Writing.

Evaluating courses to include warrants taking a hard look. You may feel it was relevant, you worked hard and your Fundamentals of Public Address class was enlightening, you may be tempted to include it. Take on the role of a Human Resources Recruiter. Will they care you took that class? Is it relevant for the Social Media Marketing position? If not, don't include that class.

Paula Christensen, CPRW, CCMC, CJSS

A visual pictorial or infographic educational section can help distinguish a student from other candidates. Visual images are retained and can have a lasting impression.

Tina Kashlak Nicolai, PHR, CPBA, CARW

Employment History

Your employment history section is a list of work experience, internships, and accomplishments during college. In reverse chronological order, describe your job experiences in a coherent and continuous manner.

Begin with details on the most important items: current company/employer's name, job title, job function, and dates (e.g. Summer of 20XX). Use the official name of the company. Because many companies have names or initials that may make it difficult to identify what kind of a company it is, use a short tagline to describe each company: industry position, dollar volume, customer base, products, and/or recognition. For example, NAME OF COMPANY: "An international retailer of personal care products with $70M in annual sales."

Job Scope Description

For each position or internship, write a two to three sentence description of your duties and responsibilities. This could include information regarding the position, function, and responsibilities. In essence, describe what you did and your responsibilities. Mention notable accomplishments. This is where your accomplishment history comes into play.

This section can have other titles:

- Summer Work Experience
- Employment Background
- Relevant Experience

What the Coaches Say:

When you create the employment history section on a college graduate's resume, what is your approach? What are you thinking?

When creating a client's employment history section, I begin by including a brief description of the duties performed. I draft 1-2 sentences of a mini job description. Next, I list 4-5 bullet points of accomplishments, results, and proof. So many new graduates simply list the job duties they performed. Digging deeper, identifying how you made in impact is crucial. What did you do differently than every other person who has held that role? When you worked as a Mechanical Engineering Intern and completed the medical device project, what was the benefit to the company, team, or customer?

Before: Assisted engineers with new customer projects.

After: Increased speed to market by two months for Greenfield project. Used Fused Deposition Manufacturing (FDM) and cycle testing equipment to prove functionality and reliability when designing components.

Paula Christensen, CPRW, CCMC, CJSS

I determine if the employment experience is related to the job search goal. If it is, I will include it in the Professional Experience section and showcase accomplishments that demonstrate qualifications for the job the student is seeking. If work experience is not related to the career goal, I put it in a Work History section that lists the job title, employer, location, and dates. The purpose of the Work History section is to show the student has held a job and understands what it means to arrive on time and work toward achieving company goals—two of the attributes employers look for when they hire a new employee.

Lorraine Beaman, MA, ACRW, CARW, NCRW, CEIC, MCD

Other Credentials

Depending upon your unique circumstances you may have additional credentials. The following sections can add depth to your resume.

1. Affiliations/Associations

Affiliations and associations can be impactful on a resume by indicating your involvement in your chosen industry and the community. Include groups you are a member of. An Affiliations section may look like this:

College Marketing Association

American Red Cross

Consider whether or not you want to include groups that could possibly create a bias. Any groups that are religious, race-related, or political are those that immediately come to mind.

2. Languages

The world is getting smaller. Being fluent or proficient in a foreign language can be a significant differentiator, depending on the kind of positions you are pursuing. A Language section generally appears this way:

Fluent in Spanish

Proficient in Portuguese

3. Technical

Understanding technology is becoming indispensable in today's world. Include your proficiencies with technology here. List those that are unique. A Technical section generally appears this way:

C++, Commvault, VMWare, Windows Servers, Microsoft Active Directory

4. Certifications

Depending upon your field of study, you could have started the completion of a certification or licensing (e.g. actuarial exams). These certainly need to be listed on your resume even though they are not complete.

Starting the process of achieving a professional certification while still in college is a significant differentiator from others. It demonstrates your commitment to your field of study and career. It will get an employer's attention.

If you have the time and are willing to make the commitment of effort, identify a relevant professional designation and start the certification coursework. Many can be achieved online.

What the Coaches Say:

There is a variety of additional information that can be included on a resume such as campus activities, athletics, fraternity or sorority, clubs, honors, languages, among others. How do you treat this information on a resume?

Extracurricular activities are important to add to show a well-rounded student. Students may also benefit if they held leadership roles, broke records (sports), experienced learning abroad, held multiple jobs (paid for college), or any other achievements.

A student involved in multiple activities tells a story to the employer that "time management" and "agility" are organic core competencies. When the resume is strategically designed and written, we can convey the branding with an impact stronger than using words. It's a balancing act.

Tina Kashlak Nicolai, PHR, CPBA, CARW

Extra-curricular activities are beneficial to include. Prioritize them based on importance for future jobs and the criteria below.

1. Recent leadership experience.

2. Honors or awards.

3. Languages preferred for your target industry, role, or company.

4. Volunteerism that aligns with the targeted company's values.

Paula Christensen, CPRW, CCMC, CJSS

Use of Recommendations on a Resume

When properly used, recommendations, testimonials, and endorsements appearing on a resume can be impactful. These affirmations capitalize upon the persuasion principle of social proof mentioned earlier in the book.

Due to a resume's limited space, a statement of recommendation (appearing in quotes, italics, or both) must be short, relevant, and direct. Testimonials and endorsements from others are more powerful than what you say about yourself.

To be effective, the person providing the recommendation must be identified by name and title. Get permission from the individual offering the recommendation prior to including it on your resume.

Example:

"We were proud to have Jessica as our summer intern. She quickly caught on to our cost accounting methodologies and helped our accounting department notably."

—Elizabeth Jones, VP of Accounting

You can also close a resume with an impactful recommendation:

"As a part-time service representative in our call center, Katy was clearly the most client-focused representative on our staff!"

—Bob Johnson, Call Center Director

Again, for effect, consider putting the recommendation in italics. Identify the source of the recommendation by name and title and get permission. Remember, since it is a recommendation, this technique is using the persuasion principle of social proof.

What the Coaches Say:

What is your opinion about including recommendations on a resume?

Recommendations may add value depending on the relevance to the candidate and the position he/she is seeking. When using recommendations, be sure to get approval from the person writing the recommendation prior to including in your document. Also, be sure the recommendation states something unique about you and your achievements and/or brand.

Tina Kashlak Nicolai, PHR, CPBA, CARW

Well-chosen excerpts of recommendations can be very effective, providing valuable word-of-mouth advertising. They are most credible when attributed by name and title or relationship. Don't overdo it or the effect will lack sincerity.

Mary Jo King, NCRW

Highlighting a Unique Qualification or Achievement on Your Resume
(Use with Discretion)

This technique can be effective but it must be used with caution and good judgement. What you do is use the highlighting function of your computer (Microsoft Word, for example) and highlight a particularly strong or truly unique qualification or achievement on your resume. The same idea works for paper resumes. The highlighted words become part of the document and immediately stand out.

This technique can alert the employer of a particular match that exists between what the employer is looking for and your collegiate background. Use this technique sparingly and only in those situations where it is truly warranted. Otherwise, your resume may look gaudy and will not make a positive first impression.

Information NOT to be Included on a Resume

• Do not put "References Upon Request" at the end of your resume. It is naturally assumed that you will furnish references if asked.

• Don't include the reasons for leaving your different jobs. (summer or part-time)

• Don't include compensation on your resume.

• Do not put personal or legally protected characteristics, such as age, marital status, race, state of health, social security number, height, weight, and so forth on your resume.

Testing the Impact of Your Resume

After your resume is complete, see if it makes the initial impression or impact you want. Give your resume to a couple of friends and the professionals in the career services office. Ask them for their evaluation.

If the "impact" points of your resume are not what you want them to remember, you may need to revise it. On the other hand, if your review group remembers what you want to communicate with your resume, it's ready for use! Have your "quality control" group do the same for your other job-search documents or online profiles, as well.

What the Coaches Say:

When you visually look over a resume, what are you looking at or looking for that confirms in your mind that it is "a good one?"

It is quickly scannable and its message easily received (skills section). Information provided is relevant, expresses a brand (headline) and has enough white space to allow the eye breathing room to digest the print. It does not tell the reader what the candidate wants (objective statement), but what the candidate offers (career summary). It is crafted without spelling/grammar errors or repeated active verbs so it showcases the writer's command of English language and written communication skills. It has section titles divided by divider lines with easy-to-read font large enough to read, but not so large it appears elementary.

Dr. Cheryl Minnick, NCRW, CCMC, CHJMC, CAA

---

1. A clearly defined target (industry, functional expertise, and job title). Many hiring managers report "I'm not even sure what this person is looking for."

Candidates sometimes lack focus and their message gets muddled.

2. Recent and relevant accomplishments. Too many job seekers waste valuable space on their resume with information that is not relevant. You might be proud that you made it to the state tennis tournament in high school however, when you're applying for engineering positions, your co-op, internship, and job experiences are more critical. Take a hard look at every sentence you include and ask "Why would a hiring manager care about this?" If you cannot answer that question, you shouldn't add that information.

3. Succinct and error-free documents.

4. A modern format that includes color and/or a graphic element, if appropriate. Don't get too crazy. HR professionals and hiring managers still prefer to have resumes with information formatted in a familiar, organized manner.

Paula Christensen, CPRW, CCMC, CJSS

Attaching Your Resume to Your Online Profile

It is entirely permissible to attach your resume to your online profiles, namely LinkedIn. The potential exists that your resume could be printed off or electronically forwarded to a hiring executive by an internal company recruiter or any other source.

However, you may want to skip attaching your resume to your profile, as a conscious strategy. Communicating directly with hiring executives is pivotal to your job-search success, and the desired goal. A well-constructed online profile creates interest on its own, triggering the talent acquisition professional to reach out and communicate with you. After communication starts, then send your resume.

Infographic Resume

An infographic resume is a colorful, high-resolution document that visually presents your background and accomplishments by using graphics, pie charts, bar graphs, and timelines in creative ways. They can be particularly impactful when displaying notable achievements, high-level recommendations, and college activities, among other things.

The impact of an infographic resume comes from the fact that readers are drawn to colorful images. That attention can set you apart in today's crowded job market.[47] There's a tendency to remember things better when they are presented with images.

An infographic resume can, *in very limited circumstances*, replace the traditional resume. This is most often the case in the creative fields like design, marketing, advertising, digital media, and so on.

However, for the vast majority of time, an infographic resume should be used as a *supplement or differentiation tactic* in conjunction with a traditional resume.

There are advantages, disadvantages, and considerations for using an infographic resume in a job search. Let's start with a few advantages:

It differentiates you. An infographic resume is clearly a differentiation tactic. Although the idea of an infographic resume has been around for a while, they are not widely used and therefore seldom seen by employers in most industries. A well-thought-out, well-prepared, and well-presented infographic resume can make you stand out compared to other college job seekers.[48]

It works well as a networking tool. You can use an infographic resume alongside (or instead of) your traditional resume and business cards when you network at an event.

One unique approach would be selecting your most persuasive college achievements and creating an infographic "handbill." Create a four-inch-by-six-inch infographic handbill and put it on thicker paper or use it as a large business card. This is truly unique and seldom seen; it's guaranteed to create conversation.[49]

It provides insight into your thinking and presentation skills. One interesting advantage to an infographic resume is it opens the door of insight into how you think and creatively present ideas and concepts. This can be very persuasive if the position(s) you are pursuing require presentation skills.[50]

It vividly presents your collegiate background. Infographic resumes are colorful, high-resolution documents. Unlike your LinkedIn profile (which is an online template) and your resume (which has expected and accepted sections), an infographic resume is a

---

47 Pamela Skillings. "The Ultimate Infographic Resume Guide." *Big Interview.* June 18, 2013. http://biginterview.com/blog/2013/06/infographic-resumes.html (accessed February 17, 2016).

48 Ibid.

49 See also, ibid.

50 Ibid.

blank canvas. It is a platform to creatively present your college experiences any way you choose, using color and graphics.

Although the advantages of an infographic resume are attractive, there are considerations that may turn into a disadvantage if not handled properly:

How will it be received by hiring executives? This is a serious consideration. An infographic resume is a neat idea and can be very intriguing. It can open your mind to all sorts of creative thoughts on how to present your information. This is especially true once you start viewing examples. However, it may not be the best strategy for every industry or an entry level position.[51]

It must contain impactful information. If an infographic resume is not persuasive or is poorly constructed, it will hurt your job search. It can be a distraction, reflect negatively on your candidacy for the job, or eliminate you as a contender for the position.

It must look great! Not just good. Your final product must have a "holy cow this is really cool" factor. Otherwise, it will not have the persuasive and differentiating effect you are looking for. One interesting concept you could explore is creating an "infographic" section to your traditional resume. This would be a form of a showcase resume using color and graphics as your showcase section. Then, resume information would follow in the usual style.[52]

A Few Final Thoughts about Infographic Resumes

It is highly recommended that you speak to professionals who create these documents. Seek their opinion as to whether you have the caliber of college credentials and activities to have an impactful infographic resume (with the understanding that they will have the incentive to persuade you to buy their services). Since creating the document on your own can take countless hours, explore the costs and hire a professional to do it for you. The time required to create an infographic resume is better spent pursuing other job-search activities.

If you create an infographic resume (or have one created for you), get it out there! One easy thing to do is attach it to your LinkedIn profile. Obviously you want to have it to hand out during networking events, career fairs, and as a supplement to interviews. Since you put the time, effort, thought, and money into this tactic, look for ways to leverage it in your job-search activities.

---

51 Ibid.

52 See also, ibid.

Caution: Creating an infographic resume can be a distraction or become busywork stopping you from moving your job search forward. Be aware of your time and use it wisely. An infographic resume is a differentiator, but it will not get you a job all by itself.

Discovering examples of infographic resumes and professionals (vendors) who create them is as simple as conducting a Google search for "infographic resumes."

What the Coaches Say:

When or under what circumstances would you recommend the use of an infographic resume for a recent college graduate?

Infographics are situational and depend on the position the candidate is targeting as well as having pertinent information to fill an infographic. Infographics work well independent of a traditional resume as well as in addition to a traditional resume. Some candidates use the infographic as an introduction to who they are as they convey bite-sized elements of information in an easy-to-retain snapshot. Studies show that strong visual messaging has a much higher retention rate, recall, and comprehension than use of words alone. For this reason, when authors write books, or resume writers write traditional resumes, we are using descriptive words to paint an image in the reader's brain. The reason this is so is to retain, recall, and enhance comprehension.

Tina Kashlak Nicolai, PHR, CPBA, CARW

I would recommend it for someone in product marketing, advertising, and other fields that require artistic creativity. The infographic resume becomes not only information about student's qualifications, but also a sample of their work.

Lorraine Beaman, MA, ACRW, CARW, NCRW, CEIC, MCD

Creating Your Own Resume

To grow, you must be willing to let your present and future be totally unlike your past. Your history is not your destiny.

— Alan Cohen[53]

Although an employer reads a resume for content, they also draw conclusions based on its appearance. If you are comfortable with your word-processing skills, create your own resume. Spend the appropriate amount of time building an impactful resume, but don't grind over its creation. Normally four to eight hours of concentrated effort on a resume should suffice, if you do it yourself. Any more than that may be busywork disguised as being productive. Don't make this mistake. You have other important things to do! Once your resume is satisfactorily written, move on to other important tasks that can move your job search forward.

53 "Self-Limiting Beliefs." *Quotes from the Masters.* http://finsecurity.com/finsecurity/quotes/qm103.html (accessed May 28, 2015).

What the Coaches Say:

When you begin composing a resume (blank computer screen), what thoughts or writing philosophies are in your mind?

I strive for a balanced approach weaving together facts with personal branding. I set out to create a marketing tool featuring my clients top differentiators, much like a marketing person creates a marketing campaign for a product. I create everything from the key messaging points to the label of the (product) client. A comprehensive plan works best; including both traditional approach and online presence.

Tina Kashlak Nicolai, PHR, CPBA, CARW

Before I ever sit down at the keyboard to write a resume, I ask several questions and do not start writing until I have the answers. What is the graduate's career goal? What in his/her academic, life, and work experience will showcase his/her qualifications for the job/career he/she is seeking? How do I create a powerful document that sends a clear message to the prospective employer who needs to interview this candidate?

Lorraine Beaman, MA, ACRW, CARW, NCRW, CEIC, MCD

If you are uneasy about creating your resume, seek out a resume-writing service. It is recommended to find a resume writer who is certified by a resume credentialing organization:

- **CPRW** (Certified Professional Resume Writer), designation sanctioned by the Professional Association of Resume Writers (www.parw.com).

- **NCRW** (Nationally Certified Resume Writer), designation sanctioned by The National Resume Writer's Association (www.thenrwa.com).

- **CARW** (Certified Advanced Resume Writer) and **CMRW** (Certified Master Resume Writer), designations provided by Career Directors International (www.careerdirectors.com). They also have awards for resume writers.

Websites for these organizations provide a listing of resume writers by location. Designations of some kind (there are others) offer some assurance that the writer has the prerequisite level of expertise to create a resume to your satisfaction. There are other talented resume writers who do not have a designation. Simply ask to see samples.

A well-written, professionally prepared resume is one of the best investments you or your parents can make in getting you off to a good start in your job search. However, it will not get you a job. It can only help you get noticed, help you get an interview, and then operate as a guide for hiring executives to ask questions during an interview. Don't underemphasize or overemphasize its role.

Too many job seekers (collegiate or otherwise) erroneously believe that a "great" resume is the ticket to a great job. It's not! A resume is a tool, one of several.

Resume Checklist

When your resume is complete, put it through this final checklist.

Item	Comments	Check off
Name	The name you go by is on your resume	◯
Contact Information	Is your telephone number and email address correct?	◯
Title	Does your resume announce who you are as a professional?	◯
Branding	A statement of your distinct talents, professional qualities, traits	◯
Summary	If you use a Summary, is it an accurate description.	◯
Education	Major, Minors, GPA (if 3.0+), scholarships, activities, date of (anticipated) graduation	◯
Employment	Accurate dates, duties, responsibilities, accomplishments	◯
Font-Consistency	Consistent use of font size, bolding, italics	◯
Over-used emphasis	Not too much bolding, italics, shading, etc.	◯
Amount of information	Not too much or too little	◯
Length	One, maybe two pages, for most graduates	◯
Spell checked	May not pick up all errors	◯

Item	Comments	Check off
Connection	Does the content generally support branding words or phrases?	◯
Format	Uniform and consistent.	◯
No prohibited information	No personal or discriminatory information	◯
Appearance	Appealing, easy on the eyes, enough white space	◯
Final assessment	Do you feel good about it? Does it have the wow factor you want?	◯

There are sample resumes provided by experienced and credentialed resume writers later in this book. They are the very same resume writers who have been providing you advice.

Chapter 4

LinkedIn

Active participation on LinkedIn is the best way to say,
'Look at me!' without saying 'Look at me!'
— Bobby Darnell[54]

Please Note: LinkedIn changes its format, features, appearance, and functionality regularly. These changes enhance the LinkedIn experience as well as restrict some of its functionality. Some of the functional instructions could be different due to these changes and influenced by the level and kind of the LinkedIn account of the user.

This topic on LinkedIn was as current as possible at the time of writing.

LinkedIn is the most used and effective professional networking website on the planet,

---

54 Jerome Knyszweski. "How to Use LinkedIn as a Student—And Nail That Dream Job." *LinkedIn Pulse*. April 28, 2015. https://www.linkedin.com/pulse/how-use-linkedin-student-nail-dream-job-jerome-knyszewski (accessed May 28, 2015).

with more than 500 million members in two hundred countries and growing.[55] In the United States alone there are more than 128 million members. At present, LinkedIn adds "more than two new members every second."[56] "Over 25 million profiles are viewed on LinkedIn daily."[57]

In today's job market, it is imperative to your job search to have a complete and robust LinkedIn profile. LinkedIn is the overwhelming resource (87 percent) most frequently used by HR recruiters to identify and evaluate candidates.[58] By having a complete and robust LinkedIn profile, you significantly increase your chances of being contacted by an HR talent acquisition recruiter. In fact, "Users with complete profiles are 40 times more likely to receive opportunities through LinkedIn."[59]

Having a complete LinkedIn profile is **imperative** to your job search.

What makes your profile complete? Generally speaking, your profile is "complete" when it has the following:

- Your location and industry (of interest)
- A current position (we will discuss a technique to address this)
- Two past positions (summer jobs, internships)
- Your education
- Your skills (minimum of three)
- A profile photo
- At least fifty connections[60]

55 Smith, Craig. "133 Amazing LinkedIn Statistics." Last updated November 17, 2016. http://expandedramblings.com/index.php/by-the-numbers-a-few-important-linkedin-stats/. See also, Smith, Craig, DMR, "200+ Amazing LinkedIn Stats," Last Checked/Updated October 2016, http://expandedramblings.com/index.php/by-the-numbers-a-few-important-linkedin-stats/. Downloaded November 28, 2016).

56 "About LinkedIn." *LinkedIn Newsroom.* https://press.linkedin.com/about-linkedin (accessed May 29, 2015).

57 Dexcreumaux, Geoff. "Top LinkedIn Facts and Stats [Infographic]." *We Are Social Media.* July 25, 2014. http://wersm.com/top-linkedin-facts-and-stats-infographic/ (accessed May 29, 2015).

58 Ibid. See also, Craig Smith, DMR, "200+ Amazing LinkedIn Stats," Last Updated October 2016, http://expandedramblings.com/index.php/by-the-numbers-a-few-important-linkedin-stats/. This source indicates that 94% of recruiters use LinkedIn to vet candidates.

59 Foote, Andy. "Why You Should Complete Your LinkedIn Profile." LinkedInsights.com. December 7, 2015. https://www.linkedinsights.com/why-you-should-complete-your-linkedin-profile/ (accessed November 22, 2016).

60 Ibid.

If your profile is incomplete, it won't register as high in searches as those that are more robust.[61] It cannot be overemphasized. LinkedIn should be your primary online professional networking and job-search tool.

In many cases, your LinkedIn profile could be the first impression a talent acquisition professional has of you. A strong profile is a must. It projects professionalism and gives you credibility even as a recent college graduate.

Before we begin discussions on specific LinkedIn topics, and if you already have a profile, it is recommended that you turn off the network notification function of your profile until you have completed making all changes to your profile. Here's how: Go to your Profile page. Click on the "Me" icon at the top and from the drop down, select "Settings and Privacy."

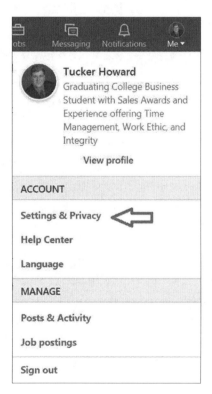

Then, select the Privacy option.

61 Reynolds, Marci. "How to Be Found More Easily in LinkedIn (LinkedIn SEO)." *Job-Hunt.org*. http://www. job-hunt.org/social-networking/be-found-on-linkedin.shtml (accessed June 4, 2015).

Scroll down and click on the "Sharing Profile Edits." Slide the toggle to No.

By doing this, your network (regardless of its size) will not be alerted regarding changes you may be making. You can reactivate the announcements later if you choose.

Use of Keywords

It is estimated that there are more than a billion searches annually on LinkedIn.[62] Companies and recruiters search on LinkedIn by keywords to find candidates.

Let's take a quick review of keywords. As you know, keywords are specific words or phrases that reflect your education, experiences, abilities, interests and are frequently buzzwords, or terms-of-art that are applicable to you professionally. Like your resume, your profile must contain certain keywords to get attention and communicate that you are qualified for a particular position.

Keywords can include the following:

• Position title you are interested in or qualified for

• Education (school name, degrees, G.P.A.)

• Character traits, qualities

• Professional designation you may be pursuing

• Skills, knowledge, competencies

• Industry terms-of-art (and abbreviations)

• Licenses, certifications (if any)

---

62 Frasco, Stephanie. "11 Tips To Help Optimize Your LinkedIn Profile For Maximum Exposure and Engagement." *Convert with Content.* https://www.convertwithcontent.com/11-tips-optimize-linkedin-profile-maximum-exposure-engagement/ (accessed June 10, 2015).

• Location (state, city)

• Software and technologies you're familiar with

We will have an extended discussion later in this chapter about the use of keywords when we talk about optimization of your LinkedIn profile.

What the Coaches Say:

What is your advice and strategy regarding the use and location of keywords in a LinkedIn profile?

Placing keywords in these five areas (listed in order of importance) will help optimize your LinkedIn profile: Headline, Summary, Most recent job experience, Skills, and Status updates.

Paula Christensen, CPRW, CCMC, CJSS

LinkedIn algorithms use keyword density (frequency) to rank search results. This means that the most important keywords should be used multiple times throughout the profile, including headline, summary, job descriptions, skills, and course list.

Mary Jo King, NCRW

Your LinkedIn Profile - Sections

Before we begin our discussion on building an impactful profile ("optimization"), let's briefly introduce the major components of your profile.

1. Photo

Your photo is important.[63] It shows that you are a real person. Since LinkedIn has a professional focus—and you are looking for a job—it is recommended to have a photo taken at a studio by a professional or, at a minimum, a close-up photograph of you professionally dressed. Some college career centers offer taking LinkedIn profile photos are part of their services. According to experts, "profiles with a photo are fourteen times more likely to be viewed."[64] Moreover, having a photo makes you thirty-six times more likely to receive a message on LinkedIn.[65]

Here are some Do's and Don'ts when it comes to your LinkedIn photo. Many of these have been cited in a study by PhotoFeeler[66], while others should be common sense considering that LinkedIn is a professional networking site.

Do:

Be professionally dressed

The photo should be of your head and shoulders

Look directly into the camera. Make eye contact

Smile

Don't:

No sunglasses (clear eyeglasses are fine)

No party pictures

No shopping mall glamour shots

---

63 "Jobvite Recruiter Nation Report." *Jobvite.* 2016. http://www.jobvite.com/wp-content/uploads/2016/09/RecruiterNation2016.pdf (Accessed March 15, 2017).(41% of recruiters believe that seeing a picture of a candidate before meeting them influences their first impression)

64 Smith, Jacquelyn. "The Complete Guide To Crafting A Perfect LinkedIn Profile." *Business Insider.* January 21, 2015. http://www.businessinsider.com/guide-to-perfect-linkedin-profile-2015-1 (accessed June 4, 2015).

65 Smith, Craig. DMR, "200+ Amazing LinkedIn Stats." Last Updated October 2016. http://expandedramblings.com/index.php/by-the-numbers-a-few-important-linkedin-stats/ (Downloaded November 28, 2016).

66 "New Research Study Breaks Down The Perfect Profile Photo. *PhotoFeeler.* May 13, 2014. https://blog.photofeeler.com/perfect-photo/ (accessed November 7, 2016).

It is highly recommended that your LinkedIn profile photo be professionally taken.

2. Name

Use the name you commonly go by. If your given name is Richard, but you go by Rich, use Rich. It is permissible to put both your given name and the name you use in quotation marks or in parentheses. If you have a common name, you may want to add your middle initial.

What the Coaches Say:

What is your opinion about the name the graduate should use on their LinkedIn profile? Should they use their birth name, the name they go by, or their birth name with the name they go by in quotation marks?

Use the name you wish to be called in a professional setting. Using your formal name comes off as a bit stiff. Above all, be consistent. Use the same name for your personal webpage, LinkedIn profile, and your resume. Make yourself easily searchable and discoverable for hiring managers.

There is some research that suggests you should place your middle initial on your resume, that James T. Clark seems smarter then James Clark. Psychologists Wijnand A.P. Van Tilburg of the University of Southampton and Eric R. Igou of the University of Limerick studied the use of middle initials in documents. They concluded, "The display of middle initials increases the perceived social status of these people and (it) positively biases inferences about their intellectual capacity and performance." http://www.businessinsider.com/middle-initials-make-you-look-smarter-2014-5

Paula Christensen, CPRW, CCMC, CJSS

Use the name that you go by. There is no reason to list your formal birth name unless you use it in business. Don't send people down a rabbit hole trying to determine you are who you say you are. Make it easy. If you use Susie Smith, then list Susie Smith. Don't use Suzanne Maria Smith. Additionally, if you use P.J. Jones but your birth name is Robert George Jones, III, use P.J. Jones on your LinkedIn profile.

Tina Kashlak Nicolai, PHR, CPBA, CARW

3. Headline

Under your name is your Headline area. It is the first thing someone reads about you.

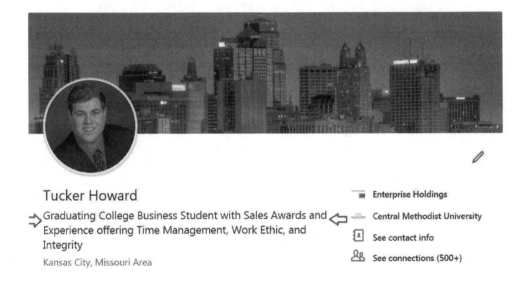

You have 120 character spaces in your headline. Make it impactful (which will increase the number of views you receive) by describing yourself with keywords or short phrases that best describe you. "What do you want to be known for?"[67] Or found for? Avoid superlatives or flamboyant adjectives in your headline (E.g. World's Best College Graduate).

The headline ultimately attracts viewers with the intention that they continue to read your profile and be impressed with your education, internships, experience, campus activities, skills, and accomplishments. When we discuss optimization, we will delve much deeper into the strategic use of your headline.

---

67 Whitcomb, *Job Search Magic*, p. 68.

What the Coaches Say:

How do you view the Headline section (the section immediately below the name)? What is your advice to create an impactful Headline for a recent college graduate?

There is space for 120 characters in the headline. This is valuable real estate, heavily weighted in LinkedIn search algorithms. Pack this space with keywords that people will use to find someone who does what you do. Use as much of the allocated space as possible, and begin branding yourself:

Student-Focused Leadership in Learning Delivery ▶ Instructional Design, Content Development and Program Management

Customer Service Excellence ▶ Dedicated to Improving Process, Conquering Challenges, and Delivering on Commitments

The Passionate Data Analyst – Specialist in JMP Data Analysis Software, Product Formulation, and Numerical Storytelling

Dedicated Accountant and CPA Candidate | Accurate Full Cycle Accounting, Payroll, Taxes, and Financial Analysis

Creative Brand Development ▶ Strategic Planning & Implementation in B2B & B2C Marketing for Emerging Media

Mary Jo King, NCRW

There are two schools of thought.

1. Load your headline with keywords for your target industry. These are mainly nouns that a recruiter would use to search for candidates. You can find these keywords by searching job postings, exploring O*NET https://www.onetonline.org/, and researching LinkedIn profiles of individuals who hold your targeted position.

> Aspiring Sales Representative, Enterprise & Consultative Sales, Motivated Relationship Builder, Negotiator, and Trainer
>
> 2. If you decide not to take the keyword approach to your headline, another idea is to craft an engaging tag line that explains how you're different and what you aspire to be.
>
> Manager Trainee with Multiple Sales Awards Offering Leadership, Customer Service, Negotiation Skills and Work Ethic
>
> Paula Christensen, CPRW, CCMC, CJSS

4. Location and Industry

The Location section appears below your Headline.

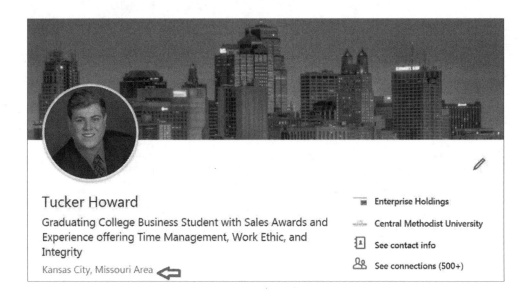

Tucker Howard
Graduating College Business Student with Sales Awards and Experience offering Time Management, Work Ethic, and Integrity
Kansas City, Missouri Area ⇐

Enterprise Holdings
Central Methodist University
See contact info
See connections (500+)

LinkedIn lists every significant metropolitan city in the country (more than 280 geographical location phrases at last count). Your location (or one very close) is likely listed.

It is important to put an accurate metropolitan city location on your profile. When employers and recruiters conduct searches, they often look for profiles of individuals who live in a particular city or region. Listing no location or a generic "United States" makes you almost invisible to employers and recruiters who may be looking for a recent college graduate located in your metropolitan area or region.

When selecting a city, use a major metropolitan area instead of a suburb. This increases your odds that a HR recruiter will find you.

Choose an industry that interests you. LinkedIn lists 145 industry phrases (at last count), so choose the one that best fits your interests. Your industry specialty is only viewable to HR recruiters that use advanced platforms of LinkedIn. When employers and recruiters conduct searches, they may look for profiles that identify particular industries.

Including an industry on your profile has the potential to get you fifteen times the amount of views than those who do not list an industry.[68]

To access your Location and Industry, click "ME" at the top of the LinkedIn page. From the drop down, select Settings and Privacy. Then click Account. Scroll down and select Name, Location, and Industry.

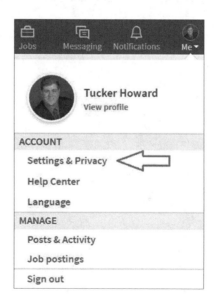

---

68 "10 Tips for the Perfect LinkedIn Profile." *LinkHumans, Slideshare.* Published July 1, 2014. http://www. slideshare.net/linkedin/10-tips-for-the-perfect-linkedin-profile. (accessed November 11, 2015).

5. Contact and Personal Information

LinkedIn allows you to provide contact information. Your Contact and Personal Information is located down the right side of your profile. It looks like this:

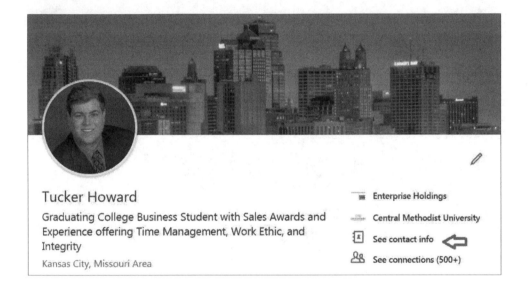

Click "See contact info" and you're in. This is a good place to put your personal email address and your cell phone number. Make it as easy as possible to be contacted.

6. Summary Section

The Summary section is an area where you can write a narrative of your education, internships, campus activities, background, experience, achievements, and use of character traits. To edit or create a Summary, click on the pencil icon in the upper right hand corner of your profile.

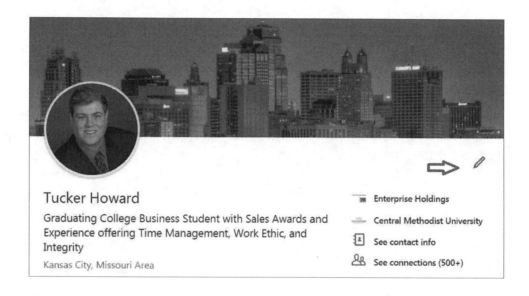

Tucker Howard

Graduating College Business Student with Sales Awards and Experience offering Time Management, Work Ethic, and Integrity

Kansas City, Missouri Area

Enterprise Holdings

Central Methodist University

See contact info

See connections (500+)

Your Summary section has a significant impact on optimizing your LinkedIn profile and will be discussed at length in the pages that follow.

What the Coaches Say:

What advice or what strategy would you recommend when writing the Summary section for a recent college graduate's LinkedIn profile? And, how does it differ from the Summary section of a resume?

LinkedIn summary sections are different than resume summaries. They should be engaging and tell a story. They still need to be professional, include results and keywords but it's also acceptable to add some professional stories and a bit more background. Profiles also have a warmer feel because they are written from the first-person point of view. Here are some questions you can use to ensure your LinkedIn profile is engaging:

What drew you to your field?

Are there parts of your personality that make you perfect for your job/field of study?

What are your three biggest natural talents/strengths?

Are there times when a mentor, teacher, or coach influenced you? How did that contribute to your career path?

Finish this sentence. People are drawn to me because I am _____.

Another tip: Complete a free questionnaire from the University of Pennsylvania helping you identify your character strengths. Use these strengths and descriptors to weave into sections of your profile, resume, and cover letter.

https://www.authentichappiness.sas.upenn.edu/questionnaires/survey-character-strengths. The questionnaire identifies character strengths which help tell your impactful story.

Paula Christensen, CPRW, CCMC, CJSS

Try to engage the reader with a dynamic summary. Write your summary in first person, be professional, and give a little more personal touch . . . Why are you good at what you do, why did you pick that major, and what are you looking forward to accomplishing in your career? All personal things appropriate to add to the summary on LinkedIn.

Ellen Steverson, NCRW, GCDF, CEIC

7. Experience

This is reasonably straightforward. Think resume and include internships. Use relevant keywords. Remember that your LinkedIn profile and your resume must match in general content. According to LinkedIn, "add[ing] your two most recent work positions . . . can increase your profile views by twelve times."[69] Strategic use of the Experience section will be discussed with optimization.

69 Ayele, Daniel. "Land Your Dream Job in 2015 with These Data-Proven LinkedIn Tips." *LinkedIn Blog.* January 29, 2015. http://blog.linkedin.com/2015/01/29/jobseeking-tips/ (accessed June 9, 2015).

8. Education

Your education should align directly with your resume, including use of G.P.A. Review the Education section of the Impactful Resumes portion of this book. LinkedIn users "who have an education on their profile receive an average of ten times more profile views than those who don't."[70]

Additional sections of your profile. LinkedIn has additional sections to further customize your profile. Depending on the HR recruiter or hiring executive, these areas may have an impact on their impression of you. To find these additional sections on your profile, look for a large blue box containing "Add profile section" that should appear below your Headline and Location.

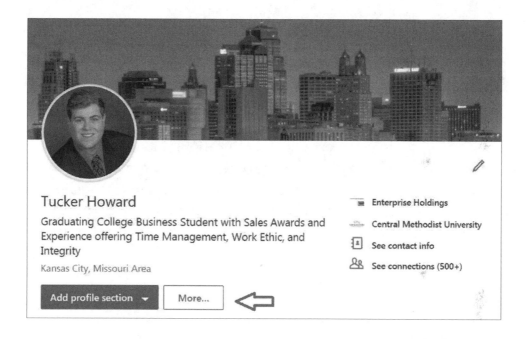

Tucker Howard

Graduating College Business Student with Sales Awards and Experience offering Time Management, Work Ethic, and Integrity

Kansas City, Missouri Area

Add profile section ▾   More...

Enterprise Holdings
Central Methodist University
See contact info
See connections (500+)

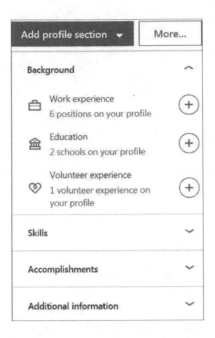

Click it and you will see an option regarding Background which will allow you to add information regarding your work experience, education, and volunteer experience. You will also see an option to add Skills. The next option is Accomplishments. This will give you a drop down list that includes publications, certifications, courses, projects, honors and awards, patents, test scores, languages, and organizations. We'll discuss some of these additional sections in a moment. The last option is Additional information which will allow you to ask for a recommendation.

9. Volunteer Experience

Many employers look favorably upon profiles of those who volunteer or are involved in civic causes—it speaks to matching the culture of the company. "In fact, according to LinkedIn, 42 percent of hiring managers surveyed said they view volunteer experience equal to formal work experience."[71] If you have volunteer experience in college, list it here.

10. Skills (and Endorsements)

LinkedIn allows you to list fifty skills. As a recent college graduate, you will list only a specific few. Think through your internships and summer jobs. List the skills you used. Try

71 Dougherty, Lisa. "16 Tips to Optimize Your LinkedIn Profile and Your Personal Brand." *LinkedIn Pulse*. July 8, 2014. https://www.linkedin.com/pulse/20140708162049-7239647-16-tips-to-optimize-your-linkedin-profile-and-enhance-your-personal-brand (accessed November 11, 2015).

to list five, but no more than ten skills. According to LinkedIn, listing five or more skills in your profile will get you up to seventeen times more profile views.[72]

Endorsements are a nice LinkedIn feature. They add credibility and a compelling nature to your profile as others agree with the skills you have listed (they can add others). Once you have listed your skills, reach out to your friends that you are connected to, as well as other networking connection and ask for endorsements of your listed skills.

Endorse others. Remember, LinkedIn is a networking mechanism and a two-way street.

11. Honors and Awards

List all notable honors and awards you have received, signaling to an employer that others have recognized you for your leadership, performance, scholastic achievement, and so on.

12. Organizations

Listing your memberships in collegiate professional associations can have an influence on employers because it reflects that you have a serious interest in the industry.[73]

13. Ask for Recommendations

Remember that having others say good things about you is better than you promoting yourself.[74] Recommendations are mini testimonials that people give you who know you or have worked with you. You can request them via LinkedIn. It's another way to build credibility.

Many talent acquisition professionals review recommendations as part of their evaluation protocols. As a minimum goal, get at least three recommendations posted on your profile from former bosses from summer jobs and internships, colleagues, professors, and so on.

14. Groups

LinkedIn groups are valuable for your job search. They help you get plugged in and give you insight and knowledge. "Your profile is five times more likely to be viewed if you join and are active in groups.[75]

---

72 Smith, Craig. DMR, "200+ Amazing LinkedIn Stats." Last Updated October 2016. http://expandedramblings.com/index.php/by-the-numbers-a-few-important-linkedin-stats/ (Downloaded November 28, 2016).s

73 Yate, *Knock 'em Dead*, p. 86.

74 Matt, "Brag Book."

75 LinkHumans, "10 Tips."

HR talent acquisition professionals and hiring executives search LinkedIn, and they also interact in LinkedIn groups.[76] With more than two million groups on LinkedIn,[77] there is no reason not to join a group relevant to your industry of interest or location. Eighty-one percent of users surveyed were in at least one LinkedIn group,[78] meaning hiring executives and recruiters—maybe even the one who will give you your first job—are likely already members of, and might even be active in, a LinkedIn group. In a survey of LinkedIn users who found a job within three months of focused searching, 82 percent interacted with a group on LinkedIn.[79]

LinkedIn allows you to join 100 groups, but only join those pertinent to your interests, background, and location. Determine a group's membership—larger ones offer more exposure. You will need to request membership to join a group.

To explore possible Groups to join, click the Work icon at the top of your profile.

From the drop-down options, select Groups.

76 Pollak, Lindsey. "How to Attract Employers' Attention on LinkedIn." *LinkedIn Blog*. December 2, 2010. http://blog.linkedin.com/2010/12/02/find-jobs-on-linkedin/ (accessed June 4, 2015).

77 Arruda, William. "Is LinkedIn Poised To Be The Next Media Giant?" *Forbes*. March 8, 2015. http://www.forbes.com/sites/williamarruda/2015/03/08/is-linkedin-poised-to-be-the-next-media-giant/ (accessed June 5, 2015).

78 Vaughan, Pamela. "81% of LinkedIn Users Belong to a LinkedIn Group [Data]." *Hubspot Blogs*. August 11, 2011. http://blog.hubspot.com/blog/tabid/6307/bid/22364/81-of-LinkedIn-Users-Belong-to-a-LinkedIn-Group-Data.aspx (accessed June 8, 2015).

79 Oswal, Shreva. "7 Smart Habits of Successful Job Seekers [INFOGRAPHIC]." *LinkedIn Blog*. March 19, 2014. http://blog.linkedin.com/2014/03/19/7-smart-habits-of-successful-job-seekers-infographic/ (accessed June 9, 2015).

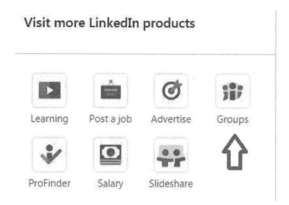

Then click the Discover option. LinkedIn may provide some possible groups of interest to you.

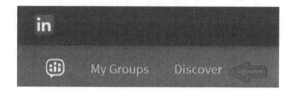

Once you join a group, it is much easier to relate to people. You have something in common. Common ground is a good thing when starting a networking communication.

15. Other Enhancements

You can also use a variety of media to showcase your skills (video presentations including Slideshare, pictures or screenshots, and text documents). These are optional and not required to get you found by an HR talent acquisition recruiter. However, they can add credibility to your candidacy. Upload a video if you did public speaking. If you're skilled in graphic design, showcase your portfolio. Consider adding anything unique or impactful to prove and reinforce your ability, experience, or achievements.

★ **Introducing LinkedIn Optimization**

Optimization is taking full advantage of how the LinkedIn algorithms and programming work to be discovered for your first job. It means effective use of your keywords, putting those keywords in the correct areas of your profile, proper use of repeating those keywords, profile completeness, adequate number of connections, and making your profile compelling.

All of these elements, pulled together, optimize your LinkedIn profile for maximum effectiveness. An optimized LinkedIn profile makes you more discoverable and more desirable when a talent acquisition professional uses LinkedIn to find a college graduate. Since 87 percent of HR recruiters use LinkedIn to identify and recruit candidates[80], having an "optimized" LinkedIn profile could help significantly in your job search.

How Does It Work . . . How Does an HR Recruiter Use LinkedIn to Find Candidates?

There are numerous ways an HR recruiter can use LinkedIn to locate recent college graduates. To illustrate one method, go to your LinkedIn home page or profile. Along the top next to the LinkedIn logo is a Search box with a spyglass.

Put the following words in that space just as written: insurance AND sales. Click the spyglass. Your results will be thousands of profiles appearing on the page (and potentially a couple of job openings). The example terms used were overly broad but it gives you a concept of how a talent acquisition professional uses LinkedIn by refining search terms (keywords) to identify candidates. The purpose of this section is to teach you how to optimize your LinkedIn profile so you are one of those top candidates!

The Goal of Optimization

Now that you have a general understanding of the functionality of the LinkedIn algorithms and programming, you need to know what you are striving for by optimizing your LinkedIn profile. Your goal, in descending order is: (1) to be listed (ranked) as the number one profile on the first page (the ultimate achievement), (2) to be on the first page, or (3) to be on the first three pages.

These goals can be achieved, provided you have adequate information and you follow the instructions for optimization. Depending upon your circumstances, you may need to evaluate your ranking by limiting it to cities that you are interested in living.

The components for optimizing your LinkedIn profile are:

---

80 *Jobvite 2016 Recruiter National Survey* www.jobvite.com (accessed February 4, 2017).

1. **Keywords**—where they appear on your profile and proper repetition.

2. **Completeness**—having enough information to register as "complete" according to LinkedIn.

3. **Connections**—being connected to other professionals and being a member of LinkedIn groups.

4. **Compelling**—intellectually or emotionally moving the employer to contact you.

Keyword Location

Where your keywords appear on your profile does matter. The sections listed below are the primary areas where the algorithms and programming look to match keywords:

1. Headline
2. Summary
3. Job Title
4. Experience/employment descriptions
5. Skills

There are advanced platforms that employers can purchase from LinkedIn that could expand this list, but these are the primary sections where the algorithms and programming match keywords.

Headline

You have one hundred twenty character spaces available to you in your headline, which is actually a lot of room. Since we know that this is a section where the algorithms and programming goes to match keywords, make sure they appear here.

The headline section provides an excellent opportunity for you to create a branding statement describing yourself. What do you want to be known for or found for?[81]

Here's a convenient formula that works well for many recent college graduates:

Recent College Graduate + [A bridge phrase or action verb (e.g. "with summer job experience in" or "utilizing")] + [Keywords, including transferable skills and professional character traits]

---

81 Whitcomb, Susan Britton. *Job Search Magic: Insider Secrets from America's Career and Life Coach.* Indianapolis, IN: JIST Works, 2006. p. 68.

For example:

> Recent College Graduate with dual degrees in Marketing, Advertising offering experience from internships, Ambitious

> Graduating College Business Student with Sales Awards and Experience offering Time Management, Work Ethic, and Integrity

Summary

You have 2,000 character spaces available to you for your summary,[82] which is a ton of room. Do not get "long winded" when writing your summary. Your summary is just that . . . a summary of your college experiences, not an autobiography. Think about the summary of your resume. Expand it using your best judgement.

An effective technique is to start your summary by restating your headline, word-for-word, and then expanding upon it to include other keywords that would not fit or were of secondary importance in your headline (perhaps more of your soft skills).

Remember, LinkedIn is looking to match keywords *and* tracking the number of times they appear when ranking you against other similar profiles. By restating your headline you create an introductory statement (banner) running along the top of your summary. The HR recruiter does not think twice about it but you have taken advantage of the programming by stating keywords twice between your headline and your introductory banner statement in your summary.

After your introductory banner statement, write one to three paragraphs that summarize your college experience. This will likely include reference to your education, college activities, duties and responsibilities from internships and summer jobs, and keywords (college achievements are handled separately, read on). As you write, be aware that this paragraph(s) must read smoothly. A good approach is to write the paragraph(s) then insert keywords as appropriate. It's also a good technique to write your summary paragraph(s)—and other sections—in a Word document and then copy and paste it into the appropriate section. This will catch grammar errors and misspellings. This is important. A survey conducted by Jobvite indicated that 72 percent of HR recruiters view typos negatively on social media.[83]

---

82 Foote, Andy. "Maximum LinkedIn Character Counts for 2016." December 10, 2016. https://www.linkedin.com/pulse/maximum-linkedin-character-counts-2016-andy-foote. (Accessed November 22, 2016).

83 "Jobvite Recruiter Nation Report." *Jobvite.* 2016. http://www.jobvite.com/wp-content/uploads/2016/09/RecruiterNation2016.pdf (Accessed March 15, 2017).

The next component of your Summary, following your college summary paragraphs, is your college accomplishments. These are your achievements you are most proud of. Start with "College Accomplishments Include:" and then list your top three or four. If you are not sure whether to include a particular achievement, hedge toward not including it. You want these achievements to be your best ones.

This discussion on accomplishments fits directly into one of the tenets for optimizing your LinkedIn profile—Compelling. The concept of "compelling" will be woven throughout the rest of this discussion as we address other topics and strategies.

Once you have your accomplishments listed in your Summary section, either use the programming on your computer or go to the Internet and copy and paste an icon and place it in front of each of your accomplishments. When choosing an icon, choose something dark, like a bullet-point • a black diamond ◆ or black pennant ▶. These dark icons draw the eye of the HR recruiters and highlight, in their minds, your achievements. Whatever icon you select, use it consistently throughout your profile. Using different icons makes your profile look jumbled or gaudy. Below is an example of this approach:

Graduating College Business Student with Sales Awards and Experience offering Time Management, Work Ethic, and Integrity—Exploring Sales and Business Opportunities.

Professional Qualities Include:

Time Management Skills—Balancing academics with college athletics.

Work Ethic—Once assigned a task, I pursue it fully and with the best of my ability.

Curiosity—I will ask questions.

Honesty and Integrity—These qualities are ingrained into my value system. I spent two summers counseling and working with youths at Christian camps (Kanakuk Kamps and Sky Ranch).

Sales Successes Include:

I have successful sales experience with Enterprise Rent-A-Car (summer internship) and Waterway Gas and Wash (summer job). I was locally and regionally ranked for my sales results:

▶ Enterprise — Awarded 3rd place college intern scholarship program (Out of 11 interns locally)

▶ Enterprise — Achieved Platinum Club as an intern — July, 20XX (#3 sales representative out of 185 sales representatives regionally)

▶ Waterway Gas and Wash — #1 Monthly Sales Consultant in the Metropolitan Market multiple times.

▶ Waterway Gas and Wash — #1 Monthly Sales Consultant Regionally (Kansas City, Denver, Cleveland, and St Louis markets) multiple times.

youremail address@gmail.com
(123) 456-7890

Finally, at the end of your summary, provide your personal email address and cell phone number. This is a good strategy because people that are not connected to you cannot see your Contact and Personal Information.[84] You want to make it as easy as possible for an HR recruiter to contact you and providing this information at the end of your Summary makes it easy to do so.

Job Title (and Company Name)

We are now in the Background section of your LinkedIn profile. LinkedIn provides 100 character spaces for your title.[85] We know that your job title and job description is where LinkedIn looks for matching keywords. But, how can you leverage the LinkedIn programming since you currently do not have a professional-level job? Easy. Your "job search" is going to be your current job.

For a title, you are going to modify what you created for your headline. You have 100 character spaces so you can be creative. Some examples:

Recent College Graduate with dual degrees in Marketing, Advertising Seeking First Professional Level Job

---

84 Pearcemarch, Kyle. "SEO for LinkedIn: How to Optimize Your LinkedIn Profile for Search." *DIYGenius.* March 19, 2015. https://www.diygenius.com/how-to-optimize-your-linkedin-profile-for-search/. (Accessed November 22, 2016).

85 Foote, Andy. "Maximum LinkedIn Character Counts for 2016." December 10, 2016. https://www.linkedin.com/pulse/maximum-linkedin-character-counts-2016-andy-foote. (Accessed November 22, 2016).

Graduating College Accounting Student with Intern Experience Seeking Entry-Level Accounting Role

For your employer (company name), you also have 100 character spaces, but you likely will not use all of them. Here are some options:

Exploring First Career-Level Job in Sales

Seeking a Position with an Accounting Firm

Transitioning from College to the Field of Engineering

Position Description

Your position description provides for more creativity. A unique and effective approach is to write a short cover letter in this area. You have 2,000 character spaces. By its nature, your position description / cover letter will be generic. But this approach gives you the opportunity to speak to the talent acquisition professional and provide information they would not otherwise know. Read the Effective Written Communications chapter of this book for additional instructions on this technique.

When you are done writing this "letter," have someone from your career placement office review it. Make adjustments as recommended.

Skills

List your keywords as skills. Think through your internships and summer jobs and list the skills you used. Although LinkedIn allows for fifty skills, as a recent college graduate, you will list far fewer—five and certainly no more than ten. Just so you know, and according to LinkedIn, the number of times you are endorsed for a skill has no weight on how many times the algorithms and programming recognize that particular skill / keyword. In other words, having ten people endorse you for a skill (keyword) does not mean the algorithms see that keyword appearing ten times on your profile.

What the Coaches Say:

What strategies do you recommend to optimize or make the graduate more discoverable as a result of a LinkedIn word search?

Keyword density (frequency) is the primary factor in LinkedIn. Develop a strong headline, a unique summary, and a complete list of skills (there is space for 50 keywords and keyword phrases in "Skills and Endorsements").

Join groups, follow companies that interest you, and gather recommendations. Log in at least once a week to review or work on your profile and participate in groups. If you have something relevant to say, do it in status updates. Make at least 100 connections. Let recruiters know you're "open" with the dedicated switch available in Career Interests (under Jobs tab). All of these practices contribute to search engine optimization (SEO).

Mary Jo King, NCRW

The most important thing to become more discoverable is to optimize your LinkedIn profile. Many new graduates don't take the time to fill in each section. Complete all your sections (Summary, Experience, Education, Volunteer Experience, Skills, Recommendations and Accomplishments). Profiles with complete information come up higher on searches. If a recruiter is searching LinkedIn and 15 candidates come up meeting their specifications, candidates with optimized profiles (and the most keyword hits) come up first.

The second recommendation to increase your discoverability is to include industry, job title, education, and soft-skill keywords to help recruiters find you.

Thirdly, include results, measurables, and accomplishments. This is proof that you made an impact and differentiates you from others. Take accomplishments directly from your resume and transfer them to your LinkedIn summary and experience sections.

Paula Christensen, CPRW, CCMC, CJSS

Keyword Stuffing

Keyword stuffing is *abusively* over using your keywords throughout your profile to increase your ranking.[86] It's a strategy designed to game the system. Sadly, this is a strategy too often suggested by some LinkedIn profile writers and career coaches. According to discussions with LinkedIn Customer Service, the algorithms and programming are now (supposedly) designed to detect this strategy and can actually reduce your ranking.

The far better approach (and the one promoted in this book), is to construct a profile using accepted and common sense optimization strategies that present your college background and experience in a genuine and sincere manner to make the most positive impression possible on the talent acquisition professional.

Let's now move the discussion to the next tenet of optimization—Completeness.

Completeness

The more complete your LinkedIn profile is, the higher it will rank compared to other profiles. According to LinkedIn, "Only 50.5 percent of people have a 100 percent completed LinkedIn profile."[87] Consequently, by having a complete profile you can outrank many other competing college graduate profiles.

The LinkedIn algorithms and programming *display* search results (How you rank compared to other profiles) based on the following:

1. Profile completeness
2. The number of shared connections

---

86 "Practices to Avoid When Optimizing Your Profile For LinkedIn Search." *LinkedIn*. https://www.linkedin.com/help/linkedin/answer/51499/practices-to-avoid-when-optimizing-your-profile-for-linkedin-search?lang=en. (Accessed November 23, 2016).

87 Foote, Andy. "Why You Should Complete Your LinkedIn Profile." *LinkedInsights.com*. December 7, 2015. https://www.linkedinsights.com/why-you-should-complete-your-linkedin-profile/ (Accessed November 22, 2016).

3. Connections by degree (1st, 2nd, and so on)

4. Groups in common

Profile completeness is the "trump card" with the LinkedIn algorithms and programming.[88] The other factors of ranking do not matter as much if your profile is not complete. If you need a refresher of what constitutes a complete profile, here are the components:

• Your location (and industry)

• A current position (with a description)

• Two past positions

• Your education

• Your skills (minimum of three)

• A profile photo

• At least fifty connections"[89]

You are already well down the road to completeness (and compelling) as you work on your profile using keywords. However, LinkedIn has additional sections that can be added to your profile beyond those that are most commonly used. They include:

Volunteering Experience

Publications

Certifications (Professional Designations)

Courses

Projects

Honors and Awards

Patents

Test Scores

Language

Contact and Personal Information

Organizations (College Professional Associations and Affiliations)

Posts

---

88 Ibid. "Profile Completeness is a trump card in the search engine."

89 Ibid.

Volunteering Experience, Organizations

There are a couple of considerations regarding these sections. First, volunteering experience is favorably viewed by employers, but it must be substantive. Standing behind the card table selling brownies at the Marketing Club Social doesn't count. However, being a local volunteer for the Red Cross does. Second, avoid any reference to any organization or cause that could be viewed as controversial. This would generally mean anything regarding politics, religion, race, and so on. Of course there are exceptions if you are pursuing a career in politics, religion, and race relations.

Honors and Awards

It is perfectly acceptable to restate your college-level accomplishments and achievements in the Honors and Awards section. This is especially true if the achievement resulted in an award. Repetition of your achievements affirms in the mind of the talent acquisition professional that you are a well-qualified college graduate.

Language

If you live in the United States and English is your native language, do not list it. It is assumed that you are fluent. This section is used for foreign languages.

Personal details

Avoid providing any personal information that would be legally protected or inappropriate for a talent acquisition professional to ask in an interview.

Connections

The more connections you have, the better the probability you will rank higher than others profiles.[90] Your ranking is, in part, influenced by how closely connected you are to a talent acquisition professional (or anyone else looking). The difficult part is you have no idea who could be looking on LinkedIn and how closely connected you are to them.

The best strategy to combat against or take advantage of this connection factor is to increase your connections and join industry-relevant groups. Also try to get connected to as many professionally relevant people as possible. These are professionals that can hire you or help you. This would include talent acquisition professionals, former bosses, your

---

90 Pearcemarch, Kyle. "SEO for LinkedIn: How to Optimize Your LinkedIn Profile for Search." *DIYGenius.* March 19, 2015. https://www.diygenius.com/how-to-optimize-your-linkedin-profile-for-search/. (Accessed November 22, 2016).

references, and even friends of your parents. If you want to work for a particular company, seek connections within that company (yes, that will mean reaching out and asking to be connected with people you do not know). Strive to get a minimum of fifty professionally relevant connections (even more if you can). The more professionally relevant connections you have, the higher the probability that you will be more closely connected to the talent acquisition professional who is searching on LinkedIn. The closer the connection, the higher you will appear in the ranking of profiles.

When you invite someone to connect on LinkedIn, customize the invitation. Doing so increases the probability of the invitation being accepted and sparking communication.

You have 300 character spaces for a customized invitation. Below is an example to get you thinking about your customized invitations:

I'm a recent graduate from State University, pursuing an entry-level sales role, 3.4 G.P.A., would like to connect.

Extending a customized invitation (containing a brief description of yourself like the example above) to a HR talent acquisition professional should get you connected with many of these people. Once the connection is made, you can start communication about your job search.

When it comes to groups, you are allowed to join up to 100 groups on LinkedIn.[91] Since your ranking is influenced by the number of common groups you have with a talent acquisition professional, it is very important to join relevant and well-populated groups, especially those groups that are in industries you are interested.

Compelling

A profile is compelling when it intellectually or emotionally moves the talent acquisition professional to contact you. There are several factors that can make a profile compelling. They include your education and academic credentials, knowledge and skills, accomplishments, recommendations, the overall appearance and completeness of your profile, and anything else that makes you unique in the eyes of the talent acquisition professional.

Your profile can be compelling based on your education and academic credentials. You have been educated in areas that a talent acquisition professional is looking for or is

---

91 "General Limits for LinkedIn Groups." *LinkedIn*. https://www.linkedin.com/help/linkedin/answer/190/general-limits-for-linkedin-groups?lang=en (Accessed November 23, 2016).

impressed by. You have experience through internships and summer jobs and character traits in need by the talent acquisition professional. This can range from being educated, and having experience with a particular software program to having previous customer service experience with a large organization. There are thousands if not millions of things a talent acquisition professional could look for that are education, knowledge or skill-based, including character traits.

Documented accomplishments are clearly compelling. The most influential accomplishments are those that come from internships and summer jobs, especially when they can be quantified with numbers, percentages, dollars signs, savings (in time and money), and the list goes on. More often, though, accomplishments will come in other forms such as leadership roles, high academic achievement, scholarships, and so on. Accomplishments can heavily influence a talent acquisition professional to contact you. Your accomplishments communicate that you are unique and a high quality college graduate candidate.

Recommendations can influence the compelling nature of your profile. Once your profile is identified as a "probable" qualified college recruit by a talent acquisition professional, the number and content of the recommendations can influence the talent acquisition professional to contact you. As a general rule of thumb, try to get two to three positive recommendations on your LinkedIn profile.

And finally, the overall completeness and appearance of your profile can be a compelling factor. When HR talent acquisition professionals see that you have taken the time and put in the effort of creating a professional profile, it projects the image and creates the mental impression that you are ready to enter the professional world.

There are millions of graduating college seniors who fail to appreciate the job search and career enhancing power of a LinkedIn profile. Potentially life-changing opportunities pass those people by through their failure to have a complete and professional-looking LinkedIn profile. However, to your benefit, you will have a complete, professional, and compelling profile that will open your career to opportunities that others will not have, or ever know about.

> ### *What the Coaches Say:*
>
> **In your opinion, what strategies would you recommend to make a college graduate's LinkedIn profile compelling or persuasive?**
>
> ---
>
> Start with an interesting summary. Add narratives under jobs that showcase what you have learned and accomplished. Ask for and include recommendations. Join groups in your field, post projects, your resume, and other media that showcases your skills. Include a professional photo. Include all the applicable information LinkedIn prompts you to include: volunteer activities, languages, and education. Also, build your network; your number of contacts reflects your ability to network effectively.
>
> Lorraine Beaman, MA, CEIC, ACRW, CARW, NCRW, MCD

Job Alerts

LinkedIn will send you Job Alerts, through email or mobile communications, when an open position is advertised on LinkedIn that matches a job profile you create.

To create a job profile and to start receiving these alerts, begin by accessing your LinkedIn page and click the Jobs icon.

You will now see a page title, "Jobs you may be interested in."

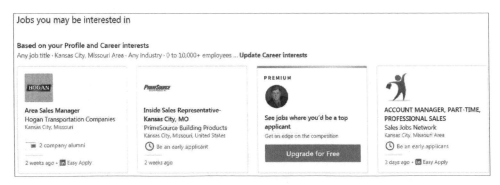

These are posted openings on LinkedIn that the programming believes you might be qualified based on the information contained in your profile (This is yet another reason to have a complete and robust LinkedIn profile). Click on any of the job(s) of interest to you to read more or to apply.

To create Job Alerts, go to the top of the page where you see "Search jobs" and fill in the box with the criteria you are focused on.

Then, fill in your location in the "City, state, postal code or country" box. Once you have filled in the information, click "Search."

You will now see a page with listed jobs. You will also see at the top of the column an option to "Create search alert."

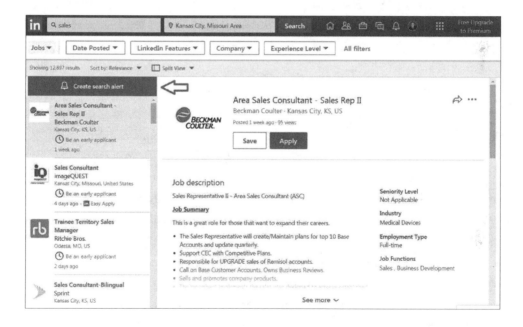

When you click "Create search alert," you will be taken to a page where you can select the frequency and method of notification. Make your selections and click "Save"

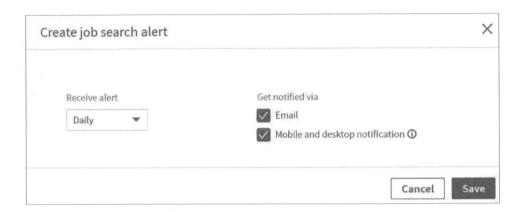

You can repeat the process for other job opportunities you are interested in. LinkedIn allows for several saved searches. Your saved searches will be shown under the search bar as "Saved jobs."

When you look into several jobs in one week, the LinkedIn programming concludes that you are a job seeker (Although the exact number is guarded by LinkedIn as proprietary, seven is the number often referenced). When that happens, you should automatically begin receiving emails from LinkedIn about jobs similar to the ones you researched.

★ The Open Candidates Feature on LinkedIn

LinkedIn has a feature where you can signal talent acquisition professionals that you are open to new opportunities. This feature is called "Open Candidates."

How to Access the Open Candidates Feature. To access this feature, click the "Jobs" option at the top of your LinkedIn profile.

From there you will see "Jobs you may be interested in." Close to that will be a link entitled "Update Preferences." Click it.

Scroll down and begin answering the questions about location, experience, industries (LinkedIn may offer suggestions), company size, and availability. When you activate the feature you are also given an Introductory section with 300 character spaces.

Finally, let talent acquisition professional recruiters know you're open by activating the feature to "On."

Who can see your Open Candidate profile? Only talent acquisition professionals who have paid for and use LinkedIn's premium "Recruiter's Platform" (prices begin at around $8,000 per license) can see that you have filled out the Open Candidates questionnaire.[92] As a recent college graduate, you should certainly use this feature. However, for employed professionals LinkedIn provides this disclaimer, "We take steps to not show your current company that you're open, but can't guarantee that we can identify every recruiter affiliated with your company."

Strategies for using the Open Candidate feature. As a recent college graduate, using the Open Candidates feature is a great idea and another way to get noticed. Talent acquisition professionals can screen recent college graduates not only based on qualifications, but to those that are actively open to new opportunities. This can place you toward the top of their contact list! According to LinkedIn, "open candidates" are more likely to be contacted by recruiters.[93] Use the Introductory section of the questionnaire to emphasize education, skills, background and accomplishments. Sell yourself. Remember, you only have 300 characters spaces so you have to be succinct. Modify the summary paragraph of your resume (using the three-step formula) as a starting point. For example:

---

92 Uzialko, Adam. "LinkedIn's Open Candidates: How to Search for a New Job, Quietly." *Business News Daily*. October 6, 2016. http://www.businessnewsdaily.com/9468-linkedin-open-candidates.html (Accessed November 25, 2016).

93 Bell, Karissa. "LinkedIn will now help you secretly tell recruiters you want a new job." *Mashable*, October 6, 2016. http://mashable.com/2016/10/06/linkedin-tell-recruiters-you-want-a-new-job.amp (Accessed November 25, 2016).

"A college graduate with a 3.7 GPA in Accounting. Proven ability from summer internships in forecasting, analysis, audit, and reconciliation. Conscientious, self-motivated, and service-oriented professional who enjoys solving problems through the application of accounting principles."

Measuring the Effectiveness of Your LinkedIn Profile

Having a complete profile, implementing optimization strategies, and making your profile compelling are necessary steps to maximizing the use of your LinkedIn profile in your job search. But the true effectiveness of your profile is the number of views and search appearances it gets. If you are in a full-blown, active job search utilizing all the tools at your disposal, one measure of success is getting a minimum of twenty views and search appearances (from those professionals who can help you or hire you). Twenty is not a scientific number but rather a minimum threshold number to use as a benchmark for evaluating both the effectiveness of your LinkedIn profile as well as your job search efforts as a whole.

You can track the number of views and search appearances from your profile page. Look for "Who viewed your profile" and "Search appearances" that appear on your Profile page (under your summary introduction).

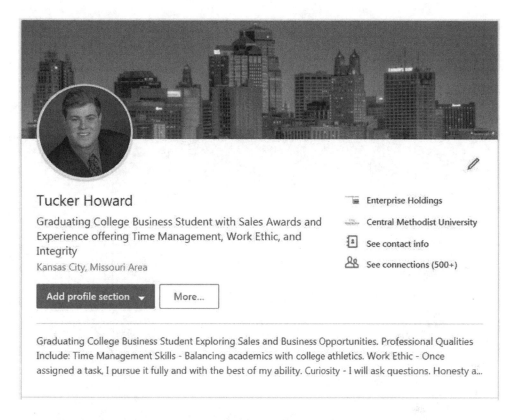

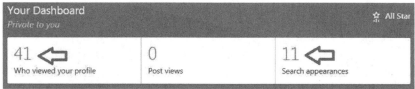

Clicking on the "Who viewed your profile" will show you the people that viewed your profile. "Search Appearances" will display the names of the companies from which people have searched and found your profile. Do these people and companies happen to be those you are reaching out to (or should be reaching out to)?

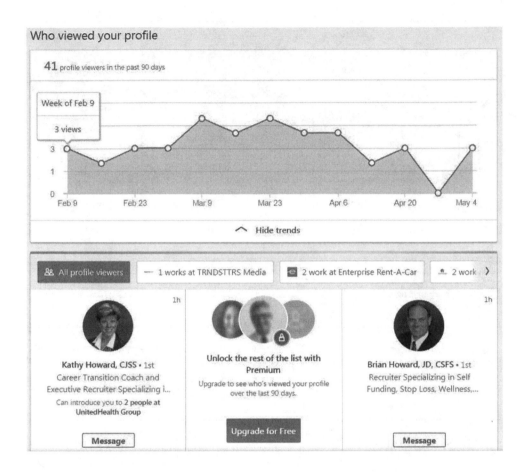

Below the list of companies are the titles of the people who have found your profile. Hopefully they are hiring executives, internal company HR, and external recruiters.

These LinkedIn features can give you valuable insight on how well your LinkedIn profile is working for you (based on its content) and is also a measurement regarding the progress of your job search.

What Do You Do with Your LinkedIn Profile After You Get a Job?

Once you land a job (and you will!), you have a couple of choices with your LinkedIn profile. First, you can create your Experience section using real job information referencing duties, responsibilities and eventually accomplishments you achieve in that position.

There is another approach to consider. Understand the construction of your profile has been focused on you. It has been written to showcase you as a high potential college graduate with the purpose of a job search. When you get a new job, you may want to shift that focus to your new employer. This is achieved by putting a paragraph in your current employment that describes the company, its products, services, value proposition, etc. You can often get this information from the company website or company LinkedIn page.

After you insert the company description, follow the same advice as previously instructed with a paragraph about your duties and responsibilities, followed by accomplishments as they occur.

Keep Your Profile Current

Update your information and keep it current so it doesn't get stale over time. According to LinkedIn, keeping your positions up to date on your profile makes you eighteen times more likely to be found in searches by recruiters and other members.[94]

LinkedIn is a dynamic site that changes frequently, adding some features and functionality and taking others away. Be aware of the programming changes and their possible implications for your profile use.

Sample of an Optimized College Graduate LinkedIn Profile

Once you have implemented all of the optimization strategies, your LinkedIn profile should look similar to the sample profile that follows.

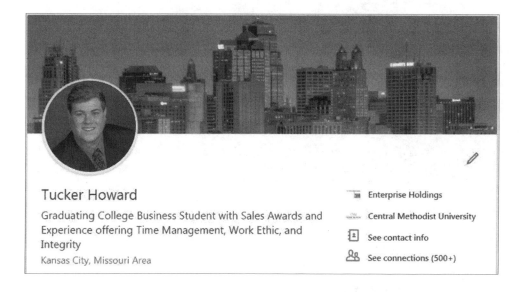

94 Smith, Craig. DMR, "200+ Amazing LinkedIn Stats." Last Updated October 2016. http://expandedramblings.com/index.php/by-the-numbers-a-few-important-linkedin-stats/ (Downloaded November 28, 2016).

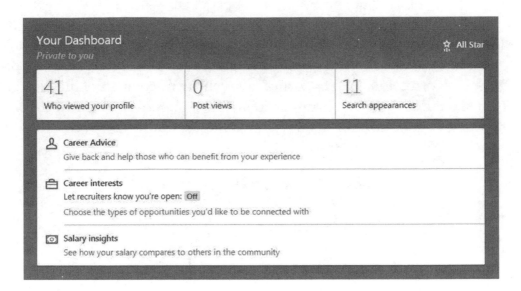

College Summer Intern
Enterprise Rent-A-Car
Jun 2016 – Aug 2016 • 3 mos
Overland Park, KS

Worked in a fast paced business environment interacting with with both individual and corporate clients.
Persuasively communicated with clients offering additional services while balancing client's needs and corporate business interests.
Worked effectively in a team-based competitive environment

Accomplishments include:
▸ Awarded Third Place Scholarship (Out of 11 Interns)
▸ Achieved Platinum Club in July, 2016 as an intern (Ranked as one of the Top 10 sales representatives regionally out of 185. Ranked #3.)

Activities Team Lead
Sky Ranch
Apr 2015 – Jul 2015 • 4 mos
Van, Texas

Activities Team at a Christian summer camp.
▸ Supervised and responsible for athletic activities for kids 10 to 16 years of age.
▸ Interacted with all campers to create a safe Christian atmosphere.

Youth Counselor
†KANAKUK Kanakuk Kamps
Jul 2014 – Aug 2014 • 2 mos
Lampe, Missouri

Youth counselor at a Christian summer camp.
▸ Worked with and supervised six groups of 9 to 12 boys from seven to nine years in age.
▸ Directed campers to scheduled activities on time while creating a safe, fun, Christian atmosphere.

Business Owner

Tucker's Lawn Service

Mar 2006 – Aug 2013 • 7 yrs 6 mos

Overland Park, Kansas

Owned and operated neighborhood lawn mowing business
Was responsible for client satisfaction.
Was responsible for all equipment manitenance.
➤ 4-5 lawns per season – April through November

Sales Consultant, Line Associate

Waterway Gas & Wash

Nov 2011 – Jul 2013 • 1 yr 9 mos

Overland Park, Kansas

Sales Consultant (Promotion from Line Associate)
Greeted customers and informed them about services offered by Waterway.

Accomplishments include:
➤ #1 Monthly Sales Consultant in the Kansas City Market multiple times.
➤ #1 Monthly Sales Consultant Regionally (Kansas City, Denver, Cleveland and St Louis markets) multiple times.

Line Associate - Cleaned vehicles both exterior and interior after exiting car wash.

Education

Central Methodist University

Pursuing Bachelor's Degree in Business, Sales and Marketing

2013 – 2017

Activities and Societies: Central Methodist University Baseball Team Fellowship of Christian Athletes (FCA)

Academic and Athletic Scholarship Recipient
➤ Eagle Academic Scholarship
➤ Athletic Baseball Scholarship, Dual Position Player

Blue Valley North High School

2009 – 2013

Activities and Societies: FCA (Fellowship of Christian Athletes) Baseball Team, Swim Team, Soccer Team

Ranked as the #1 Academic High School in the State of Kansas

➤ Dean's List
➤ President's Community Service Award (100+ Hours of Community Service) – 2012, 2013
➤ Blue Valley North High School Baseball Team 2009-2013
2012 Class 6A Kansas State Baseball State Championship Team

Volunteer Experience

K-7 Missions Week
 Kanakuk
2010 – 2013 • 3 yrs
Children

- Kanakuk Camps - Mission Service Week (Christian summer camp) – 2010, 2011, 2012, 2013
- President's Community Service Award (100+ hours of community service) – 2012, 2013

Skills & Endorsements

Time Management · 6
Ian Harvey and 5 connections have given endorsements for this skill

Customer Service · 6
Endorsed by **Ian Harvey, who is highly skilled at this**

Leadership · 5
Ian Harvey and 4 connections have given endorsements for this skill

Industry Knowledge

Sales · 3

Interpersonal Skills

Team Building · 2

Accomplishments

2 **Honors & Awards**

College Summer Intern
Jul 2016 • Enterprise Rent-A-Car

➤ Awarded Third Place College Scholarship (Out of 11 Interns)
➤ Platinum Club – July, 2016 as an Intern - (#3 sales representatives out of 185)

Sales Consultant
2012 • Waterway Gas & Wash

➤ #1 Monthly Sales Consultant in the Kansas City Market multiple times.
➤ #1 Monthly Sales Consultant Regionally (Kansas City, Denver, Cleveland and St Louis markets) multiple times.

Interests

 Enterprise Holdings
48,728 followers

 The New York Times
2,992,380 followers

 Engaged Companies
376 followers

 Time Magazine
1,316,998 followers

 Enterprise Rent-A-Car
125,951 followers

 Mark Cuban
President
4,162,835 followers

Chapter 5

Cover Letters and Other Written Communications

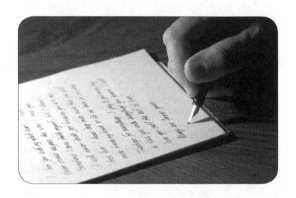

Dost thou love life? Then do not squander time,
for that is the stuff life is made of.
— Benjamin Franklin[95]

Understand that most cover letters do not get read. Hiring executives and talent acquisition professionals tend to bypass it and go straight to the resume.[96] If the resume is strong, some employers will then go back and read the cover letter. Regardless of how an employer treats the letter, make sure that you invest an appropriate amount of time writing an impactful cover letter. A well-written cover letter immediately begins to differentiate you from other recent college graduates by highlighting strong points in your education and experience and provides a sample of your writing ability.

It is a good strategy to write a template cover letter that can be customized for different job opportunities.

---

95 Franklin, Benjamin. "The Way to Wealth," *Poor Richard's Almanac*, July 7, 1757.

96 Cain, Aine. "Why you should still spend time perfecting your cover letter, even though most hiring managers won't read it." *Business Insider.* http://www.businessinsider.com/why-you-still-need-to-write-a-cover-letter-2016-10 (Accessed August 27, 2017). (Only 20% of private sector managers even read cover letters)

What the Coaches Say:

Do you have any tricks-of-the-trade when writing a cover letter for a recent college graduate?

Cover letters can be intimidating. Avoid using standard wording that has no personality and is just like every other new grad cover letter. Personalize your cover letter, tailoring it to the position in which you are applying. Pull out 2-4 keywords from their job posting and briefly explain your results/accomplishments/proof in these areas.

To increase engagement, include one sentence describing what makes you different from your peers applying for the same position. The trend for cover letters is short. Some experts say 150-250 words is ideal because HR professionals are bombarded with cover letters. They appreciate letters that are brief and to-the-point. End your letter with a robust call to action— "I would appreciate the opportunity to interview. Thank you in advance for your consideration, I will follow up early next week."

Paula Christensen, CPRW, CCMC, CJSS

If the new graduate does not have job-related work experience (e.g., an internship), I use one or two academic assignments as examples of the skills/experience the employer is seeking.

Lorraine Beaman, MA, CEIC, ACRW, CARW, NCRW, MCD

Types of Cover Letters

In general, cover letters (including emails) fall under three categories:

A **letter of application** is used to match your credentials to a specific employment position.

A **letter of inquiry** is written (frequently to HR) when you are exploring whether the employer may have a possible open position within the company.

A **marketing letter** is written to quickly grab the attention of a talent acquisition professional or a hiring executive. The goal of this "attack" strategy is to showcase your qualifications and create enough interest so the talent acquisition professional or a hiring executive reads your resume and engages you in conversation. You are proactively marketing yourself directly to a potential employer who could likely hire you for the position you seek (regardless of whether there is a known or posted opening).

The Cover Letter Success Formula

Getting your cover letter read increases the odds of getting your resume reviewed and it differentiates you. Be concise. With your cover letter (as well as all your written communications), proofreading is mandatory. Executives are reading not only for content, but for sentence structure and how you express your thoughts. Spelling or grammar errors broadcast that you either don't pay attention to detail or are careless. Have someone who is unfamiliar with your letter read it. You could also let your writing sit overnight. Some claim that reading it backward helps. And when it comes time to send your letters, don't send the same one to every executive. Having a template is fine, but customize each one. And don't mention salary, compensation, or benefits in a cover letter.

To maximize your effectiveness when writing cover letters, use the following approach, which has proven effective over the course of time:

- Create interest
- Match
- Showcase an accomplishment/qualification
- Provide additional information (as needed)
- Close

Here's an in-depth look at how to do this:

Create interest

You must quickly get the attention and interest of the employer. Personalizing the letter with their name (found by searching LinkedIn or the company website, or calling the company) will go a long way. Adding a "RE:" line (meaning "regarding") lets the executive know what your letter is about, and the position you're interested in. Generating interest increases the time the executive spends on your letter. All too often, college graduates do the opposite by beginning their letters with the following type of opening paragraph:

> *I am writing to apply for the position of Management Trainee, which I saw advertised on Jobboard.com. I believe my education and college experiences make me the perfect candidate for this position at your company.*

This type of opening sentence is ineffective. Instead, begin your letters with something that will grab the attention of the talent acquisition professional or be thought-provoking. Some examples are:

1. **Mention a personal or professional referral**. *Our mutual friend, Peter Huggins, suggested that I reach out to you.* Mentioning a common acquaintance is one of the most effect ways to capture a reader's attention (using the persuasion principle of social proof).

2. **Come out swinging with one of your top achievements**. *I am a recent graduate from State University with dual degrees in Accounting and Finance, a 3.7 G.P.A., and experience from a summer internship.*

3. **Identify yourself by a unique or highly sought-after skill or knowledge base.** *I have just completed my Master's degree in Accounting from Well-Known University.*

4. **Refer to a statistic.** *According to the most recent polling, 43 percent of small businesses will increase their marketing and advertising budgets, up from 21 percent just a year ago.*

5. **Ask a relevant business question.** *Have you found it difficult to hire college graduates with the work ethic to advance your business? If so, I have the work ethic and recommendations to back it up.*

6. **Mention a recent company event or a news release that is significant**. *Congratulations on your acquisition of Plate Co., Inc.! I understand this could increase your market share significantly.*

7. **Use a quotation**. *Jeremy Johnson of the United Marketing Association recently found that redefining target markets can increase effectiveness by almost double.*

8. **Cite a relevant industry trend**. *It is a well-known fact that national healthcare legislation will create a demand for wellness software platforms. During my internship, I assisted in the development of these software platforms.*

9. **Refer to a recommendation.** *Lauren Springs received the highest evaluation scores we give for her student teaching rotation during the Fall of 20XX. [Identify person providing the quoted recommendation]*

What the Coaches Say:

What technique would you recommend to quickly capture the attention of the reader of a cover letter?

Begin a cover letter with a "carrot," an opening statement (sentence) that attracts and holds the reader's attention. Then, write strategically and hold attention by focusing on the employer's needs and challenges. Identify your ability to fill their needs and solve their challenges, then tell them!

Dr. Cheryl Minnick, NCRW, CCMC, CHJMC, CAA

Tell the reader, in the first paragraph, why you should be considered as a top candidate. There are several strategies for this. Find the approach which you are the most comfortable. There is the question approach, "Are you looking for a (job title) who (an example of a job-related skill you excel at)? If so, we need to meet."

There is the statement approach, "As an undergraduate, I excelled in (your strongest job-related skill) and am prepared to use this knowledge to help (name of company/organization) achieve its goal of (you can usually find this in their mission statement).

If someone has recommended you, "(name of person recommending you) encouraged me to apply for this position. He/she felt I would quickly become a key contributor to your organization."

Lorraine Beaman, MA, CEIC, ACRW, CARW, NCRW, MCD

Match

After you have the hiring executive's attention, hold it by very briefly identifying the job you would be interested, which matches one the company already has (best case), using their exact wording, if possible. This makes you relevant and encourages the hiring executive to read on.

Here are a couple of examples:

> *As a recent college graduate with a degree in Marketing and minor in Psychology, I am exploring an entry-level marketing position.*

Or,

> *I am an entry-level client services professional who recently graduated from State University.*

If necessary, consider using the word cloud technique to match wording of the employer.

Showcase an accomplishment/qualification

The accomplishment paragraph is important after you have created interest and matched a known company role. Make this paragraph impactful by focusing the executive on key points, but do not repeat your resume. Make your accomplishments relevant by identifying the position's most important requirements (including transferable skills and character traits), link your qualifications to them, and then show your accomplishments in as many of the job functions as you can.

One approach is to list your coursework that would apply to the position (include grades if they are strong). Start the sentence with "Relevant coursework include:"

The point is to tell a prospective employer you are qualified for the job, and then sell them on the fact that you have the collegiate background (activities, internships, grades, etc.) to do it well. These "showcase" techniques can also help to get your resume read.

What the Coaches Say:

What makes a cover letter persuasive or impactful?

An attention-grabbing opening statement goes a long way. This is the beginning of the "sales process" and the cover letter should drive the reader forward to learn more about you.

Target the letter to the specific employer and position at hand. Even if you begin with a template, make the necessary adjustments to reflect your knowledge of the company. Keep it brief and focus the content on the ways you can meet their needs.

Mary Jo King, NCRW

Cover letters with a "bold and brag" approach with 3-4 bullets that address the top 3-4 required skills or challenges the employer faces can be persuasive. Using shading or colored ink draws the eye in.

Detailed Organization. As a highly-organized professional, I believe in doing things thoroughly, right, and on time the first time, juggling projects and changing priorities with a positive attitude. I have a strong work-ethic and deliver excellence in payroll administration.

Dedicated Support. My professionalism has been demonstrated throughout my internships offering confidential HR support in terms of hire paperwork, correcting payroll errors, collecting wage overpayments, and completing data entry.

Diligent Work Effort. I am diligent in all efforts including responding to internal audiences to analyze salary discrepancies, make corrective action, and detailed payroll transactions. I stay at my desk until the work is done . . . done well and done correctly.

Dr. Cheryl Minnick, NCRW, CCMC, CHJMC, CAA

Provide additional information

In the following paragraphs of the letter, elaborate on your college experiences, skills, background, achievements, and character traits. This is where you have a fair amount of latitude on what you want to showcase. Choose those topics you feel are the most relevant or impressive to the employer. Once again, inform the employer what you did, in addition to how this produced positive results.[97]

> *I am a motivated entry-level sales professional who knows what it takes to succeed in sales. As a summer intern at Ins. Co., I worked in the sales department. I assisted the sales representatives in identifying new clients and broker-dealers, setting appointments, and assisted in the sales calls and presentations. I understand the work and perseverance required to succeed in sales.*

Another approach is to add a strong recommendation. This paragraph should be indented and single-spaced. To achieve this technique's full impact, identify the person providing the recommendation by name and title. Here's an example:

> *My supervisor, Susan J. Smith, Director of Operations, Cyban, Inc. states:*
> *Jane worked part-time for us during college. She has excellent communication skills. In addition, she is extremely organized, reliable, and computer literate. Jane can work independently and is able to follow through to ensure that the job gets done. She is flexible and willing to work on any project that is assigned to her. Jane was quick to volunteer to assist in other areas of company operations, as well.*

Remember, it is always more influential when others speak well of you than you promoting yourself.

Another technique you can use in this section is to reveal an insight about yourself to personalize the letter. It must be something relevant or important to the employer.

This paragraph can start with a phrase such as: "I am passionate about . . .", "I am personally rewarded when . . .", "I have always been intrigued by . . .", and so on. For example:

> *I am passionate about wellness. During my internship at BeWell, LLC, I got a great deal of satisfaction knowing that the wellness services the company provided will have a personal impact on the health and well-being of the customer.*

---

97 See also, Safani, "Tell a Story."

Use these paragraphs to inform the employer about any other piece of information relevant to your job search, such as relocation.

I will be moving back to Chicago (home) in the next 30 days.

Close

Conclude your letter by using a brief closing statement, followed by your intention to follow up:

Based on my education, academic performance, collegiate leadership experience, and summer internship, I believe I have the qualifications to succeed as a [entry-level position title]. I look forward to discussing this and will contact your office next week.

Don't restrict yourself to paper cover letters. Other effective methods include marketing emails (*See* Proactively Marketing Your Professional Credentials and Appendix), with embedded videos and YouTube (discussed later). Use both, as appropriate, in your self-motivated job search to gain greater visibility with employers and increase opportunities for interviews.

The Cover Letter Success Formula provides you with an effective framework from which you can create your cover letter communications. Keep these concepts in mind as you write your letters. Doing so will increase their effectiveness, differentiate you from others, and result in a better success rate (getting your resume reviewed, interviews, and so on).

What the Coaches Say:

Do you employ or recommend a formula or strategy when crafting a cover letter for a graduate? If so, what?

I recommend a one-page letter using the following formula:

The first paragraph includes the title of the job, how you found out about the job, a positive comment about the company, and how your education/experience/skills make you a top candidate for the job.

The second paragraph shows how your experience/education has prepared you to assume the responsibilities of the job. Include one or two examples of your work/academic experience.

The third paragraph highlights your soft skills using examples of when you used them. For example, "The team I worked with on my senior project and my faculty advisor told me my ability to communicate clearly with other team members and take a leadership role, when necessary, were critical in the success of the project."

The fourth paragraph is a call to action. Let the employer know you are looking forward to meeting to discuss the contributions you will be able to bring to the organization. Then state you look forward to hearing from the employer OR you will call to set up an interview. Include your email address and phone number in this paragraph.

Other suggestions: Address the letter to a specific person. If one is not listed in the job listing, use LinkedIn or do an Internet search of the company to find the person who supervises the position for which you are applying.

Use the same font and heading on your cover letter as you do on your resume. It looks very professional to have both documents match, and it puts your contact information at the top of the letter where it is easy to find.

End your letter with "Sincerely" on one line, leave space for your signature, and then type your full name. On the bottom line of the letter, type Enclosure: Resume

Lorraine Beaman, MA, CEIC, ACRW, CARW, NCRW, MCD

Research the company before you write your cover so you can demonstrate your compatibility with their needs, goals, and culture. Most cover letters should be brief, using three paragraphs to:

1) Identify the position at hand and the reason you are a great match for the role. If you have a name to drop, do so in this first paragraph.

2) Describe the breadth of your qualifications as related to their needs. To the best of your ability, make this about them, and how you can solve their problem or meet their need. Use achievements to demonstrate your claims.

3) Ask for an interview and promise to follow up in a few days. (Then follow up in a few days if you don't hear anything.)

Mary Jo King, NCRW

Below are a couple of unique sample cover letters using techniques not often used by recent college graduates.

Using a recommendation

Mr. Strutz:

Would you be interested in a Management Trainee candidate with a strong work ethic? I am a recent college graduate from State University and below is part of a recommendation from my supervisor at TechCo. (Summer internship):

> "Katherine Johnson demonstrated the strongest work ethic and 'can do' attitude of all of the interns we had last summer. She tackled every assignment with energy to complete the tasks on time."

I graduated with a dual degree in Management and Psychology and a cumulative G.P.A. of 3.4. From reading your website news releases, I understand that Blue Hills Technology is poised to significant growth as a result of you recent acquisition Gadet LLC. Congratulations!

From your job posting, you are looking for a Management Trainee that can lead small teams. I have leadership, delegation, and management skills that were developed while serving as Rush Chairman, and later as President, of my sorority.

My college and work experience, education, and work ethic make me a strong and qualified candidate for this position with Blue Hills Technology. I can make a positive impact quickly with your organization.

I look forward to communicating with you soon. I will follow up with you within the next week.

Best Regards,
[your name]

Comment: The effectiveness of this letter is the indented and italicized recommendation at the top of the letter. It is unusual and eye-catching. When the hiring executive reads the impactful recommendation, the odds grow that the rest of the letter gets read, your resume gets reviewed, and you increase your chances of getting an interview.

Job match format

Ms. Hawke:

I am submitting my resume for the Staff Account position which is advertised on your company website. From my research, Drake & Leonardo is a family owned accounting firm dating back to 1983. This is appealing to me as my family also owns a small business.

Postition Requirements	Qualifications of (Your Name)
Bachelor's Degree in Accounting	Degree in Accounting received from State University, May 20XX
Eligible to sit for the CPA exam	Scheduled to take part I of the CPA exam on June 20th
Experience with tax returns, audits,	Experience with tax returns, audits, and financial statements and financial statements from summer internship and part-time job
Working knowledge of Excel, Word, Outlook	Several years of experience using all of those program including PowerPoint and other office software
Work independently	During summer internship, managed several assignments simultaneously with minimal supervision. Demonstrated time management skills

I also founded the State University Future CPAs Club (through the Institute of Management Accountants). Formed a leadership committee and provided activities and speakers for club members.

I'm excited about the opportunity to meet you and join Drake & Leonardo. Thank you for your time and consideration. I will follow up with you next week.

Sincerely,
[your name]

Comment: This cover letter has a traditional introduction but the hiring executive will immediate notice the unusual format that matches what the company requires in the position with your qualifications. It is an easy read to determine that you are qualified for the position.

Adding a P.S. (Post Script)

One technique that can enhance the effectiveness of your written communications is adding a P.S. It's eye-catching and often gets read even when other parts of your letter do not. An interesting P.S. can get your entire letter read. The key to this technique is your statement must be very short and impactful. One approach is to state one of your top accomplishments. Here are a couple of examples:

P.S. Last summer, I was the only summer college call center representative at Major Technology Co. to receive a performance bonus.

P.S. I have maintained my 3.2 GPA while volunteering 20 hours a month for the last two years at a Cancer Treatment Center.

The best P.S. is a statement that is something distinct about your qualifications, achievements, or you as a person (like volunteering at the cancer treatment center in the above example).

If your communication is a paper letter, you could hand write your P.S. for more impact.

Thank-You Letters

The primary purposes of a thank-you letter are to express your appreciation, reiterate your relevant background, qualifications, successes, and differentiate yourself from other college job seekers. Most hiring executives appreciate a thank-you correspondence after an interview.[98] And "some employers may expect a job interview thank-you card."[99] However, it has been said that only 20 percent of all job seekers take the time to write a thank-you note.[100] If so, writing a thank you note can differentiate you from many other recent college graduates. And not sending a thank you note may reflect negatively on your candidacy.[101]

An important secondary purpose is to make sure the hiring executive remembers you. In a survey by *The Ladders*, a combined 76 percent said a thank-you note was "somewhat important" or "very important" to their hiring decision.[102] That's three out of every four! Therefore, capitalize on this opportunity to reinforce your education, experience and collegiate accomplishments. Write a thank-you note after every interview. And keep it short. This is a thank-you letter, not a written interview summary.

What the Coaches Say:

Should a graduate send letters by email or regular mail?

I often get asked if thank you notes should be sent by email or regular mail and if they are sent by regular mail should they be typed or handwritten. If the interviewer told you the company would be making a decision within 24 hours, send an email. If the decision will not be made for a week or longer, you need to decide between email and regular mail. If the person who interviewed you had nothing on his/her desk and all of the contact with you was by email, use email. If the interviewer had papers on his/her desk, send a hard copy thank you note.

---

98 "Farewell to the Handwritten Thank-You Note? Survey Reveals Email, Phone Call Are Preferred Methods for Post-Interview Follow-Up." *Robert Half.* June 14, 2012. http://accountemps.rhi.mediaroom.com/thank-you (accessed July 9, 2015).

99 "Do Employers Expect a Job Interview Thank-You Card?" *CVTips.* http://www.cvtips.com/interview/do-employers-expect-a-job-interview-thank-you-card.html (accessed July 10, 2015).

100 Helmrich, Brittney. "Thanks! 20 Job Interview Thank You Note Tips." *Business News Daily.* June 23, 2015, http://www.businessnewsdaily.com/7134-thank-you-note-tips.html (accessed July 9, 2015).

101 "Thank-You Note Etiquette." *CareerBuilder.* http://www.careerbuilder.com/JobPoster/Resources/page.aspx?pagever=ThankYouNoteEtiquette (accessed July 9, 2015).

102 "Give Thanks or Your Chance For That Job Could be Cooked." *TheLadders.* http://cdn.theladders.net/static/images/basicSite/PR/pdfs/TheLaddersGiveThanks.pdf (accessed June 5, 2015).

Whether you type the note or hand write it depends on two things. If your handwriting is illegible, the person you met with was very formal during your interactions, or you want to correct an error by providing additional information not covered during the interview, type the note. If the interviewer was very relaxed, send a handwritten note.

The last time researchers conducted research on thank you notes, it was found that 50% of all candidates send thank-you notes; 90% of the people who got offers had sent thank-you notes. Do not miss the opportunity to impress an employer with your professionalism and interest in the job. Always send a thank you note!

Lorraine Beaman, MA, CEIC, ACRW, CARW, NCRW, MCD

To maximize the impact of your thank-you letter, use the following approach:

1. Express your appreciation
2. Match and emphasize collegiate background
3. Close

Let's look at each step in more detail:

Express your appreciation

Thank the hiring executive for their time. Then, move to rapport-building, depending upon the circumstances. Your first paragraph could look something like this:

Thank you for taking the time yesterday to meet with me regarding your assistant implementation consultant position. I enjoyed learning how you derived the concept behind your state-of-the-art system. (This is a compliment, therefore using the persuasion principle of liking.) *As we discussed, my education and internship experience could assist your department with the challenges it will face in the coming months.*

Or,

Thank you for meeting me on Tuesday regarding the financial analyst position. I appreciate your time. And, by the way, good luck to your son during tryouts for the starting quarterback position!

Match and emphasize collegiate background

Because you were interviewed, you should know what the hiring executive is looking for in the position. Briefly restate and match your qualifications to the need.

During our plant tour last week, I was very impressed with your use of robotics in the manufacturing process. I can honestly say I have never seen such an impressive manufacturing plant! My degree in industrial engineering with a minor in statistics, strong G.P.A. (3.6) and experience as a summer intern with Smith & Jones Engineers has prepared me for the challenges of this position.

Close

Here, express your continued interest and a plan to contact the hiring supervisor. This final paragraph could look something like:

I am interested in pursuing this opportunity with Sinc Company! I will follow up with you next week, as you requested, to discuss additional steps.

What the Coaches Say:

What suggestions would you pass along about writing a post interview thank-you letter?

Better than a written letter, take a video and send it to the interviewer. This way, you can be heard and the unique thank you will be appreciated as being different. Video thank you's are effective.

Tina Kashlak Nicolai, PHR, CPBA, CARW

Here's what's interesting about thank-you letters. Some hiring managers and HR professionals love them and expect thank-you letters; some do not care about them at all. The problem is . . . you don't know if your interviewer falls in the first or second category. Always send a thank you letter. I've heard stories from hiring managers indicating a thank you letter made the difference between two candidates.

Here are two suggestions for making them impactful: 1. Immediately following your interview, write notes of what was discussed so you can include something specific to help them remember who you are and the position in which you interviewed. 2. Express that you are really interested in the job.

When some job seekers interview, their nervousness comes across as indifference – they just don't seem that interested. It's always helpful to state how impressed you were with their team and your excitement for the opportunity.

Sample Thank-You Letter:

Thank you all for meeting with me today. It was a pleasure learning about COMPANY NAME OR DEPARTMENT NAME and how proud your team is with its success. SOMETHING SPECIFIC THAT YOU LEARNED OR NOTICED OR DISCUSSED. I want to express my interest in becoming a member of your team. My strengths in LIST 2-3 SKILLS/KEYWORDS align with the qualifications and qualities you are looking for. I look forward to the opportunity to play a role in your company's continued growth and success.

Sincerely,

Paula Christensen, CPRW, CCMC, CJSS

Thank-You Letter When You Are Not Selected for the Job

This letter builds bridges for the future and is a very strong networking technique. It will differentiate you from almost all other collegiate job-seekers and create a favorable impression with the employer. There are two good reasons for doing this. First, it can leave the door open for future opportunities with the company. It is not uncommon for employers to revisit previous candidates when new opportunities become available.

Additionally, since professionals within an industry often run in the same circles of influence, the letter distinguishes you and could lead to other business relationships with the company. It could also lead to future opportunities with the hiring executive should he/she move onto another company and remember your professionalism.

Writing a professional correspondence after a decision not to hire you shows character and professionalism. You don't know where, when, and in what way your paths may cross again with the hiring supervisor, talent acquisition professional, and everyone involved in the interviewing process. The letter sets up a positive engagement for the next time—be it business or personal.

Here is a sample letter:

"Thank you so much for the opportunity to interview for the Junior Financial Analyst position. I understand that I was not chosen for the position. Although disappointed, I want to express my appreciation for your consideration throughout the interviewing process. ABC Company has a bright future and your leadership team is impressive!

I hope that we run into each other over the course of time.

Laurie, it has been a true pleasure meeting you and the other members of your team! Please keep me in mind should your hiring needs change in the future.

Sincerely,
Susie Student

Email Follow-Up Letters

When following up through email, the same considerations and rules apply as previously mentioned. Things to remember: make your subject line relevant, omit a street address, and always include your telephone number.

What the Coaches Say:

What advice would you give a graduate who wants to send a letter by email?

Hiring managers report receiving hundreds of email messages with "Resume" as the subject line and no message in the email body (just an attachment). When sending a resume as an attachment, you should also write a message in the email accompanying the file, an e-note.

The e-note is the email message — not an attachment, helping the recipient decide if they want to read your resume. E-notes are usually 1-2 paragraphs and provide less information than traditional cover letters. Briefly, spell out up to three relevant qualifications or accomplishments. Resist the urge to copy and paste accomplishments straight from your resume, reword them so you're sharing the same information in a different way.

To increase the likelihood that your message is opened, in the subject line, include the title of the position you're seeking (re: Human Resource Assistant) or the name of the person who referred you (John Doe suggested I contact you).

Paula Christensen, CPRW, CCMC, CJSS

Something to Think About

Some suggest that sending hard-copy cover letters, resumes, and thank-you letters is no longer as effective as it once was. People think, "It's all done by email these days." Perhaps that's true, but consider this: There are some hiring executives and talent acquisition professionals that receive one hundred or more emails a day. Obviously, not all of these emails are from job seekers, but the point is, these people are busy and they receive lots of emails.

Here's the concept: Due to the sheer volume of emails that these people receive, one possible technique to differentiate yourself (which is a goal in your job search), is to send a cover letter, resume, or thank-you note by US mail. *That which was old may be new again*. It's an idea you may wish to explore with some of your target companies and target contacts.

Another Idea

If you decide to send a cover letter, resume, or thank-you letter by US mail, consider investing in customized envelopes. Since there is a lot of open space on an envelope to use, consider noting two or three of your top collegiate achievements in the lower left corner of the envelope. How often does a hiring executive see this? Never . . . and that might be just the differentiation you need for him/her to open the envelope. Consider using a large envelop so the contents do not need to be folded.

Some Final Words about Written Communications

As you know, communication skills (written, verbal, and listening) are highly sought after.[103] Being able to write effectively and persuasively is a very important element in your job search, and it will be evaluated (as well as whether you've proofread your materials). What you write about, how you communicate it, your sentence structure, word choice, grammar, and punctuation are evaluated against other college graduate job seekers. By following the Cover Letter Success Formula and proper thank-you letter writing techniques, you can feel confident that your written communications will differentiate you from others, grab the attention of the employer, and result in a higher success rate.

Shifting Gears

So far the topics we have been discussing have been preparing you to engage in job-search activities that lead to interviews by helping you establish the right mindset and set up templates and to-do lists for success. At most, these preparatory activities should take **two weeks** (as a *maximum*) if you stay focused—ideally less. Anything beyond that could be just busywork or a diversion for you to avoid the necessary work of engaging the job market and beginning your job search in earnest.

We are now going to shift gears into topics related to generating job leads and interviews.

---

103 Hanson and Hanson. "What Do Employers *Really* Want?" https://www.coursehero.com/file/7350405/What-Do-Employers-Really-Want/.

PART II

Generating Job Leads

Chapter 6

On-Campus Career Fairs

Passion is what gives meaning to our lives. It's what allows us to achieve success beyond our wildest imagination. Try to find a career path that you have a passion for.

Henry Samueli[104]

On-campus career fairs are one of the most effective and time-efficient job search strategies available to you. For employers, the sole purpose of a career fair is to meet you, a soon-to-be college graduate (and possibly summer internship candidate) from your college or university. There is already a general interest in meeting you, otherwise the employer would not be attending. To be successful, and make the best possible impressions on employers at a career fair, take the advice and insight that follows.

Get Mentally Prepared

Mentally prepare to "put yourself out there," meet new people, and promote yourself as a potential new employee. For some, this may require some internal courage. Take heart,

---

104 "Henry Samuel." *Brainy Quote*. https://www.brainyquote.com/authors/henry_samueli (accessed November 2, 2017).

this is normal and you are not alone. Most of your peers feel the same way. Fortunately, the company representatives are sensitive to these apprehensions. They understand and are empathetic to your feelings. All of the company representatives will be naturally friendly and really do want to talk to you.

Quite literally, what you have to do at an on-campus career fair is simple:

1. Walk up to the company representative
2. Shake their hand
3. Introduce yourself

It's easy! You can do this and you can do it well, especially when you are prepared by reading the practical advice that follows!

Use of Resumes and Business Cards

Bring several copies of your resume. In fact, bring more than what you anticipate needing. You don't want to run out for some unforeseen reason.

Some employers are now not accepting paper resumes at career fairs. Instead, they ask that graduates download their resumes on their website or special portal. One strategy to leverage this situation is to bring a thumb-drive that only contains your resume. Ask the booth representative if she/he has a laptop. Then ask them to look over your shoulder as you download your resume. Taking this approach creates differentiation from others. You came prepared with an electronic version of your resume and you continued the interaction with the company representatives by working on a task (loading your resume into their system) together.

Bring plenty of business cards as well. Exchange business cards with every company representative you encounter. Having business cards elevates you in the eyes of the company representative. Not every college graduate has them—but you do and it will make you stand out. Get the company representative's business card so you have a contact name and email address when you follow up later. Exchange business cards even if you provide a resume.

Elevator Speech

Come ready with your elevator speech. Virtually every conversation you have with a company representative will require you to say something about yourself. Make the most of that moment (and opportunity) by delivering a well-rehearsed and conversational elevator speech. The company representative will recognize the speech for what it is and you will score points compared to your peers, who are unprepared and stumble through with an awkward response. When delivering your speech, make eye contact. You dilute the effectiveness of your speech if you stare off into space to recall your memorized words. Practice, prior to using your elevator speech, is the key to an effective delivery.

Do Your Research

Research all of the companies you are interested in, just like you would for any interview. This includes reading their website, any news items about the company, announcements, as well as knowing the company's products and services, consumers, and whatever else you can research that will make you knowledgeable about the company. It is very common for a company representative to ask you, "What do you know about our company?" And, ' Why are you interested in our company?" Having some working knowledge of the company along with why you are interested in the company will differentiate you from others who did not research the company and do not have a coherent and reasoned response.

Prepare a script of answers to those possible questions and others you might receive and prepare a handful of questions to ask. Review the topic on *Interview Preparation* in the interview chapter of this book for additional insight for career fair preparation.

Dress Appropriately

Dress for a career fair like you would dress for an in-office interview with an employer. As you will soon read, the very first thing a company representative will notice and evaluate is your appearance—how you are dressed. First impressions are vitally important and when you are conservatively dressed in business attire you are sending the message that you are ready for employment in the real world. Generally speaking, conservative dress for guys is a dark suit or a blue sports jacket over nice slacks, a starched shirt, tie, and hard-soled dark shoes. For the ladies, a business suit in a solid colors or mild patterns, leather high-heeled shoes (not the ones that are sky-high or when you go to the bars), and a stylish blouse would be appropriate. Do not take your purse.

Although styles change, you should get the idea of the image you want to project from this wardrobe description. If you are pursuing a career in the creative fields (marketing, advertising, and so on), you have more latitude on your wardrobe selections.

Get a Portfolio and Take Notes

Invest in either a leather or fabric portfolio. Most office supply stores carry a selection to choose from. There are several advantages to having a dark (black) portfolio. First, it projects a professional image, especially when you are conservatively dressed. A portfolio is very practical. You can put copies of your resume in it and most have small pockets where you can store your business cards.

Be prepared to take notes, especially if you are given instructions by a company representative about any action items you must do. Write down anything you believe is important that you may need later, like information you may want to mention in a thank you or follow up email.

What the Coaches Say:

What preparation would you recommend prior to attending an on-campus career fair?

Focus your participation in on-campus career fairs based on your situation and your goals. For example, if you are still exploring options, your goal for a career fair should be tailored to making connections with companies that interest you now, or in the future. Make a connection that you can follow up with over the course of time, to build a relationship with that recruiter and company.

If you have identified target companies or positions, make sure to meet with those representatives at the fair, and either strengthen the relationship you've already developed or get started on creating one.

Always do preliminary research before the career fair, reviewing their website, and searching for additional information through news sites and LinkedIn. Your research will show your interest, and help you have a conversation with the people you meet.

Bryan Lubic, M.A., J.D., CCMC, CJSS

Know your audience, dress appropriately, arrive early, take copies of your resume, have a firm handshake and prepare questions tailored to each recruiting company.

Know where the company is, what they are hiring for, and have a strategy about which employer you wish to talk with and why. Do not attend the career fair simply to wander through and look around. If you are not interested in the employers at the fair, use the opportunity to practice your "pitch" and to ask about the industry as a whole.

Say "thank you" for coming to campus—you may not be interested in the companies on campus, but if no one attends, and no one says thank you, why would employers ever return to campus to recruit.

Dr. Cheryl Minnick, NCRW, CCMC, CHJMC, CAA

Hit the "B" List First to Warm Up

At the career fair and as a matter of strategy, approach a couple of companies that are on your "B" list before those you are most interested. This will help you get into an interviewing frame of mind. Hopefully you will get the opportunity to deliver your elevator speech, have a substantive interaction, and otherwise warm up and get into the flow of things. Once you feel you're ready, go visit the employers that most interest you.

Since career fair conversations are interviews, you are highly encouraged to read the interviewing chapter in this book as a part of your preparation. That chapter goes into topics that will benefit you greatly during a career fair.

What the Coaches Say:

What strategies would you recommend to recent college graduates to get the most from attending an on-campus career fair?

If there is a list of employers handed out at the event, take a minute to determine if the employers you are targeting are in attendance and if any additional employers you might want to visit have been added.

Walk up to each of the employers you selected, use your self-introduction to introduce yourself, ask the company-specific question you developed, wait for an answer, hand over your resume, and pick up/ask for the recruiter's business card.

During career fairs, top candidates are often asked to step out of line and participate in a mini interview. Be prepared to answer the "Tell me about yourself" and "Where do you want to be in 5 years?" questions. If you do a mini-interview, ask how you follow up with the recruiter if he/she does not provide that information.

At the event, collect as many business cards as you can. Write notes on the back of the cards to jog your memory about topics you discussed. Within 24 hours, send "It was wonderful meeting you" notes that include a reference to what you spoke about to everyone you met.

Lorraine Beaman, MA, CEIC, ACRW, CARW, NCRW, MCD

What Career Fair Company Representatives Look For

There is a wide range of qualifications, professional qualities, and character traits that a company representative can look for in recent college graduates. Those qualifications, both educational and soft skills, vary from employer to employer. However, below are five that company representatives look at.

What you are wearing. This is obvious and logical. The very first thing they see is how you are dressed. Even though you are a college student, when you present yourself as crisply and professionally dressed, you project an image that you are ready for the business-world.

Your ability to communicate in conversation. How you verbally communicate is a soft skill virtually all employers look for. Speaking with confidence while holding eye contact is how professionals in the real world communicate. Putting this skill on display will differentiate you from others.

Ask questions. Company representatives are impressed by those who ask questions, especially questions based on company research. The more insightful and company-specific the question, the better you will be viewed by the representative. Good questions can make you memorable.

Be prepared to state what you're looking for. This will likely be asked of you frequently. Be prepared to answer using your elevator speech and a shortened version.

An alternative approach is "an entry level position [in the employer's industry]." It is a good fallback position if you are unclear on the specific directions of your career. If you take this approach, be prepared to state why the employer's industry interests you.

Evidence of professional qualities and character traits. As you know, professional qualities and character traits are very important in a job search and employers look for them in recent college graduates. This is especially true for new college graduates who lack specific experience. You can differentiate yourself from your peers by providing examples of sought-after professional qualities and character traits. A list of those qualities and traits are contained in the topic "Job Skills, Professional Qualities, and Character Traits" discussed earlier in the book. You can state your professional qualities and character traits as a component of your elevator speech. For example, "I have a strong work ethic having worked summer and part-time jobs through high school and college."

You can also make a stand-alone statement at the end of an engagement with a company representative. For example, "One other thing I like you to know . . . " Then identify the quality or trait with a statement that supports or proves the existence of the quality or trait."

Regardless of what approach you use, including information about professional qualities and character traits in a conversation with a career fair company representative should score you points and make you stand out compared to others.

What the Coaches Say:

In your experience, what are company representatives evaluating when meeting recent college graduates on-campus?

Company representatives are excited to be on campus. Recruiters love the energy a university provides and they're excited to speak with you about your passions and credentials. With this being said, they're on campus to learn about you, to see you in your element, and to learn about what you've been working on in regard to preparing for industry. They want to see in a brief interaction how you communicate, how you articulate yourself professionally, how you shake their hand. All of this is an assessment of soft skills and analyzing your potential fit with their organization. That's why a 30-second pitch is important to develop, to practice. The more you practice, the more comfortable you'll feel and the more likely it will turn into an engaging conversation with a company representative.

Jered Lish M.S., Gallup-Certified Strengths Coach, GCDF

They are looking for students who present themselves professionally, show initiative, and seem interested in working for their company. They determine that based on the student being dressed professionally, delivering a strong self-introduction, asking company-specific questions, and providing a copy of an achievements-based resume.

Lorraine Beaman, MA, CEIC, ACRW, CARW, NCRW, MCD

Chapter 7

Professional Networking

Networking is an essential part of building wealth.
— Armstrong Williams[105]

For many of you, networking will play a significant role in your career. Whether used for business, the gathering of industry information, or a job search among other purposes, it is important that you have a firm understanding of what professional networking is and how it works.

Due to its importance, we will discuss the basic concepts of networking as a professional along with its use during your job search as a recent college graduate. Understanding these basic concepts and putting them into practice will pay dividends for your entire career.

---

105 Williams,,Armstrong. "A Few Simple Steps to Building Wealth." *Townhall.* June 13, 2005. http://townhall.com/columnists/armstrongwilliams/2005/06/13/a_few_simple_steps_to_building_wealth/page/full (accessed May 28, 2015).

What the Coaches Say:

Networking for a job can be difficult for recent college graduates because they do not have an established professional network to tap into. What advice do you have for graduates regarding networking for a job?

Ask your inner circle of older adult family/friends where they network, can you go with them? Do research, join associations. Every city and town has a Chamber of Commerce, most have Young Professional Associations . . . attend! If you tell the Chamber you are a recent grad, they typically let you go for free!

Ellen Steverson, NCRW, GCDF, CEIC

Use both social media and personal contact to develop a network. I often have graduates say they do not know anyone they can ask for help in their job search. Then we make a list of their friends, parents' friends, and relatives, and I ask what each one does for a living and where they work. It is not long before we have 3 to 5 people who work in the field the student wants to enter.

Using the self-introduction, the student contacts the people working in the field and asks if they could provide some job search advice. From this base of contacts, the student will be able to build a vibrant network fairly quickly.

I also recommend using LinkedIn to search for alumni who work in the graduate's field. In their request to connect, I suggest using their self-introduction, identifying themselves as a fellow alumnus, and requesting advice on their job search.

Lorraine Beaman, MA, CEIC, ACRW, CARW, NCRW, MCD

Defining What Networking Is

Let's define what networking means now that you are entering the professional world. Here is a good working definition:

> Professional networking is developing and maintaining reciprocal relationships with other professionals that over time could result in career or business opportunities. The power of your network is measured by the number and quality of relevant relationships you have.[106]

Let's examine some of the important words and concepts in this definition:

Developing—Professional networks are not granted to you, they are built.

Maintaining—Once a professional connection or relationship is created, it must be nurtured. There must be some appropriate level of interaction.

Reciprocal relationships—Networking is a two-way street. The foundational concept of networking is to give or help. Each person in the relationship gives with the understanding that they can receive when the time is right. "Those who give . . . get."[107]

Measured by the number—To be useful or powerful, a network must be populated with enough contacts for your purposes.

Quality of relevant relationships—Your network must have the right kinds of connections. When your network has enough quality, relevant relationships, it becomes truly powerful when properly used.

BusinessDictionary.com defines networking this way:

> Creating a group of acquaintances and associates and keeping it active through regular communication for mutual benefit. Networking is based on the question "How can I help?" and not with "What can I get?"[108]

---

106 See also, Phillips, Simon. *The Complete Guide to Professional Networking: The Secrets of Online and Offline Success.* London: Kogan Page Limited. 2014. p. 1.

107 Van Vlooten, Dick. "The Seven Laws of Networking: Those Who Give, Get." Science Mag. May 7, 2004. http://www.sciencemag.org/careers/2004/05/seven-laws-networking-those-who-give-get.

108 "Networking." *BusinessDictionary.com.* http://www.businessdictionary.com/definition/networking.html (accessed November 12, 2015).

The most important concept in this definition is offering to help. As we proceed, we will examine and discuss steps you can take that fulfill these definitions and make you a skilled professional networker. Being skilled adds depth and quality to your network. You will be "going about it" in the right way. This will, in turn, shorten your job search. It will also make you a resource that others will turn to over the course of your career.

Why Networking Is So Effective in a Job Search

There are several reasons why networking is an effective way to find your first job:

1. **It taps into the "Hidden Job Market."** By definition, the Hidden Job Market is a term used to describe jobs that are not advertised. It is estimated that sixty to eighty percent of all jobs are not advertised or posted online.

2. **It decreases the time it takes to land your first job.** Networking is a proactive job search tactic. People you know or can be introduced to are more likely to speak or meet with you personally. And, the more communications you have, the closer you get to a job lead and a job offer.

3. **It reduces competition.** Job postings tend to draw a pile of resumes. Networking makes you a candidate of a much smaller pool.

4. **It introduces you through a common connection.** People interact primarily with people they know and like.[109] As your network begins to expand, so will your opportunities as you meet more and more people.

5. **It helps you practice for interviews and builds self-confidence.** Networking creates phone conversations, lunch dates, and interviews. These are opportunities to practice your interview skills. This will boost your self-confidence, awareness that your job search is moving forward, and feelings of success as you improve overall, leading to better interviews. Having confidence translates into better communications, which creates more interviews, eventually leading to job opportunities.[110]

---

109 Byrne, *Attraction*, quoted in Kurtzberg and Naquin, *Essentials*, p. 35.

110 Moynihan et al. "A Longitudinal Study." Quoted in Kurtzberg and Naquin. *Essentials*. p. 30–32.

Embrace a Networking Mentality

To successfully network for a job (or in the real world), it is imperative that you embrace several attitudes to make your efforts effective:

Being Sincere—skilled professional networkers show genuine interest in relationships and communication with others. That means taking the time to have meaningful engagements properly gauged by the depth of the relationships. As a recent college graduate, this means being open, honest, and humble in all of your networking communications.

Being Helpful—This goes straight to the heart of proper professional networking. Offer to help. This may be difficult as a recent graduate. What do you have to offer? Likely not very much on the professional level. The key, however, is the *offering*. You never know when you might be able to do something of value for your networking contact. Give others what they need and they will try to return the favor (Persuasion principle of reciprocity). Always be on the lookout to provide value to others whenever you can, with the expectation of receiving nothing in return. Rewards will come as the level of trust and rapport grows over time. You'll also learn what is of interest to your connections. If you discover an item (an article, referral, or business lead, among many others) that you feel very confident would have substantial value to your connection, pass it along to them.

Staying Present—As you network, be present in the moment. Whether interacting face-to-face, by telephone, or online, give your undivided attention to your contact.

Listening—The best networkers do one thing very well: They listen. They quiet themselves, are present in the moment, and listen to learn. The more you listen and ask questions, the more rapport you build. This creates or adds to the value of the relationship. By actively listening, you will often learn what others need so you can help them later.

Having a Positive Attitude—Always approach your networking with a positive attitude. People enjoy being around those who are positive and have an optimistic view of life. Your connections will want to engage with you and look forward to doing so. Nobody wants to talk to a "sad sack."

Having Patience and Playing for the Long Term—Approach your job search networking as an investment that will grow in value over time. Done correctly, it can pay dividends for the life of your career.

Following up—Following up after an engagement is critical to the development of the relationship. Timely and professional follow-up will differentiate you from others and elevate your status in the mind of your contact.[111] For the purposes of your job search as a

---

111 See also, ibid., Chapter 4, "How to Work the Room in Five Easy Steps."

recent college graduate, proper follow up could be nothing more than a well-written thank you note after a conversation or communication.

When you embrace these attitudes as you network for a job, you'll approach every step and every networking communication with the right frame of mind. You will develop more quality relevant relationships faster that will last longer, potentially for your entire career. Good networking shortens job searches.

Types of Networks

Conceptually there are two job search networks: personal and professional. Your personal network includes family, friends, college classmates, and neighbors. It also includes doctors, your dentist, and your parents' financial advisor, accountant, members of church, synagogue, mosque (faith based organizations), civic, or philanthropic groups. Everyone you interact with in your personal life is also included here. Websites in your personal network include Facebook and Twitter, among others.

Your professional network is likely very small or non-existent. However, it will grow as a result of your job search and eventually consist of people who are work colleagues, connections at other companies, former bosses, senior management, association contacts, and so on. The leading online site for professional networks is LinkedIn.

To fully grasp the scope and reach of networking for a job, understand that each one of your contacts connects you to their network. And any member of that network could know about an available job opening. Conceptually, think of it this way: Let's say you have solid relationships with twenty people in either your personal or professional network. Now let's say they each know twenty people. That's four hundred people you can get to know reasonably quickly without much effort.

As your career progresses, twenty connections will be a very low number. It's possible that your network, especially on the professional side, could be in the hundreds-plus range. You do the math on how large your extended network could be—chances are you'll be pleasantly surprised.

Who to Network with as a Recent College Graduate

Networking for a job as a recent college graduate involves connecting with people you know and then the people they know to lead you to a job. This could include the people your parents know. It also includes reaching out professionally to those you don't know for the same purpose.[112] It generally involves three types of contacts:

---

112 Claycomb, Heather, and Karl Dinse. *Career Pathways—Interactive Workbook.* (1995), Part 7.

1. Those people who can lead you to others who can assist you in your job search.
2. Those people who can introduce you to someone who can hire you.
3. Those people with the authority to hire you.

Job search networking can take place in a wide variety of situations including face-to-face, online through professional networking sites (LinkedIn), social networking sites (Facebook and Twitter), professional associations, alumni events, and even a dinner gathering with friends.

In a job search context, networking increases your "find-ability." It is estimated that for professionals engaged in their careers that between 60 and 80 percent of all jobs are found by networking.[113] Furthermore, surveys indicate that job seekers who are referred to a hiring executive have a one in seven chance of landing a job offer compared to one in one hundred if they apply online.[114] Getting referred to a job is a function of networking.

This next concept is very important and goes straight to the heart of professionally networking for a job: It's not how many people you know, but rather how many people know you. Ponder that for a moment to understand the concept. As a recent college graduate, how many people can you get introduced to and get to know well enough that they would refer you to someone else or possibly go out of their way to help you, even if it's in a small measure? This is your challenge and this is the kind of relationship-networking that drives a job search.

Fear of Networking

Unfortunately, many recent college graduates hesitate to take full advantage of networking because they're intimidated or are afraid of being viewed as a "pushy upstart," annoying, or self-serving. Put those feelings aside. Networking is not annoying to others or about arrogant self-promotion. Instead, it's about building relationships. When you think about networking as building relationships—or creating professional friendships—many of your fears will disappear.[115]

---

113 LinkedIn, "Using LinkedIn to Find a Job"; Beatty, "The Math Behind the Networking Claim"; Rothberg, "80% of Job Openings."

114 "Jobvite Social Recruiting Survey Finds Over 90% of Employers Will Use Social Recruiting in 2012." *Jobvite.* July 9, 2012. http://www.jobvite.com/press-releases/2012/jobvite-social-recruiting-survey-finds-90-employers-will-use-social-recruiting-2012/ (accessed November 10, 2015).

115 Ibid., p. 1.

Accept this next statement as gospel truth: Whether your networking is formal or informal, online or offline, there are people out there who want to help. It's your job to get out there and let them!

Do the thing you fear, and the death of fear is certain. — Emerson[116]

Networking and the Use of LinkedIn

LinkedIn conducted a six-month study of senior level professionals (Vice President titles and above) and their use of LinkedIn during their job search. The results clearly indicated that these senior level professionals knew "the value of building and nurturing professional relationships in order to be successful in their job search"[117] (networking). The study found that "80 percent were sending connection requests, 50 percent were participating in groups, 40 percent were engaging on LinkedIn via shares, likes, and comments."[118] The take-away for you as a recent college graduate is if senior-level professionals see the value of networking to find a job, the same line of thinking can apply to you as a new college graduate.

Here are some strategies and notes to keep in mind:

1. **Use good judgment when connecting or extending invitations.** Determine whether a potential connection could be helpful or a center of influence for you. Connect with those who are in your field of interest.

   Extend invitations to HR talent acquisition professionals in your field of interest or companies of interest and those in a management position who could potentially hire you.

   If you extend an invitation that is not accepted, it's okay. Do not to take it personally.

---

116 "Ralph Waldo Emerson Quotable Quote." *Goodreads.* www.goodreads.com/quotes/60285-do-the-thing-you-fear-and-the-death-of-fear (accessed May 28, 2015).

117 Ayele, "Land Your Dream Job." http://blog.linkedin.com/2015/01/29/jobseeking-tips/.

118 Ibid.

2. **Join Groups.** There are over two million LinkedIn groups.[119] Statistically, there are groups that will be in your field of interest—join them.

Once you are in a group, it is easier to connect and get introduced to people of interest to you. Whenever possible, customize your invitation for a better response and success rate.

3. **Follow target companies.** Look up the company page for any company you are interested in. Click the "Follow Company" tab. All activity from that company's page, including possible job postings, will appear on your LinkedIn home page. This is a great feature to track the company's activities and potential hiring needs.

★ Spreading the Word—Networking for a Job as a Recent College Graduate

Identifying Contacts

Now that you have a basic understanding about networking, it is time to use the knowledge for practical use in your job search.

The first step in networking for a job as a recent college graduate is to identify who you can reach out to. As previously mentioned, this includes family, friends, friends-of-the-family, and so on. If you are fortunate enough that your parents are socially active, this can open the door for wide ranging connections including civic, philanthropic, fundraising among others. These organizations are populated by people who, often by their very nature, enjoy networking. They are often more than willing to help in some measure if they can.

Don't forget to tap into your parents' network of vendors: Doctor, banker, insurance agent, financial planner, dentist, etc. You want to reach out and network with those people who can get you connected with a company or executive who can hire you. The wider you cast the net, the greater the chances of job leads coming your way.

Messaging

Once you have identified some potential networking "targets," you must have a clear message when you contact them. In other words, you have to know what you are going to say (verbally or in writing). Put serious thought and the necessary time into this step. What you say and how you present yourself is vitally important. It must be well-thought, succinct, and professional (think elevator speech). Below is an example to get you thinking as you create your own messaging.

---

119 Arruda. "Is LinkedIn Poised." http://www.forbes.com/sites/williamarruda/2015/03/08/is-linkedin-poised-to-be-the-next-media-giant/.

"Mr. Johnson, my name is Brent Cooper. You may know my parents, Bob and Betty Cooper, from the Iota Foundation.

The purpose of my call [or email] is I will be graduating in May from State University with a degree in Business Marketing. I worked as a summer intern at Burris & Haltom, a marketing and advertising firm in Dallas, where I received experience in the real working world.

I am starting a job search for my first professional-level position. My parents felt that you would be a resource for some insight and advice about my job search. If you can make yourself available, I would like to set up a brief appointment to speak."

Engaging in Conversation

Once interest is established to engage in conversation, it is incumbent upon you to kick off the conversation. Start with a re-statement of your graduation, major, internships then the types of positions, company-types, industries that are of interest to you. Ask if they have heard of any particular companies that are hiring or have hired new grads. You can ask questions relevant to the industry, general economy, job market, and so on. Do what you can to get the conversation to flow. Build rapport. Listen. Gather information.

At the end of the conversation, be a good networker and offer to help. You may not have much of anything to offer, but it is the "offering" that will make you a good networker. Your offer to help could sound something like this:

I truly appreciate the time you spent with me. I know, given my circumstances I may not have much of anything to offer you in return for you speaking with me, but should you think of something, I hope you'll reach out to me.

Networking as a recent college graduate can be intimidating. It will require you to step out of your comfort zone and show courage. But take heart! Research shows that your networking contacts have a strong desire to help you! They are forgiving if you stumble or come across awkward in your messaging.[120] Most all of your contacts recognize what you are doing and the power that networking may have played in their own careers. Being perfect in your networking is not your goal. Reaching out and giving your best effort is.

---

120 "Networking 101 for New Grads." *U.S. News and World Report.* http://money.usnews.com/money/blogs/networking-101-for-new-grads.

Alumni Associations

Depending upon your college or university, tapping into the alumni association can provide rich networking opportunities. Some alumni associations are active, others are not. Occasionally, alumni will volunteer to be a networking resource for recent college graduates—especially to those graduates with a common degree.

Depending upon the school or the alumni association, you may need to join. If there is a membership fee, it is normally affordable. Membership gives you access to the alumni directory—a potential treasure trove of networking contacts.

What the Coaches Say:

What is your advice about using an alumni association as a part of a graduate's job search?

The Alumni association is one of the greatest resources a student can have from their college education and unfortunately it is often ignored by students and graduates. Alumni are always happy to help students from their alma mater.

Tapping into the alumni association gives the student easy access to resources that would be more difficult and costly to access otherwise. Many managers in the workplace will reach out to their alma mater first to find qualified candidates for a position. Many alumni associations provide free resources for career coaching, resume writing, interview coaching and other career services. If a college graduate is not connected to the alumni association, these are opportunities they will be missing.

Juliet Murphy, MBA, MA

The alumni association of your college or university is a built-in network that was designed to help people make connections during and after their time at the institution. Participating in events is an easy way to build and strengthen your network. And the best part? Most alumni association events are designed to be fun!

Another overlooked benefit to participating in alumni association programs is that active participants are willing to help—after all, that's why they've joined and become involved in their alumni association. By participating in your alumni association, you get the opportunity to take advantage of an accessible network of people who are willing to help.

Bryan Lubic, M.A., J.D., CCMC, CJSS

Identify alumni that based on their profile, might be able to help you. Look for alumni that are early in their careers (they have just gone through what you are going through now). Alumni that are in mid-career are also great contacts. They have developed networks that could expand your reach for potential jobs. Alumni that are later in their careers are a mixed bag. Some could be helpful while others are too far removed to assist.

Start reaching out right away. Like all networking, it takes effort to get started; build momentum, and establish rapport.

An easy way to get dialed into the alumni network is to socialize locally. Some alumni form local chapters and have social events. Reach out, get connected, and start attending. For your first alumni function, ask for a chaperone to introduce you to others. This can ease the initial anxiety of your first function.

Most alumni associations have an online presence (occasionally through the college of university website). Use their website to connect and network with alumni.

To successfully approach alumni, you must have a purpose and a well-thought message (or script). Do not approach alumni with "I need a job." Instead introduce yourself and ask for job search advice, market insight, referrals to others and so on (using the scripting concepts of previous examples).

The script below is an example for a recent college graduate reaching out to an alumnus located in a different city:

Mr. Blakestead, my name is Liz Ryan and we are both graduates of State University with degrees in Marketing. I'm looking to re-locate to New York to pursue a career in apparel marketing. Could you share a few minutes with me about [a topic related to apparel, marketing, job market, etc.]?

Use your script as a verbal call, email, or a face-to-face interaction. Always say thank you and send a thank you note. Depending upon the exchange, offer to send your resume and grant permission for the alumnus to forward it to others based on their judgment.

If your college or university does not have a well-organized alumni association, you can run a search on LinkedIn for alumni.

What the Pros's Say:

What successes have you seen from graduates that have tapped into the alumni association of a particular college or university?

At a previous institution I was employed at, they had a very robust alumni association online tool that enabled students to connect with alumni for advice on their resumes, a mock interview, or discuss career advice. It was an amazing platform that yielded great opportunities for connections between alumni and students.

One day, I had a particular student with a very specific career objective to work at Amazon in Seattle, Washington, with his end goal becoming a solutions architect for the company and he was struggling on how he could network into it. After speaking with him, I knew the alumni advisor network powered by the alumni association would be a great tool for him utilize. His eyes lit up when he saw there were over 50 alumni who worked at Amazon in the Seattle area. In our coaching session, we talked about how to introduce himself, the importance of being specific with why he was conducting the outreach, how to be professional and engaging, and after our coaching session, he went home and outreached with all 50 alumni. After engaging with roughly half of the alumni, he coordinated three follow up in person informational interviews, and one of those informational interviews landed him an internship. I was thrilled this student was able to network into a role using the alumni association's technologies, and it goes to show you the power of connecting people to one another in the context of career.

Jered Lish M.S., Gallup-Certified Strengths Coach, GCDF

I have a client who is about 25 years into his career. Whenever he decided to change jobs, the first thing he did was reach out to his alumni association. He always got information and introductions that led to new jobs. He offers the same support to fellow alumni who reach out to him.

Lorraine Beaman, MA, CEIC, ACRW, CARW, NCRW, MCD

Professional Associations

If you know the direction of your career path, professional associations are a powerful networking tool. Even as a recent college graduate, one of the best things you can do to shorten your job search is to join and be (reasonably) active in a professional association. Professional associations exist to promote the interests of the industry it serves *and* the careers of its members—through networking!

Some of the most connected and networked professionals you'll ever meet will belong to professional associations. These people get a "charge" out of being connected in their industry. So, as you discover them, connect with them, network with them, and (professionally and diplomatically) leverage them as a resource for your job search.[121]

The way to get connected and involved in a professional association is not as difficult as it may appear. It starts with nothing more than an email or phone call to a representative of the association, normally the membership chairperson. When speaking to this person, express your interest in the association and your purpose for wanting to join. Your purpose is to broaden your industry knowledge beyond the classroom, network, get acquainted with the membership, and network for a job.

Professional associations are mostly volunteer organizations. With the exception of a select few positions in large national associations, an association depends on its members volunteering to help. This is achieved through various committees tasked with certain functions. With your job search in mind, ask to be involved on a committee in the association. Which committees could bear the most fruit from networking? Two committees in particular can be most helpful:

Membership Committee—Makes sense given your current circumstances. This committee gets you involved and interacting with potential new members as well as

---

121 Yate, *Knock 'em Dead*, p. 86.

current members. It's a terrific committee to be involved with for easy introductions and networking.

Program/Speaker Committee—This committee identifies and approaches industry leaders to speak at association events. Being involved with this committee is a great way to get connected to thought-leaders in your industry.

Being a volunteer as a recent college graduate for a professional association normally involves some "grunt" work. Accept that. The interactions with others at the functions will far outweigh the tasks you are assigned.

Finally, being a member of a professional association gives you access to the membership directory. This directory is a goldmine of information! It can be easily used to identify professionals in your industry for job search purposes. Properly handled, your membership in an association will frequently, though not always, give you something in common with a networking contact and gain you a brief networking conversation.

Joining and being a member of a professional association will impress future employers. It shows your interest in the industry, your initiative to develop new skills, and understand industry trends. It also shows you can step out of your classroom comfort zone and into your career. And, don't forget to put your association membership on your resume and LinkedIn profile.

The more deeply connected you are (or can become) in professional associations, the greater your chances of shortening your job search.

★ Association/Industry Conferences

Most recent college graduates don't think about attending an industry conference as a part of their job search networking. If you know the direction of your career, attending an industry conference, and networking correctly, will expose you to more employers and give you a distinct advantage over other college graduates. It's similar to attending an on-campus career fair—numerous potential employers all together in a confined area. The key to this job search strategy is you must have a clear interest in the industry, be reasonable qualified for positions in that industry, and have a plan on how to get the most from the conference (for your job search).

Association and industry conferences are great events for job-search networking. They present an opportunity to meet face to face with industry professionals and hiring executives. You can learn which companies are potentially hiring recent college graduates. Occasionally you can get insider information on companies of interest to you. You will learn this next point in the course of time, but there's no time like the present: most seasoned professionals who attend professional conferences know there is as much covert recruiting and informal interviewing taking place at conferences as actual business interaction with potential clients and customers. Realizing this fact should make your attendance at a conference less intimidating.

Conferences can be expensive (not just the registration fee, but also travel and lodging). Depending upon your circumstances, you may need to ask your parents for some financial assistance. It is probable that any conference you attend as a recent college graduate will be local or a drivable distance. Sometimes speaking with a conference official and explaining your circumstances ("a poor recent college graduate looking for a job") can get you a discount on the registrations fee—try it. It can work.

Use the following strategies to get the most out of attending a professional conference to further your job search:

1. Do research using lists of attendees and exhibitors. Every industry conference requires you to register. Registrants often get advance notice listing the attendees and exhibitors (potential employers). Look at both lists for any hiring executives who will attend. This is invaluable information for you. Make it a goal to introduce yourself and speak with them. Research the executives on LinkedIn, and see if you have anyone in common who can introduce you via e-mail or LinkedIn before the conference. This is not likely given your circumstances, but check to make sure.

Research the companies who will be at the conference as well. Too many job seekers (even tenured professionals) come to conferences unprepared. Your presence, initiative, and research will make you stand out. Check out each company online, as well as their jobs page, if one exists. See if they are looking to hire any recent college graduates and entry-level professionals. Also, find out from the conference materials when the exhibit hall is open. You'll probably do most of your job-search networking during those hours when people are at their booths.

2. Come prepared with your elevator speech, resume, and business cards. Be ready to use your elevator speech. Bring plenty of resumes, but only offer one if asked. Consider having your resumes in an envelope with your name on it so it can be transported easily (and discreetly) in a suit or portfolio. Business cards are a must, especially for circumstances that don't allow for an extended discussion about employment. Make the contact, have a good conversation, and exchange business cards. You can communicate more fully later and supply a resume (if appropriate). Make sure you put a short note on the back of each business card you receive so that you can remember something about the person or your conversation with them. This is a lifesaver when following up later.

3. Keep your attire conservative and employ a solid conference game plan. First impressions are critical, so conservative business attire is a requirement. Overdressed is better than underdressed. Dressing in conservative attire portrays professionalism and taps into the persuasion principle of authority.

Survey the layout of the conference before you arrive (using the conference materials). Map out the companies that interest you and put them in order of your personal preference, high interest to low interest. Keep in mind that your order may have to change if a lower-priority company has a booth very close to a higher-priority one. As a matter of convenience, you may drop in on a lower-priority company before the next higher-priority one.

When you arrive at the conference, see if any new companies registered too late to be included in your materials, and see if any of them need to be included on your "company hit list."

4. Make contact. Accept the fact that you will be walking up to booths and introducing yourself to new people. Walk up to the booth, extend a handshake, introduce yourself, and give them your elevator speech. You will be pleasantly surprised how friendly and helpful these people will be. Most people will help you if they can.

It is perfectly acceptable to identify hiring executives from the attendees list whose companies will have booths at the conference. Reach out to them via email or InMail indicating that you will be attending. Ask whether you can swing by their booth and introduce yourself.

5. Remember: Every conversation is an interview. Remember these three things to kicking off a good interview or conversation: make eye contact, offer a firm handshake, and show enthusiasm. Be prepared with a few questions for the person you are speaking with. Do what you can to spark a conversation.

6. Following up is crucial to your success. You'll likely use e-mail to do this, and contacting every relevant connection you made at the conference may take a lot of time. But you never know which connection will lead to your next job. Use all of the business cards you collected and create a brief follow-up e-mail (or LinkedIn InMail) to each. This is where the notes you recorded on the back of each card pay dividends.

The idea of walking into a conference filled with strangers can be intimidating, especially as a recent college graduate. That's completely understandable and you are not alone in that feeling (tenured professionals have those feeling too!). However, networking is very important to your job search and your career. It's a necessary skill. If you get the opportunity to attend an association or industry conference, follow the steps in this section. Research. Plan your strategy. Bring your business cards and practice your elevator speech. And then, muster the courage and meet people. After the first few engagements, initiating conversations will get easier and you won't be able to wait to talk to the next person!

Associations – Local Chapters

Discover whether the association has local chapters. Some do, and they frequently hold regular monthly meetings. Local chapter meetings tend to be breakfast, lunches, or after-hours meetings. The cost for these local meetings is usually little or nothing, if you are a member of the national organization. Try speaking to the local chapter president and explaining your circumstance. It could get you in for free at least for a while (until you get a job, then you have to pay like anyone else. Sometimes your employer will cover the costs of association memberships.). Attend as many as possible and build your network.

When it comes to attending a local function, ask for a chaperone—a person that can show you around and introduce you to others. You can ask for a chaperone (a different one) for the first couple of times you attend a function. After that you need to be your "own professional" and attend and introduce yourself.

Icebreaker Questions for Conferences and Events

Often the most intimidating part about networking at a conference or event is starting a conversation. After an introduction, it's uncomfortable to deal with that awkward moment of silence. The trick to overcoming that awkwardness is to be prepared with a handful of conversation starters—icebreaker questions.

When engaging in a conversation, be present in the moment and focus. Use open-ended questions starting with "what" and "how" whenever possible. Start all networking conversations with the idea of creating a "conversation surplus" for the other person. Let them fill the "conversation bucket" about them, their company, or anything else they want to talk about. Be a good, interested listener. Only speak of yourself when they ask, and eventually they will. Otherwise, keep the focus on them. Let them create the surplus in the conversation by way of your questions.

More often than not, a networking conversation balances out and ends up being equal in terms of the sharing of information and time spent in conversation.

If the conversation ends with a significant surplus in your fellow attendee's favor, that's fine. Praise yourself for being a good listener. You don't know how that seemingly lopsided conversation might benefit you in the future.

Here are some good icebreaker questions to spur conversation:

- What do you do? (Follow up with a request for their opinion on an industry issue, trend, event, or something else—this is where industry research shows you are tuned into the industry trends)

- What motivated you to come to this conference/event?

- What do you think of the lineup of speakers?

- What did you think of the breakout session topics?

- What are you finding most interesting (or valuable) about this conference/event?

- Attendance looks good. Do you come every year (or every month if a local event)?

- What's your organization's competitive edge over your competitors?

Once the conversation begins and the initial discomfort dissipates, an engaging conversation can start to develop. As a good networker, always offer to help a contact whenever you can with the understanding that they will do what they can to help you. You may not have much of anything to offer, but it is the "offering" that will make you a good networker.

Goals of a Networking Conversation

Your primary goal in a networking conversation is to display and utilize professional networking techniques. Yes, you are networking with the purpose of advancing your job search, but you will gain more traction and advance your search further by being patient and strategic.

Display networking skills first: Be present in the moment, actively listen, ask questions, and so on. By using your professional networking skills and engaging in conversation, you have built rapport. Then, when you state your situation, there is more likelihood the contact will help you!

Listen carefully and learn—what you discover may help advance your job search (you never know how at the moment). You could also pass onto others what you discover at the conference or event that could possibly help them in a myriad of ways (even as a recent college graduate, this can happen).

Face-to-Face Networking as an Introvert

Networking can be more challenging if you are introverted. Meeting new people face-to-face just does not come as easy to you as it does for others. Fortunately, there are some very practical strategies you can use to defuse much of the anxiety of networking:

- **Remind yourself of the value networking has to your job search.** Sixty to eighty percent of all jobs are a result of some form of networking.[122] Psych yourself up the best you can (without alcohol!).

- **Go to smaller events.** Avoid conferences or association events that are attended by the thousands and look for opportunities where the attendees are more in the hundreds or less.[123] Attend local functions and ask for a chaperone.

- **Focus on groups where you have a common interest or common purpose.** For example, if you're a recent graduate with a nursing degree and you don't want to go into clinical nursing. You discover that there are nurses working in the Workers' Compensation industry, look for a group comprised of nurse case managers. Conversation will be easier because you have knowledge of nursing and will be able to relate, to a certain degree, to conversations. These types of functions often have educational sessions, which gives you a reason for being there if you feel the need to state one.

- **Before attending a function, create a list of three or four icebreaker questions.** Use the previous section on icebreaker questions as a guide. Preparation is key. At an event with unfamiliar people, you may become distracted by your surroundings and forget a few things—having your list of questions will make conversations with other attendees much easier.

- **Finally, know how to close a conversation.** When the conversation has run its course and the silence begins to feel awkward, have a closing line that will politely allow you to move on. For example, "It has been a pleasure speaking with you. I'm sure you have others to meet as do I. Do you have a card?"

122 "Using LinkedIn to Find a Job"; Beatty, *LinkedIn*. "The Math Behind the Networking Claim"; Rothberg, "80% of Job Openings."

123 Townsend, Maya. "The Introvert's Survival Guide to Networking." *Inc.com*.http://www.inc.com/maya-townsend/introvert-networking-guide.html (accessed November 4, 2015).

When properly done, networking will open doors to opportunities. To be a successful networker, offer to give far more than you ever expect to receive. Over time, you will discover that you have received more than you gave.

Chapter 8

Social Media: Twitter and Facebook

There is in this world no such force as the force of a man determined to rise.

— W. E. B. DuBois[124]

Please Note: Twitter and Facebook change their format, features, appearance, and functionality regularly. These changes can enhance the experience as well as restrict functionality. This topic on Twitter and Facebook was as current as possible at the time of writing.

Social media has quickly become part of the arsenal of tools used by all job seekers when conducting a job search. It has been reported that 14.4 million job seekers have used social media to search for a job.[125] The percentage of job seekers using social media continues to increase year after year.[126] This is likely due to its increasing effectiveness and its use by you—the younger generation who have grown up with the technology.

124 Pine, Joslyn. Ed. *Book of African-American Quotations*. New York: Dover Publications, 2011. p. 51.

125 Torres, Brooke. "Job Seekers: Social Media is Even More Important Than You Thought." *The Muse*. https://www.themuse.com/advice/job-seekers-social-media-is-even-more-important-than-you-thought (Accessed November 4, 2015).

126 "Searching for Work in the Digital Era." *Pew Research Center*. November 19, 2015. http://www.pewinternet.org/files/2015/11/PI_2015-11-19-Internet-and-Job-Seeking_FINAL.pdf.

We have already discussed LinkedIn. It is clearly the most prevalent online professional networking site. We will now explore using Twitter and Facebook because their use during a job search seems more prevalent than others at the time of writing.

Twitter

Company recruiters use Twitter for talent acquisition.[127] It can be another tool you can use in your job search and to be found by talent acquisition professionals.

One very unique feature about Twitter that enhances its job-search value is that you can follow just about anyone you wish, including companies, target contacts, thought-leaders, HR, and talent acquisition recruiters, without requesting permission (unlike LinkedIn and Facebook). This openness can be a profound resource for information, identifying job leads, job opportunities, and communicating with those that can help you and hire you.

If you are new to Twitter, here are some pointers to get you started:

Create Your Twitter Account. Go to www.twitter.com and click on Sign Up. You will enter your name, email address and a password then go on to click Sign Up. You will be taken step by step to set up your account.

Create Your Twitter Username (Handle). This is nothing more than a name that appears as you tweet (a term for a posting made on the Twitter website). You're permitted fifteen characters for a username or handle.[128] You can use your own name, nickname, or any other descriptive name—so long as it is professional.

Set up Your Twitter Profile.[129] Your profile bio is limited to 160 characters including spaces, so you must be succinct but impactful with your description. Review your elevator speech, branding message, and network/resume business cards. Then, formulate your professional profile. Explore other Twitter profiles for ideas if needed.

Add a photo, likely the same as the one that appears on your LinkedIn profile. Since your Twitter profile is so short, add a link to other sites, most notably LinkedIn.

Here are a couple of partial example profiles to get you thinking:

---

127 "2016 Recruiter Nation Report fka Social Recruiting Survey." *Jobvite*. http://www.jobvite.com/wp-content/uploads/2016/09/RecruiterNation2016.pdf.

128 "Character Limit and Changing your username." *Twitter Help Center*. https://support.twitter.com/articles/14609 (Accessed 3/14/17).

129 "Setting up and Customizing Your Profile." *Twitter Help Center*. https://support.twitter.com/articles/127871 (Accessed 3/14/17).

Recent college graduate pursuing . . .

Graduating college business student . . .

Your profile statement on Twitter will be designed for a job search. Consider using or changing what you have for your LinkedIn Headline. Once your job search is over, you will want to change your Twitter profile. If you already have an established personal Twitter account, consider creating a second one solely for your job search.

Once you have an account, establish a handle, write a profile, and you are ready to go!

Identify and begin following target companies of interest to you. This can be an edge over other college job seekers, as well as a great source of information to further your search, since most major or established organizations have a corporate Twitter account. A growing trend among employers is using Twitter to announce open positions.[130] Following industry thought-leaders, hiring executives, human resource professionals, and so on can help as well.

Use hashtags well. Twitter uses hashtags (the # symbol) as an index or filing system of sorts. It's a way to search Twitter for topics or specific information. You can use this indexing system to look for job leads. Below is a short list of hashtags that can lead you to possible job openings:

#jobs

#jobsearch

#employment

#resume

#careers

#nowhiring

Think creatively with the use of hashtags and you may discover hidden openings.

You can use the hashtag indexing system to narrow your search by location or function. For example:

"#Dallas" + "#jobs"—jobs in Dallas

"#jobs" + "#sales"—jobs in sales

"#jobs" + "#accounting" + "#omaha"—accounting jobs in Omaha

---

130 "Sundberg, Jorgen. "List of 140 Employers Posting Jobs on Twitter." *Undercover Recruiter.* http:// theundercoverrecruiter.com/list-employers-posting-jobs-twitter/ (Accessed March 16, 2017).

If you choose to post content. When you create a tweet, Twitter limits you to 280 characters, including spaces and a link. You must be brief and to the point with your messages.

You can tweet and retweet (forwarding someone else's posted message) as much as you like. Just don't overdo it. The key is to create interesting and relevant content. This can be tricky as a recent college graduate. Share news, links, and professional insight. Respond to other people's shares. The most important thing is to think before you post. Since you are now a professional job seeker, your tweets reflect directly on you. Others form an opinion and an impression of you based on what you post and how you express it.

Overall, Twitter's use and acceptance can be industry specific. In other words, some industries may use it more than others. Regardless, Twitter is gaining wider acceptance by employers. Twitter is a job search tool that should be considered and used as part of your strategy, but its impact will rely on your use and your chosen industry's acceptance and use of it.

Facebook

When it comes to Facebook, the lines between social and professional networking have blurred. Facebook has historically been viewed as a purely social networking venue. That has changed. As younger professionals enter the job market and advance their careers, many have repurposed Facebook into a professional networking tool, with a personal touch. In fact, many job seekers view Facebook as a job search tool that showcases the "whole person," not just the professional.

Companies have caught on. Most larger, established, and forward-thinking companies have a corporate Facebook presence. They use Facebook to attract job seekers and to check the character of job applicants.[131]

As a job search tool, Facebook is similar to LinkedIn. You will discover similarities as we discuss Facebook. Some of these points will be shorter, because concepts have already been more thoroughly covered in the LinkedIn section. Note the similarities:

Profile. Like LinkedIn and Twitter, you need to create a professional Facebook page.[132] From the top navigation bar click the expansion arrow next to the question mark icon. You

---

131 "Number of Employers Using Social Media to Screen Candidates Has Increased 500 Percent over the Last Decade." *CareerBuilder.* April 28, 2016. http://www.careerbuilder.com/share/aboutus/pressreleasesdetail. aspx?ed=12%2F31%2F2016&id=pr945&sd=4%2F28%2F2016 (Accessed March 16, 2017).

132 "Pages." *Facebook.* https://www.facebook.com/help/282489752085908/?helpref=hc_fnav.

can then click "Create Page." Choose from the list of categories that Facebook provides. From those categories, there are subcategories to choose from. Be sure to align your Facebook page and LinkedIn profiles.

If you prefer to utilize your personal Facebook account and you have been using it socially with your friends, it's time to get out the mop and bucket and clean it up (if you haven't already)! Remove all unprofessional posts. Remove all unprofessional photos. From this point forward, all posts and photos must be acceptable to the professional viewing audience (hiring executives, corporate HR, executive recruiters, and so on).

Similar to LinkedIn, use keywords and industry terms-of-art to enhance your "findability." Consider linking to or mentioning your LinkedIn profile. Make sure it is consistent with employment, dates, and so on.

Classify your friends. From your Home page, go to the left side of the page to "Explore" and click on "Friend Lists." From there you can create a "New List." Create a list of your professional friends/contacts. The benefit of this is that you can post information directed only to your professional contacts. As you add professional friends, classify them to this list. Depending upon the number of friends you have, it could take you a while to do this, but it is worth it. Be sure that any professional contacts you add are relevant to you.

"Like" and follow target company pages. By doing this, you will receive information about job openings, announcements, news releases on your home page and your notifications list.

Searching on Facebook. You can use the search function within Facebook on a wide variety of topics (likes, interests, groups, and so on). Type your search term into the search bar at the top of your Facebook page and click enter. More than one search term can be entered into the search bar.

Once your search results load, you can then refine your search by Top, Latest, People, Photos, Videos, Shop, Pages, Places, Groups, Apps and Events, Posted By, Tagged Location and Date Posted.

If you choose to post content. Like Twitter and LinkedIn, post relevant content and pass along good information as it should come your way. Remember to think and be smart about what you post.

Privacy Options.[133] Facebook has many privacy options such as managing who can view your full profile, pages, friends lists, photos, etc. It is recommended to review and set your privacy options appropriately for a job search.

---

133 "Basic Privacy Settings & Tools." *Facebook Help Center.* https://www.facebook.com/help/325807937506242/?ref=contextual (Accessed 3/17/17).

---

212   The *Motivated* College Graduate

Some final words on Facebook. Traditionally viewed as a purely social site, Facebook is now clearly a significant resource tool for a job search. Will Facebook ever surpass LinkedIn as a professional networking site? Who's to say? What is certain is Facebook is another tool that can advance and shorten your job search.

★ Chapter 9

Proactively Marketing Your Collegiate Credentials Directly to Employers

Far better it is to dare mighty things, to win glorious triumphs, even though checkered by failure, than to take rank with those poor spirits who neither enjoy nor suffer much, because they live in the gray twilight that knows neither victory nor defeat.

— Theodore Roosevelt[134]

Introduction to the Direct Approach

Career fairs, on-campus interviews, industry conferences, networking, and selectively applying for jobs online are all effective job search strategies. There is one more technique that you should use to further maximize your exposure to the job market. That technique is the direct approach—Proactively Marketing Your Collegiate Credentials Directly to Employers.

---

134 Roosevelt, Theodore. *The Strenuous Life*. Speech. The Hamilton Club, Chicago, IL, April 10, 1899. http://www.bartleby.com/58/1.html (accessed May 28, 2015).

What the Coaches Say:

College graduates can increase the number of their job opportunities by proactively marketing their collegiate background directly to employers - hiring executives and talent acquisition professionals (HR). What insight and advice would you offer graduates who use this strategy?

Yes, being a new grad is an exciting time since so many people enjoy helping the recent grad . . . use their enthusiasm to help with your job search and talk to everyone . . . BUT, if you don't know what you're looking for or the skills you offer, no one can help. Understand the value you bring, communicate it, and proactively market yourself as a new college grad!

Ellen Steverson, NCRW, GCDF, CEIC

Your goal is to be the person the hiring managers reach out to when they have a position to fill. When using this strategy, make sure you are clear about your career goals and expectations, identify companies that offer positions that meet your criteria, then actively promote your collegiate credentials to get a meeting with the hiring manager. Do not worry if you are told there are no open positions—employers are always looking for top candidates and sometimes create positions when they meet someone they want in their workforce.

Lorraine Beaman, MA, CEIC, ACRW, CARW, NCRW, MCD

Proactively marketing your collegiate credentials is contacting an employer directly regardless of whether there is a known open position. This approach will differentiate you from the vast majority of other college graduate job seekers and can shorten your search, but it requires initiative, courage, and perseverance.

We are about to discuss two ways for directly contacting employers and proactively marketing your collegiate credentials. The first is a cold call. It involves you calling a talent acquisition professional or prospective hiring executive and presenting yourself as a well-qualified college graduate. Then, as needed, you will make follow-up communications through additional calls or email correspondence. This approach requires the emotional strength to accept some rejection or being ignored. However, it is arguably one of the quickest ways to get interviews or otherwise "get in the mix" in the job market. This technique has you hunting for a job in the Hidden Job Market.

For some, the idea of making cold calls as a part of a job search is very uncomfortable, too pushy, or too aggressive. The technique is not for everyone. There is an alternative.

The second approach can be equally effective and initially easier to execute. It requires that you create and send an impactful email to a talent acquisition professional or hiring executive, followed by telephone calls and additional emails. The follow-up calls are more of a warm call since you have reached out to the talent acquisition professional or hiring executive after email correspondence. Regardless of which approach you take, it is absolutely necessary that you pick up the phone and call executives who could potentially be hiring!

The very first thing to do when you use this job search tactic is making sure your voicemail greeting at home or on your cell phone is professional. You don't want to ruin a positive first impression with an unprofessional greeting.

To put this job search technique in action requires that you identify employers, identify the talent acquisition professional or hiring executive, communicate a compelling message about your collegiate background and how you can benefit the employer's organization.

Here are the steps to creating and executing an effective proactive marketing plan:

1. Identify your target companies.
2. Determine the talent acquisition professional or hiring executive's identity.
3. Research for a telephone number and email address.
4. Write a compelling call script or email cover letter about your collegiate background.
5. Execute. This is either starting with a call or email.

The Work

The technique of proactively marketing your collegiate credentials is an effective method of identifying job opportunities and can significantly shorten your job search once executed. Proactive marketing takes effort, but it is an effective ways to uncover opportunities that may not even exist *except* in confidential conversations among managers (The Hidden Job Market).

Your proactive efforts could represent the most labor-intensive commitment of time you invest in your search. It may take three to four days of solid research time for you to identify target companies, the right (or probable) talent acquisition professional or hiring executive (or both), and his or her current email address and phone number. It is recommended that you make the commitment of time to do this work.

The proactive method requires a shift in your thinking. You are now looking for a company you want to work for, instead of a job . . . so to speak.[135] As you discover and learn about interesting companies, put additional marketing effort toward these companies, perhaps a drip email and call strategy (discussed later).

As you identify those "high-interest" companies, follow them on both social media (LinkedIn, Twitter, and so on) as well as more traditional news sources (press releases, Google alerts, and more). Connect with relevant employees and managers on LinkedIn. Consider asking for a research interview(s), which is another technique mentioned later. The more you can learn, the more you network, and the more you make them aware of your availability and collegiate credentials, the greater your chances of getting an interview.

Determine Your Target Employers

There are a variety of methods and sources to identify target employers:

1. Lists that your career placement office may have
2. Book of Lists with major employers by industry type (most metropolitan areas have them)
3. Companies you can identify by reviewing profiles from a LinkedIn group
4. Association membership lists (an excellent source)
5. Industry conference attendee lists and vendor lists (another excellent source)
6. Purchased lists (services that sell databases of companies and contacts) including:
   - www.infousa.com
   - www.hoovers.com
   - www.standardandpoors.com
   - www.jigsaw.com
   - www.listgiant.com
   - www.goleads.com
   - www.vault.com

---

135 Whitcomb, *Job Search Magic*, p. 273–274.

Start with your shortlist of targeted companies. Then, collect information on fifty more companies. It may sound like a lot, but it might be the only fifty companies (plus your short list) you'll need to research to get an offer (or two). If you exhaust the original group of companies, research more.

Identify the Talent Acquisition Professional and the Hiring Executive

This is a process of research. You are looking for two people: a talent acquisition professional (likely in the Human Resources Department) and the probable executive that has the authority to hire you. These people can be identified in several ways:

- Company website

- LinkedIn

- Call the company and ask.

If you are in doubt, identifying and contacting two or three executives in addition to the talent acquisition professional is fine so long as you are reasonably focused on who you contact. It is acceptable to contact someone on the executive management team (like the COO). It depends on the size of the company.

Research Email Addresses

This can be tricky, but the best way is to review the company website. Go to the contact page and look for an email address. If there is not one there, go to the news and events page. Normally a press release for the company will have the marketing employee's email address. That can give you the formula that companies use for their email addresses. If you cannot find an email anywhere on the website, just use the website address and put an @ symbol before it.

Another way is to look up employees of the company on LinkedIn. Sometimes employees provide their company email address, which will give you the email formula you need.

As an alternative, use different forms of the hiring executive's name and then the company web address or the email address you have found on the website in the Google search. For instance, most companies use the formula firstinitiallastname@xyz.com. Google that and see if you have any results. If not, try different formulas: firstname.lastname@xyz.com. You can usually find email addresses this way because people sometimes use work emails for personal use.

Below are some different formulas you can use to search for email addresses:

jsmith@xyz.com

john.smith@xyz.com

smithj@xyz.com

john@xyz.com

johns@xyz.com

johnsmith@xyz.com

There are free services that can greatly increase your success rate with email address research. One service is https://hunter.io.

Using the Telephone

Some college graduates will hesitate to proactively market themselves and their credentials using the telephone or cell phone. In today's job market, it is imperative to utilize every resource and technique available to shorten your job search. Making calls must be part of your job-search arsenal.

To help ease the physical use of the telephone, consider investing in a hands-free headset or use a Bluetooth device on your cell phone. This will free up your hands so you can write and you won't have to hold the phone to your ear with your shoulder. Being hands-free will have a positive effect on your tone of voice and keep you more relaxed when making calls.

The Positive Impact of Using the Phone

There are several good reasons why you need to make calls to talent acquisition and hiring executives as a part of your job search. It helps you . . .

1. Differentiate yourself. Calling a talent acquisition or a hiring executive to discuss your collegiate background and possible opportunities sets you apart from other college graduate job seekers. Employers value initiative.

2. Create a positive mental impression. When you are on the phone, the only variables that count are your educational, qualifications, enthusiasm, and positive phone voice.

3. More quickly establish a relationship. Your call personalizes the engagement and communication. It is said that 60 percent of hires are made based on personal chemistry, according to a study by the University of Michigan on hiring managers.[136] A conversation helps build that chemistry (using the persuasion principle of liking), which can lead to an interview.

4. Create urgency and value. By calling an employer, you create the perception that you will not be on the market long. The talent acquisition and hiring executive will see that you are taking your job search seriously and are researching future opportunities thoroughly. All of this helps you create value (using the persuasion principle of scarcity).

5. Gather information to be more prepared for possible interviews. An initial phone conversation with the hiring executive may help you learn what the company looks for in a new college hire. You can then prepare answers to possible interview questions based on that information.

Excuses for Not Using the Phone in a Job Search

Over the course of time, every excuse imaginable has been raised why individuals will not use the phone. These excuses basically encompass the following:

1. "It's intimidating. Calling people I don't know."
Accept the fact that everyone (including those you will call) has faced finding their first job. It was as uncomfortable for them as it is for you now. They understand what you are doing and going through. Most will help if they can. Using the telephone to connect with employers may seem intimidating at first, but once you have a few good calls, the intimidation fades and it will actually be fun! (Honest, it'll really happen!)

2. "I have better things to do than leaving a bunch of voice messages."
Actually, you don't. And, this excuse is "task avoidance." You come up with things to do to avoid making calls.
Leaving voice messages and playing a little phone tag is all part of the process. You must show persistence. You may have to call someone a handful of times before speaking to them. A talent acquisition or hiring executive takes note of persistence—as long as you don't cross the line and become an annoyance. As a general guideline, make three attempts. If you do not get a response, it's safe to move on.

---

136 DiResta, interview by Canters, "How to Blitz."

If you keep missing an employer that has called back, ask to schedule an appointment that is convenient for both of you. Ask if an administrative assistant can contact you to set up the call.

3. "I have attended career fairs, sent a lot of emails and resumes, and networked with everyone I know. They'll be calling me!"

Conducting a job search to find the best possible position as your first job is about using every avenue available to you. This means taking the initiative to reach out to those who can grant you an interview. Failing to do could be cheating yourself from finding that best-fit first job or prolonging your job search.

4. "My resume and collegiate qualifications are strong. Employers will find me and call!"

No they won't. Employers seldom proactively reach out to college graduates asking them to interview with them. It does not work that way. Take the lead and contact employers. One simple phone could make a remarkable difference in your job search.

5. "They could hang up on me!"

This excuse is ridiculous, and so what if they do? Regardless, it is so rare that it is almost not worth mentioning. You are introducing yourself as a professional and asking people for their assistance. They will not hang up on you. And, in the very rare event it happens, that's the one company you don't want to work for anyway.

6. "I don't want to be rejected."

This excuse, for some, can be significant because the root cause is fear. Fear, whether real or perceived, is a formidable emotion. If this is an obstacle for you, you must call upon your courage to overcome it. Script what you will say, focus on those words, and say them.

No one wants to be rejected. Although you will encounter the word "no" or a statement such as "I don't think I can help you" or any number of responses that will not advance your job search, don't get discouraged. Rejection is an inescapable part of the process. But keep in mind: Rejection is not personal, it's business. They are not rejecting you as a person. And every "no" gets you one step closer to a "yes."

If you are struggling with the idea of making calls as a component to your job search because you fear being rejected, that people will hang up on you, or people will be rude to you, let's make it a game (or a challenge). Assume that you make one hundred proactive calls to talent acquisition professionals and potential hiring executives. (Recall you are supposed to find fifty companies to contact and identify two people at each to reach out to). Further assume that there exist two people that will be rude to you or will hang up on you. Your challenge is to make calls and find those two people.

Here is the reality: You will either make calls as a part of your job search or you won't. But if you do, you will reap significant rewards that will positively affect your job search and potentially your career.

If you choose not to use the phone, the following things will likely happen:

1. Your job search could take longer.

2. You risk settling for any job (just to be employed).

3. You risk slipping into a passive job search relying on posted job openings. (And by now you know, that is not the best strategy.)

Phone Zone

This is a quiet place free of distractions, where you can focus and concentrate on the task at hand. It can be your dorm room (when your roommate is gone), fraternity/sorority room, or even a room available at your college or university's career placement center. It's a place where the risk of interruptions and background noise is minimized. Prior to making calls, remove all unnecessary paperwork and nonessential items from your work surface or desktop. The only things you need are:

• Your call list
• Your script for leaving a voice message
• Your presentation of what you will say when you speak to the employer
• A script for answering common responses or objections (more on that later)
• A copy of your resume
• Success stories
• Pen, paper, maybe something to drink
• Your enthusiasm

Phone *Phear*: The Pre-Game Jitters

It is perfectly normal to have some anxiety about calling talent acquisition professionals or hiring executives. For some of us, it happens. Your entire job search won't collapse because of a case of the nerves. In fact, a healthy dose of nerves is an indication of an outstanding performance to come! Below are some tips to turn nervousness into focused effort:

1. Script and practice the delivery of your message. Know what you are going to say (more on that in a moment).

2. Concentrate on delivering your message/script with confidence. You are on the phone. They cannot see you.

3. Remember that you know everything about the subject at hand: You! In other words, there won't be a question about your background you can't answer.[137]

4. Adopt the attitude that every company you call has a possible opening. Never assume that it is a bother that you called or the answer will be "no."

Here is a suggestion that helps most college graduate job seekers: When it comes time to start making calls, generate five calls in succession, without breaks, as efficiently and effectively as you can. Remarkably, once you break the ice and create a rhythm, the reluctance fades. Progress is being made. Once you get the feel for it, you will be surprised how many quality calls you can make.

Who to Contact

For each company on your list, you will reach out to two, and maybe three, people. This includes:

1. **A talent acquisition professional**—normally a person in the Human Resource department.

2. **The hiring executive**—this is the manager or supervisor that you conclude from your research would be the person who you would report to for the position you are pursuing. Sometimes first-level managers are not easily identified. It's perfectly acceptable and encouraged for you to contact department heads (those higher up in the company) responsible for the type of position you are seeking.

3. **Another hiring executive**—this is an executive that you are not certain is the right contact, but could be. Go ahead and reach out. One extra contact may be all it takes to get someone's attention and get an interview.

137　　See also, Claycomb and Dinse, *Career Pathways*, Part 5, "Phone-phobia."

With this strategy in mind, you can feel confident that your proactive marketing efforts will alert the employer of your availability and credentials.

The Marketing Call Script

The following is a sample script that will get you thinking as you write your own marketing call script.

Introduction

The introduction identifies who you are. If you can, reference a mutual acquaintance or someone that referred you. That common ground often helps break the ice.

"Mr. Sanders, my name is Chris Watson. I was referred to you by Bob Johnson."

If you do not have a common reference point:

"Mr. Sanders, my name is Chris Watson and I am a recent college graduate with a degree in Marking from State University."

Ask permission to continue the call

Hiring executives are busy, and they will appreciate the thoughtfulness.

"I realize that I've called you out of the blue. Did I catch you at a good time?"

OR

"I hope that I can get a few minutes of your time?"

Get their attention

Similar to your elevator speech and cover letter, make a clear statement about one of your collegiate accomplishments. Grab their attention.

"As I mentioned, I just graduated from State University with a degree in Marketing. I have a 3.4 G.P.A., was the president of the Marketing Club, and was an intern last summer at Eckhardt and Taylor."

OR

"As I mentioned, I am graduating from State University with a degree in Psychology. I received academic and athletic scholarships and was a starter on the University baseball team."

What if you are a college graduate but choose not to be involved in a lot of activities and do not have a high G.P.A.? How do you sell yourself? Answer: focus of your positive character traits.

> *"As I mentioned, I recently graduated from State University with a degree in Home Economics. I have a strong work ethic having worked full time during the summer [and part time during the school year?]. I am focused and believe in 'putting my head down' to get the job done."*

If you happen to be one of those college graduates that worked full or part time to put yourself through school, most employers will be impressed with your achievement. In some cases (depending upon the employer), working while going to school can carry more weight as a collegiate accomplishment than a high G.P.A. or a long list of collegiate activities. This is especially true if the talent acquisition professional or hiring executive also worked to get through college.

Purpose for the call

Now that you have introduced yourself and gotten the talent acquisition professional or hiring executive's attention, state the reason for the call: to set up an interview.

> *"I'm looking for my first job out of college and I would like to meet (or speak) with you to discuss how I can contribute to the success of (Company Name)."*

Relate to the employer (optional)

If possible, try to make a statement (if you can) that relates to the employer. This can be a statement specific to the company, a trend, or an issue facing the industry. This is where your research or following the company on social media can give you information to use.

> *"By the way, I read that you have just rolled out a new cost containment service line."*

OR

> *"As I understand, the new healthcare regulations that take effect next year might change business."*

If you do not have enough information about the company or industry, you can omit the "relate" portion of the script.

Close

Close the script with a request for an interview (the ultimate purpose of the call).

"I am available (to meet with you or speak with you in more detail) in the afternoons next week. Which day would work best for you?"

OR

"I can make myself available Tuesday morning or after 3 p.m. on Thursday. Which timeframe might work best for you?"

OR, if you do not want to be so forward in your request . . .

"I can be flexible to your schedule to meet so long as it does not conflict with any exam dates I have."

These closing questions assume that the employer is interested, and yes, you are being a little bold here. The key is to *speak the words* then wait for a response. The purpose is to get an interview. So, ask for one!

After you finish the script

Once you finish speaking the script, you will likely encounter a moment of silence. The employer is processing what you have said. This is not the kind of call they receive every day. Remain quiet.

The talent acquisition professional or hiring executive will respond with one of two things: A question that indicates interest (a "buying sign") or an objection/deflection. If the response is a question, this is good. Provide a short, responsive answer. There could be a follow-up question, which is great. Provide a response. However, at some point you need to again request an interview, either a phone interview or in person.

"Mr. Tyrrell, it sounds like we might have some things to discuss. Let's schedule an appointment to (talk in more detail/meet in person)."

OR

"Mr. Tyrrell, it appears that there may be an opportunity where I can bring some value to your company. When could we schedule a time to speak?"

There will be calls when your script will not go exactly as written. The talent acquisition professional or hiring executive might interrupt with a question. Anticipate this happening. Simply respond the best you can.

Responses to Objections

If you get an objection (or deflection), it will likely be one of the following:

1. *"I don't have any openings."*

More often than not, this response is truthful. The first priority of any smart hiring executive is to achieve company goals through people, and be on the lookout for talented people. Offer to send your resume. If it gets read, another opportunity within the company could be a possible fit. And, most importantly, ask a question—get the hiring executive talking if you can. It is this part of the engagement where you build rapport. Something as simple as:

> *"I understand. May I forward my resume to you in the event something changes? One question: What do you see as the industry's most important trend right now?"*

OR

> *"That's all right. Can you think of another company you could refer me to that might have a need?"*

OR

> *"I understand but I certainly appreciate you taking my call. Is there any advice that you might have that could assist me in my search?"*

2. *"We don't hire recent college graduates. We only hire experienced people."*

More often than not, this response is likely truthful. But ask a question, the answer to which could give you information that might advance your job search. Here is a couple:

> *"I understand. Do you know what companies (in the area, in your industry) do hire recent college graduates?"*

OR

> *"Regarding your experienced people, do you recall what companies they may have started their careers?"*

OR

> *"If you were in my shoes, what would you do to land that first career job?"*

3. *"Can you send me your resume?"*

The response here is to agree but ask a question to hopefully get an interview or further the dialogue and continue to build a professional relationship. Responses could include one of the following:

> *"I will! Would it make sense to sit down and discuss my background so you further understand what I could bring to the table? I can make myself available to your schedule."*

OR

> *"I will! What job title or opportunity should I refer to when I send it?"*

OR

> *"I will! What specific skills or experience might you be looking for?"*

4. "I really don't have time to talk right now."

> *"I understand. Is it possible to schedule a brief ten-minute call later?"*

5. "You'll need to talk to Human Resources."

This may or may not be a brush-off, but at least get a name in HR for when you make contact. When you do contact HR, you can use the name of the hiring executive that referred you. Respond with something simple, like:

> *"Great! When I speak to HR, whom should I ask for? And what position should I tell them you asked me to contact them about?"*

Ask One Question After the Objection

If you can, ask one question after you respond to the hiring executive's objection. A good method to initiate this question is: "Let me ask you a question." There are myriad questions you could ask, but choose one that is germane to the conversation or your job search.

Dealing with Rejection

A very important point to remember when you make these calls: You will be rejected eventually (in one form or another). You need to keep telling yourself that people are not rejecting you as a person. Most of the time, it is the situation with the company—they aren't hiring, they don't hire recent college graduates, or something else. So each time you are rejected, renew your positive attitude with the next call. With each rejection you get, you are closer to an affirmative response (an interview!). It's a process of elimination.

I can summarize the lessons of my life in seven words—
never give in; never, never give in.

— Winston Churchill[138]

Handling the Gatekeeper

As you make calls, you will undoubtedly encounter a "gatekeeper" — a person whose function is in part to protect the talent acquisition professional's or hiring executive's schedule. Be ever so kind and polite to these people. Befriend them if possible. As a general rule, they will have one question for you:

"What is this regarding?"

When speaking with the gatekeeper, be straightforward and say something like:

> *"I am a recent college graduate with a degree in Finance and I am looking for my first job out of college. I want to reach out to Mr. Eisele. Is he available?"*

You may be diverted to Human Resources, which is fine. But, ask to leave a message for your intended contact if you can. Here's what you can say to the gatekeeper if she wants to send you to Human Resources.

> *"Thank you. Who should I contact? Would it be okay to leave a message for Mr. Eisele all the same?"*

If the gatekeeper insists on diverting you to HR, you can call back after business hours and perhaps leave a message through the phone system. Frequently you can enter a name and leave a message.

Leaving a Voicemail Message

Most of the time when you make your calls you will get the hiring executive's or talent acquisition professional's voicemail. You can use voicemail as an opportunity to leave a brief message. The voicemail could go something like this:

---

138 Cornerstone Coaching LLC. "What Winston Churchill Can Teach Us About Inevitable Success." February 26, 2014. http://www.cornerstoneadvisoryservices.com/blog/what-winston-churchill-can-teach-us-about-inevitable-success (accessed May 28, 2015).

"Mr. Geringer, this is Taylor Suderville and I'm a recent college graduate from State University with a degree in Anthropology. My G.P.A. is 3.1 and I worked part-time through school to help my parents pay for college. I have recommendations that say I have a strong work ethic. I would like to connect with you at your convenience to discuss my background and professional character traits and how I can contribute to the success of (Company Name). [(Optional, but could be helpful) I am interested in positions in sales or client retention] I can be reached at 123-456-7890."

How many voice messages? There is a fine line between being persistent and becoming a pest. Only you can make that determination. However, three would likely be the maximum. Vary the content of your messaging so it is not the same each time. Remember that you can reach out to the hiring executive by email as well and blend your contact methodology.

Email Marketing Your Collegiate Credentials

An alternative approach when proactively marketing your collegiate credentials is to initially reach out to the talent acquisition professional or hiring executives by email (or LinkedIn InMail). With reference to the Cover Letter Success Formula, write a compelling email cover letter.

Marketing emails essentially follow the identical formula for content as any other letter with some distinct differences that should be observed to increase effectiveness:

Subject Line. Good use of the subject line is vital. It must be short and impactful. A poor subject line would read: *"College grad looking for work."* A good subject line would read:

> *College Graduate-Animal Science Degree-2 Internships*
> *College Graduate-3.6 G.P.A. in Marketing-looking for entry-level position*

A very good approach is using your Headline from your LinkedIn profile, and then modifying it as needed using good judgment.

Street Address. This is a communication sent by email, not by the US Postal Service. Do not put a street address in the email. A date is unnecessary as well.

Attaching a Resume. It is recommended that you attach a copy of your resume. However, some companies have servers with robust firewalls that screen out all unfamiliar emails with an attachment. If your email that had a resume attached is returned with an undeliverable kickback, try again without the resume attached.

When it comes to attaching a resume, customize the name of the document. It should at least be your name with a space between your names *e.g.* John Smith.docx. A unique approach would be your name plus a branding statement *e.g.* John Smith - 3.8 G.P.A. docx.

Close. Your close should be different due to the "reply" function with emails. It is recommended that you ask the recipient to act in response to the email. An example of a good close would be: *"If you have an interest or a need for a recent college graduate with a strong work ethic, please reply or call me."*

Telephone Number. Always put your telephone number in your marketing emails. The employer may want to bypass the reply button and speak to you directly. Give them a way to do so.

Your Email Signature Block. Consider customizing your email signature block to help promote your job search. Below is one example:

> *Julie Stubblefield*
> *Business Marketing Degree, Graduation May 20XX*
> *GPA 3.7* [optional]
> *State University*
> *Seeking business operations positions in the Phoenix area*
> *(Possibly add a hyperlink to your LinkedIn profile)*

Sending Your Marketing Email

Once you have identified your target companies, identified the (probable) talent acquisition professional or hiring executive, obtained an email address, and written a compelling marketing email, it is time to send them.

Send each email individually. DO NOT send a mass email and waste your time and effort.

Instead, copy and paste your template email, and then customize each email as needed. Spell check. Give it one last look for appearance; attach your resume, pause for any last thoughts, and send.

When you get an undeliverable message on an email, don't get discouraged or distracted. That will happen. Move on. When you've completed sending the other emails in your original batch, address the kickbacks. Regarding the kickbacks, double-check the spelling and the email formula. Call the company to confirm the email address, informing the person on the phone the email address you used and that you received a kickback. This approach frequently works to get the correct email address.

Email Marketing Through LinkedIn

Sending marketing emails as LinkedIn InMail is acceptable. Depending on the level of LinkedIn account you have, the number of InMails you have is limited. Therefore, try reaching hiring executives first through their company email and use LinkedIn InMail as a secondary strategy if reaching the talent acquisition professional or executive through company email proves futile.

Follow-Up Calls

After you send your marketing emails, wait a day or two and see if you get responses. Obviously, you want to immediately follow up on any emails you receive indicating interest. After a day or so, you will need to start generating calls to the employers you sent emails to. You will use virtually the same scripts provided with a reference to the email you sent previously. Your voice message should also reflect that you sent an email a few days prior. Follow this example:

> *"Mr. Eisele, this is Jackson Masson, I'm a recent college graduate with a degree in Criminal Justice. I sent you an email a few days ago. If you recall from the email, I . . . [re-state much of the content of your marketing email.]*

These calls should seem more like a warm call, and easier to generate, since you have already reached out to the hiring executive. You are now simply following up. Remember, the ultimate purpose of the call is to ask for and get an interview.

★ Drip Email Marketing

An effective strategy when marketing your collegiate credentials is "drip" marketing, which is when you send messages to a hiring executive over a period of time. The drip concept is to send a marketing email and then systematically contact the same talent acquisition professional or hiring executive with a couple of additional emails containing different information. The goal is to generate interest to secure an interview.[139]

There are several important points to be aware of when using this technique. Be very organized, record who you have contacted, with what information, and when. Space your drip emails at least two or three days apart.

There is a variety of information you can select for your drip messages. Here are a few ideas:

1. A recommendation or endorsement.
2. A list of references—especially if there is a chance that the talent acquisition professional or hiring executive might know one of them.
3. A short success story of a character trait in action.
4. Positive comments from summer job performance or internship reviews.
5. An abridged summary from a personality assessment, if you have one.

Here is an example of how to introduce new information through the drip email marketing approach:

> *Ms. Brust,*
>
> *I reached out to you a few days ago by email [or call.] If you recall, I'm a recent college graduate with a degree in Computer Science, GPA of 3.6 and a summer internship with Hi-Tech International.*
>
> *I want to pass along another piece of information that you may have interest. Below is a recommendation I received from my summer internship supervisor:*
>
> *[Contents of the recommendation]*
>
> *I am interested in Forward-Thinking Technologies due to its work with artificial intelligence.*
>
> *Is it possible to schedule a call? I can make myself available to your schedule.*

Just remember, the purpose of drip marketing is to generate interest and secure an interview. Always offer your availability at the end of each drip email.

Most college job seekers that use the drip marketing approach find it easy to execute. The overall effectiveness depends on the talent acquisition professional and/or hiring executive. Some may respond more favorably to a follow-up call because they recognize and appreciate the initiative. For others, it makes no difference.

---

139 Hill, Paul. *The Panic Free Job Search: Unleash the Power of the Web and Social Networking to Get Hired*. Pompton Plains, NJ: Career Press, 2012. p. 203.

Blend the email marketing and phone contact approaches. Follow good judgement on the number and methods of contact. Show persistence, but again, don't become a pest. If you are not getting a response to your overtures, move on.

★ The Research Interview

This job search technique can yield promising job leads. A research interview is a very brief conversation, either by telephone or face to face, with an employee who currently works for a target company. The point of the conversation is to ask open-ended questions that elicit responses regarding their experiences working for that company. It's also a good time to ask about the industry, trends, and so on.

The reason why the research interview works so well is twofold. First, people like to talk about themselves and share their experiences with others. Just assure your contact that the conversation is confidential.

Second, as a general rule, people like to help others. Once you establish confidentiality and show your genuine interest in their responses, people tend to speak openly. Once people realize that their experiences and opinions are the focal point of the call, the information will flow.

Here is a step-by-step guide to setting up a research interview:

1. Identify an appropriate number of targeted companies in which you have a sincere interest.

2. Identify an appropriate contact within that target company. Use LinkedIn to help find someone appropriate.

3. Call, email, or use LinkedIn InMail and request an appointment by clearly stating the purpose for the conversation (to learn about the company and/or the industry). Establish an appointment time for a fifteen to twenty minute conversation.

4. Prepare, in advance, four or five open-ended questions. The key is to get them talking about themselves, the company, their position, and so on. As a rule, stay away from the topic of compensation and benefits.

5. Since you set up the appointment, be the one to generate the call. Be punctual and ask your contact whether it is still a good time.

6. Conduct the research interview by asking your questions. Keep things to fifteen to twenty minutes to be mindful and respectful of their time. If you start to run over, acknowledge it; frequently the contact will say it is okay to continue.

7. Always write a thank-you note or email. Send it promptly after the conversation.

It is not uncommon for people to ask about your job search as a part of this conversation. This is where the magic of this approach often happens. They will volunteer information about internal openings, lead you to network to others inside or outside the company, mention job leads with other companies, and so on.

If there happens to be an open position within the company, ask whether your contact could refer you to the appropriate person. Also (and this is important), ask whether the company offers referral bonuses to employees for referring qualified job seekers. If so, this creates an obvious incentive for your contact to refer you. According to recent surveys, nearly two-thirds of companies encourage employee participation in recruiting by offering referral bonuses.[140] These bonuses can exceed $1,000.[141] *However,* some companies with internal referral bonuses exclude non-experienced candidates from their program.

A research interview is a great strategy. It is an easy and comfortable call to make and the topic is safe and reasonable for the company employee.

What the Coaches Say:

What has been your experience, or what is your opinion, about using a research (or informal) interview as a part of a college graduate's job search?

Informational interviews are very helpful in several ways. You learn about current industry issues which allow you time to prepare to discuss these issues during an interview. Also you meet potential hiring managers and people who can help you meet other hiring managers. This is an especially effective job search method for students in the social sciences or humanities who want to launch a career in business.

Lorraine Beaman, MA, CEIC, ACRW, CARW, NCRW, MCD

---

140 "Jobvite Recruiter Nation Report 2016," *Jobvite.* http://www.jobvite.com/wp-content/uploads/2016/09/RecruiterNation2016.pdf (Accessed March 15, 2017). (64% of recruiters report awarding monetary bonuses to incentivize referrals into their organizations.)

141 "Bonus Programs and Practices." *WorldatWork.* June 2014. http://www.worldatwork.org/adimLink?id=75444 (accessed June 1, 2015).

I would encourage a recent graduate to set a goal to have coffee/tea/drink of choice, with as many connections per month whether known or unknown as possible in an informational interview capacity.

I had an international student who was determined to land a job in the USA, and he had specific and targeted cities he wanted to live in which included: San Francisco, NYC, Miami and LA. He set up nearly 50 coffee/connect sessions within a 2.5-week period! He jokingly told me he had the jitters for weeks after those few weeks of interviews because of the amount of coffee he had drank. He flew from coast to coast for these meetings, and through his intentional informational interviewing he was able to meet a high-level executive who connected him to one of his colleagues who eventually ended up helping him land a great job in NYC.

This student's go-getter spirit resonated with the decision maker and because of his intentionality, great 30-second pitch, and resilient process, this student landed a great opportunity! The famous phrase goes, it's not what you know but who you know, and through informational interviews you meet a lot of people and gain a lot of insightful information which can generate opportunity.

Jered Lish M.S., Gallup-Certified Strengths Coach, GCDF

Using Videos or YouTube as a Part of Your Messaging

Embedding a short video (or YouTube link) into email messages to employers is unique, effective, and can differentiate you from others, *if done correctly*.

First and foremost, your video must be professional. If it is not, you can significantly harm your job search efforts. If you decide to pursue video, consult the section on Webcam or Skype Interviews. Many of the same considerations listed there will apply to your video (your attire, look into the camera, and so on).

The purpose of the video is to introduce yourself as a "professional," create interest, and differentiate yourself from other college job seekers. Used for this purpose, it is not a lengthy video resume. Therefore, keep your video short; the recommended length is a minute to a minute-and-a-half.

The video personalizes you. The talent acquisition professional or hiring executive can see you, pick up on your personality, and learn about you. The video operates as a first impression, which is very important (see First Impressions later in this book). Remember to smile.

What do you talk about? After introducing yourself, discuss your collegiate accomplishments, and character traits. A logical starting point is your elevator speech. Start out strong with an attention-getting statement. Refer to the attention-getting recommendations listed previously. Many of those will work here. (As you may have figured out already, many of the concepts and techniques of a job search weave together, are interchangeable, interrelate, and complement each other.)

It is imperative that you script, memorize, and practice what you are going to say. Then make sure you can deliver the speech in a conversational tone and manner (just like your elevator speech). This video will be viewed by talent acquisition professional or hiring executives. It must be perfect!

Frequently, companies that design and create websites could help you produce a video with graphics. Or, you or a close friend might have the ability to do that.

When All Else Fails

There comes a point when it becomes apparent that the employer is simply not going to respond to your messages (emails or calls). If this happens, there's one last thing you can do before you "close the door" and move on. Send one last short email describing your collegiate background and ask that should the hiring executive become aware of any openings that would be a match to please pass along your information. This technique enlists the talent acquisition professional or hiring executive as a resource that could be helpful to your search.

Here is an example to get you thinking when composing your email:

Mrs. Paulsen,

I've reached out to you a few times over the past week or so. I'm sorry we have not connected.

I am a recent graduate from State College with a degree in Agricultural Business (Agri-Business). I have strong social skills having been the Rush Chairman for my fraternity (Lambda Chi Alpha). I am looking for my first professional job after college. Should you become aware of any entry-level positions with other companies, please feel free to pass along my information. My resume is attached.

Best Regards,
Your Name

Let's take a closer look at the email:

- It is short and to the point. This is important. Resist the temptation to provide too much information about your collegiate background and circumstances. You've already done that with previous communications.

- It grants permission to pass along your information. This allows them to help you, should they become aware of an opening.

- The hiring authority does not need to reply to you that your information has been passed along.

As you use this technique, every once in a while you will get a reply email acknowledging your message or a job lead. As with all job leads, it can lead to further networking and possibly your next job!

How to Honestly Measure Your Progress

The most important thing to measure regarding the progress of your job search is:

The Number of First Time Interviews!

These interviews are your first conversation with a company representative (the actual hiring executive, talent acquisition professional, or someone else), and the purest reflection of your efforts toward getting a new job. Your goal is to get as many first time interviews as you possibly can. When you get a first time interview, make it your goal to get another as quickly as you can with another company. Get on a roll!

There is a plethora of other activities you can track and you should selectively do so (namely, the number of calls you make or marketing emails you send to hiring executives). But when the day is done, first-time interviews are the honest measurement of moving your search toward getting a new job.

If you are dissatisfied with your results regarding first time interviews, frequently it is a result of your effort, or lack thereof. Are you attending career fairs, networking, making enough proactive outreaches—email, LinkedIn, calling or emailing enough talent acquisition professional or hiring executives? Are you focused and putting concentrated effort into your search? Be honest with yourself.

What is the second most important thing to measure regarding the success of your job search?

The Number of Second Time Interviews!

These are interviews beyond the initial screening. You are in the company's evaluation phase and "in-play."

If you are not advancing out of first time interviews, communicate with those employers that passed on you and get as much honest feedback as they'll give you. Remedy what you can and make changes.

Counting true, actual, and substantive interviews is the purest measure of your job search. The only way to get a job is to get an interview. And, the more interviews you have, the better your odds of landing a fulfilling position in the shortest time possible.

PART III

Interviewing and Making a Positive Impression

Chapter 10

Interviewing

To get something you never had, you have to do something you never did.

— Jose N. Harris[142]

How Much Are Interviews Worth?

Did you know that during an average round of golf, the actual amount of time the golf ball is in contact with the club face is a fraction of a second per swing?[143] Playing eighteen holes of golf results in a very short amount of ball contact overall. Remarkable! The same ratio of contact to length of an athletic contest likely holds true with other sports where there is an instrument striking an object (hockey, baseball, and tennis immediately come to mind). Now think of all the time these professional athletes spent over the course of their lives practicing, staying fit, being coached for hours, and so on to perfect, as much as possible, the technique and muscle memory to execute a swing that results in such a sliver of contact time. This analogy represents the small amount of time you spend interviewing relative to the total amount of work hours over the course of your career.

Let's do some math: Assume you work forty hours a week for fifty weeks a year (two

---

142 "Jose N. Harris Quotable Quote." *Goodreads.* http://www.goodreads.com/quotes/415120-to-get-something-you-never-had-you-have-to-do (accessed June 22, 2015).

143 "Ball at Impact." *Golfswing.com.* http://www.golfswing.com.au/139 (accessed February 15, 2016).

weeks a year for vacation and personal time off). This totals two thousand hours of work time a year. Assume that you will work for fifty years—as a society we are choosing to work longer into our lives.[144] Therefore, your total number of career working hours is one hundred thousand hours. A little staggering when you think about it.

Statistically speaking, the average professional could have as many as ten jobs over the course of their career[145] (for some it could be more, or less, but ten is representative in today's free-agent market, and it makes the math easier). Assume that it takes twenty-five hours of total interview time to secure a new position. This includes the interview process for the job you're hired for, as well as all of the positions you interviewed for that did not work out. Recently, interview processes have been lengthened for a variety of reasons.[146] So, ten jobs that took twenty-five hours of interviewing per job equals 250 hours of interview time over the course of your career. The ratio of 250 interview hours for one hundred thousand hours of career work time gets you .25 percent. When viewed this way, those interview hours take on more importance. (And we're not done!)

Consider the financial impact an outstanding interview can have on your career and personal life. Assume that you were, *on average*, able to improve your compensation by $10,000 every time you changed jobs. (It is recognized that there is a plethora of circumstances that affect this generalization. There could be times when it is less or more, but on average, assume an improvement of $10,000 per job change. Play along here; it's to prove a point.). So, ten jobs over the course of your career, with an increase of $10,000 per position, equals $100,000. Multiply that over a career of fifty years and that gets you $5,000,000. And that does not include the investment value of that money over time!

Okay, if you find yourself thinking about these numbers, the analogy, and the ways you could shoot more holes in it than a block of Swiss cheese, you've missed the point! Don't over-think it. The numbers and the analogy are not perfect! The point of the illustration is

144 Woods, Jennifer. "Working Longer—Whether You Want to or Not." *CNBC.com*. December 23, 2014, http:// cached.newslookup.com/cached.php?ref_id=105&siteid=2098&id=10359558&t=1419339600 (accessed June 9, 2015).

145 Bureau of Labor Statistics. "Number of Jobs Held, Labor Market Activity, and Earnings Growth Among the Youngest Baby Boomers: Results from a Longitudinal Survey." News release. March 31, 2015. http:// www.bls.gov/news.release/pdf/nlsoy.pdf (accessed May 29, 2015).

146 Joyce, Susan P. "After the Interview, What is Taking Them SO Long?" *Work Coach Café*. September 17, 2012. http://www.workcoachcafe.com/2012/09/17/after-the-interview-what-is-taking-them-so-long/ (accessed February 15, 2016); "2015 Candidate Behavior Study." *CareerBuilder*. http://careerbuildercommunications. com/candidatebehavior/ (accessed February 15, 2016); McGregor, Jena. "Interviewing for a Job is Taking Longer Than Ever." *On Leadership. Washington Post*. June 18, 2015. http://www.washingtonpost.com/blogs/ on-leadership/wp/2015/06/18/interviewing-for-a-job-is-taking-longer-than-ever/ (accessed February 15, 2016).

to impress upon you that interviews are critically important to your career enjoyment and financial well-being. Approaching interviews with a cavalier attitude or flying by the seat of your pants is foolish. There's simply too much at stake. When it comes to interviewing for a job, prepare! Interviews are worth a lot of money and they can mean a lot to your career, you, your family, and the lifestyle you live.

Let's review for a moment. Remember from Understanding the Employer's Mindset, an employer in the business world hires with two main goals in mind: to make money or save money.[147] In the non-commerce world it is achievement of the organization's mission. An interview is the platform that addresses those ultimate goals, through information exchange.

How an Employer Views an Interview

Employers want to answer five major questions as a result of the interviewing process:

1. Can you do the job? (skills, experience, character traits needed to perform the job)

2. Will you do the job? (motivated to actually perform the job functions)

3. Will your performance have a positive impact on company goals? (subjective prediction of future performance . . . will you be any good at it?)

4. Do you fit in? (cultural fit)

And, if those four questions are answered yes, then . . .

5. Can we offer fair compensation? (for a recent college graduate)

When the first four questions are answered affirmatively and the compensation fits, you have a shot at the position. Other college graduates may pass the criteria, too. Failing to pass any one of these hurdles will result in the employer pursuing others for the opportunity. Let's look at how you can give yourself the best chance to succeed.

Can You Do the Job?

Questions in this portion of the interview will be about your education, ability, knowledge, as well as your transferrable skills and character traits. It is an evaluation of your qualifications for the job and a determination of whether you can actually perform the functions of the position. Emphasize your education, skills, abilities and character traits and match the basic elements needed to perform the job functions.

---

147 Whitcomb, *Job Search Magic*, p. 274.

Will You Do the Job?

Motivation is pivotal to success in any job position (or job search), and is a professional quality all hiring executives want to see in a college graduate. The hiring executive needs to know whether you will be motivated to actually perform the job functions.

As a recent college graduate, you must convince the hiring executive that you have the required abilities and character traits, and are motivated to use them! This is achieved by educating the hiring executive about your passion for the job, work ethic, internal drive, and examples of taking the initiative and going the extra mile. Revealing that you have researched the company, position, and perhaps the hiring executive's background can also be a reflection of your motivation.

If the hiring decision comes down to two equally qualified candidates, the one that has demonstrated motivation and enthusiasm frequently wins.

Will Your Performance Have a Positive Impact on Goal Achievement?

Here, the hiring executive will attempt to predict your future performance on the job, and compare you to other college graduates. You may have the necessary skills and be willing to use them, but will your performance significantly and positively impact and advance company or organizational goals, be an improvement from the last person in the position, and so on? This is where competition for the position takes place in the mind of the hiring executive. It's about persuading the hiring executive that you can make things better.

It is imperative during the interview to stress education, character traits, recommendations, accomplishments, your internships and work history, and so on. Ask about how you will be measured in the position, position goals, and projects.

Generally, in today's environment (business or non-commercial), many employers are very sensitive about short-term goal achievement. They have a problem, and they want it solved yesterday. The lead-time to get quantifiable results in a position is getting shorter. Therefore, in interviews, focus your responses the best you can on providing value and results to the employer in a short period of time. (Just be careful not to over-promise and under-deliver.) Portray yourself as a quick learner, hard worker, and someone that will come up-to-speed quickly, leading to quicker ROI (return on investment) from hiring you.

Do You Fit In?

Cultural fit with the organization and personal chemistry with those you will work with is a big deal. Statistically, 60 percent of hires are based on personal chemistry.[148] Employers tend to hire who they like even though more qualified candidates may be available.

Cultural and personal chemistry questions explore likeability, connection, communication, values, interests outside of work, and dress/appearance. When the hiring executive shifts gears into more personal topics, they are assessing your cultural fit and personal chemistry.[149]

Can We Offer Fair Compensation?

Most employers that hire recent college graduates have a salary range established for their entry-level positions. If you happen to have strong credentials and do well during the interview process, you could receive an offer on the upper side of that range. Since most employers have established salary ranges for entry-level positions and you likely do not have a lot of previous experience, "fair compensation" to the employer is their pre-determined salary for the position. You probably do not have a lot of negotiation leverage on compensation. *See Negotiating a Job Offer* later in this book.

Strategy for a Successful Interview

A successful interview involves four basic elements:

1. **Uncovering the employer's need.** You achieve this through research, reading job descriptions, listening, and asking probing questions.

2. **Communicating to the employer that you can satisfy that need.** You achieve this by matching and relating education, skills, character traits, and experience to the needs of the employer.

3. **Persuading the employer to hire you.** You achieve this by differentiating yourself by emphasizing your education, activities, past accomplishments and relating all of these to the employer's need.

4. **Showing enthusiasm for the position.** It has been repeatedly shown that top qualified candidates that show enthusiasm for the position are more successful in

---

148 DiResta. interview by Canters. "How to Blitz."

149 "Jobvite Recruiter Nation Report 2016." *Jobvite.* http://www.jobvite.com/wp-content/uploads/2016/09/RecruiterNation2016.pdf (Accessed March 15, 2017).

receiving job offers.[150] Simply put, everyone wants to be wanted and the more you convince an employer you want the job, the more likely you are to get it.

As you read through the rest of this chapter, keep these four strategies in mind as their themes are woven into many of the substantive interviewing topics and techniques that follow. The concept behind this strategy is very similar to "Solution Selling," a sales methodology where the salesperson focuses on the customer's pain(s) and addresses those pains by introducing his or her product and services.[151] As it applies to your job search, you must position yourself as the solution to the hiring need.

Strategy for Opening the Interview

This is an interviewing strategy that can be very effective if the interview opens in a way that gives you the opportunity to use it. If the interview does not open in such a way to use this strategy, don't push it.

After pleasantries are exchanged, ask the interviewer verbally to describe what he or she is looking for in the open position. Listen very carefully. You are about to hear the answers to the test! Then, by reference to your education, college activities, accomplishments, and character traits (whatever might be the emphasis of the description), fulfill the employer's needs or wants.

Here is a possible opening to start your thinking when using this approach:

"Ms. Webb, thank you for meeting me today. Let me ask you, what qualifications, character traits, and results are you looking for in someone filling this role?"

This proactive approach can put you in a strategic advantage. Whatever the interviewer provides as what he or she is looking for (plus information you gathered from your research) are the "target" qualifications, character traits, needs and issues the interviewer wants or needs in the open position. You need to fulfill these targeted needs or wants by reference of your education, college activities, and so on. Successfully doing so can remove questions

---

150 U.S. Department of Labor. "Soft Skill #2: Enthusiasm and Attitude." *Skills to Pay the Bills.* http://www. dol.gov/odep/topics/youth/softskills/Enthusiasm.pdf (accessed June 19, 2015); Adams, Susan. "How to Ace Your Job Interview." *Forbes.* March 1, 2013, http://www.forbes.com/sites/susanadams/2013/03/01/how-to-ace-your-job-interview-2/ (accessed June 15, 2015).

151 "What is Solution Selling?" *Sales Performance International.* http://solutionselling.learn.com/learncenter. asp?id=178455 (accessed June 8, 2015).

the interviewer may have about your qualifications for the position. After you listen and acknowledge what was said, your initial response may start something like this . . .

"I think I understand. You need someone that [re-state what you heard]. Let me tell you about my collegiate background and how I fit much of what you are looking for (or, meet the requirements of this position). [Then match the employer's stated needs with your background, qualifications, and character traits the best you can.]"

After you give your response, the tone of the interview may relax. The interview may become more conversational.

First Impressions

Research has repeatedly shown that talent acquisition professionals and hiring executives heavily base their evaluations on their initial impressions of a job seeker.[152] Therefore, the first thirty to sixty seconds of an interview are crucial to your success. The hiring executive creates first impressions of you, positive or negative, in that quick snippet of time.[153]

If the hiring executive draws a negative first impression, there is a tendency to ask tougher questions to validate the initial negative impression. Or, the hiring executive could elect to minimize the engagement and make the interview very short.

On the other hand, if the hiring executive has a positive first impression, there is a tendency to ask easier questions and even overlook deficiencies in qualifications.

Create an initial positive impression by dressing conservatively (over 50 percent of a person's impression of you is determined by physical appearance),[154] smiling, having a firm handshake, eye contact, and by making opening remarks that demonstrate your sincere interest in meeting the talent acquisition professional or hiring executive.

Be aware of your countenance (your facial expressions) during the interview. Try to keep it positive even when you hear less favorable information about the opportunity. Gather

152 Zolfagharifard, Ellie. "First Impressions Really DO Count: Employers Make Decisions About Job Applicants in Under Seven Minutes." *Daily Mail.* June 18, 2014. http://www.dailymail.co.uk/sciencetech/article-2661474/First-impressions-really-DO-count-Employers-make-decisions-job-applicants-seven-minutes.html (accessed June 5, 2015).

153 Regis University Career Services. "Interviewing Strategies for CPS Students and Alumni." *Regis University.* http://www.regis.edu/About-Regis-University/University-Offices-and-Services/Career-Services/Student-and-Alumni/Interviewing-Strategies.aspx (accessed June 19, 2015).

154 Jamal, Nina, and Judith Lindenberger. "How to Make a Great First Impression." *Business Know-How.* http://www.businessknowhow.com/growth/dress-impression.htm (accessed June 2, 2015).

information and be slow to judge. The executive will be watching and your unintended facial impressions could portray your negative thoughts (even though you may not yet have full information). This could have a bearing on the lasting impression the talent acquisition professional or hiring executive has of you.

Creating an initial positive impression means you won't be playing catch up during your interview.

If you believe that the first impression is not positive, you have some heavy lifting to do, but it can be done.[155] Here are a couple of things you can do: First, ask questions about the job and answer using your success stories. By showcasing your use of your education, skills, and positive character traits you might be able to move the needle back in your direction. Even if your performance is superior, you may not overcome an initial negative impression or rough interview start. Do the best you can to get off to a good start.

What the Coaches Say:

First impressions are very important when interviewing. What advice would you give to help graduates to make that positive first impression?

Key factors in making a positive first impression are professional dress, a smile, eye contact, and a handshake. Many employers place a lot of weight on a candidate's handshake. I have had employers tell me they would never hire someone who did not have a professional handshake.

A good handshake requires the web between your thumb and first finger touch the web between the thumb and first finger of the interviewer, followed by a squeeze equal to the person you are shaking hands with. Sounds easy—but practice with several people to make sure you can respond to the firmness of someone else's handshake.

Lorraine Beaman, MA, CEIC, ACRW, CARW, NCRW, MCD

---

155 "Cognitive scientists say it can take up to two hundred times the amount of information to undo a first impression as it takes to make one." Zack, Devora. "10 Tips for People Who Hate Networking." *Careerealism.* May 4, 2015. http://www.careerealism.com/hate-networking-tips/ (accessed July 17, 2015).

Top five ideas for making a great first impression:

1. Dress to the culture of the company.

2. Have a prepared and captivating 30-second pitch prepared which highlights at the end of it why the company you're applying to interests you so much.

3. Prepare thoughtful questions that are specific to every one of the interviewers if you have access to their background.

4. Research the mission and values of the organization and infuse them into your answers.

5. Non-verbal communication is important to the process. Have a strong handshake, have a confident sitting posture, and remember to smile and have engaging eye contact.

Jered Lish M.S., Gallup-Certified Strengths Coach, GCDF

Interviews: Progression

Most interviewing processes have three distinct phases: Screening, Evaluation, and Consensus (Final Decision).

Screening. Screening interviews can be conducted in person or over the phone with the primary focus of determining whether you have the requisite education, qualifications, and character traits for the job. Your goal for this interview is to make the cut and move forward in the interviewing process.

Evaluation. In this phase, the hiring executive(s) will dig deep into your background by asking specific and pointed questions about your education, knowledge, leadership ability, and activities. You'll get into the nitty-gritty of your collegiate experience. In addition, cultural fit and personal chemistry are also being evaluated.

Occasionally, you will encounter an "approval" interview as part of the evaluation stage. It is with a member of senior management and can either be traditional in length or very brief. First impressions are huge here. This is an opportunity for the individual to meet you and give approval. With a certain degree of frequency, you may encounter one favorite interview question from this person, because many interviewers have one that they ask everybody. This is usually when the interview is going to be brief and the executive has limited time. Be on your "A" game—it matters.

Consensus (Final Decision). This is when the decision about who to hire is made. This meeting may not happen for a few days or even a week after all the interviews of other college job seekers are complete. It is a total assessment of your candidacy for the position, including overall qualifications and fit, compared to the others that were interviewed.

Interview Preparation

The interviewing process starts before you engage the employer in conversation. Here is a list of things you should do when preparing for an interview.

Research the company. Learn as much as you can. Get on the company's website and LinkedIn. At a minimum you must know the following:

1. The products and services offered by the company.

2. Who the buyers/consumers of these products and services are.

3. How these products and services are valued or needed by the buyer/consumer (the company's "value proposition").

4. Who a few of the company's market competitors are.

5. News, recent events, and any announcements regarding the company (often the website will have a "News" tab).

6. In the non-commercial world, knowing the goals and mission of the organization is a must.

Check out the websites Glassdoor (www.glassdoor.com) and Vault (www.vault.com). These are websites where employees of companies can post comments about the company, both positive and negative. Be aware that these websites can be used by disgruntled (former) employees to vent the frustrations and try to harm the company's reputation.

Research the position. Read the job description, if there is one. If there is not a job description, try to find a comparable one.

Research the hiring executive(s). Get on LinkedIn and research the background of the talent acquisition professional and hiring executive(s). Understand their career history and look for any common ground. Having something in common, either professionally or personally, creates personal chemistry—a principle of persuasion and an integral part of hiring. It's been shown that employers hire those they "most like being around," so establishing personal chemistry can significantly increase your odds of advancing in the interviewing process and getting hired.[156]

Research the industry. Research trends—these are the hot topics that are shaping and impacting the industry. What is the future outlook for the industry? Familiarize yourself with the companies in the industry. Determine the best you can, who the industry leaders are and who are up-and-comers. Get educated.

★ **Script answers.** Take the time to script the answers to known or reasonably anticipated questions you will be asked. Put yourself in the employer's chair and think of the likely questions you would ask and script your answers. Then, if those questions are asked, you will be prepared and will be able to succinctly provide a response.

Prepare questions. Prepare questions to ask based on your research about the company, position, the hiring executive, and the executive's area of responsibility.

The interview is a two-way street. The hiring executive is evaluating you for the position, but you are evaluating the company, position, culture, and opportunity to figure out if this job at this company matches you. It is common for hiring executives to evaluate you based on these questions you ask. So, have good questions to ask!

Here are some powerful questions college graduate job seekers have asked that sparked engaging conversation:

- Why is this position available? (Is the company growing? If so, that's good.)

- What do you see as the most important task or challenge facing this position?

- Looking back on this job and how it's been done in the past, what would you change?

- Who would you point to as a top performer in this job? What traits made him/her so good? What actions made him/her successful?

- What obstacles do you foresee the selected candidate encountering that would hamper success in this position?

- What performance standards will define success in this position?

- What does success look like in the first ninety days?

- Why do you work for this company?

Take some time to do this research and prepare. It will help you in your evaluation of

---

156 Sutton, Robert I., PhD. *The No Asshole Rule: Building a Civilized Workplace and Surviving One That Isn't*. New York: Warner Business Books, 2007. quoted in Kurtzberg and Naquin, *Essentials*, p. 18.

opportunities. An interview is an exploration of many things, but ultimately you and the employer are both looking for the best possible fit.

Interview Formats

The following types of interviews occur during the screening and evaluation stages of the interviewing process:
- **Telephone** - conducted either by the hiring executive or talent acquisition professional
- **One-on-One** - just the hiring executive or talent acquisition professional and you
- **Skype/Webcam** - can be used at any stage
- **Succession** - usually used as a second or home-office interview, this type is multiple one-on-one interviews, typically with people from different departments—tailor your questions to the area the interviewer works. For example, asking an operations executive about efficiency and cost savings
- **Group** - likely a group of managers from different departments; direct your response to the person asking the question
- **Meal** - can be over breakfast, lunch, or dinner
- **Behavioral and Performance-Based** - questions here will focus on specific examples of your past behavior as indications of your future performance

★ Practice (Mock) Interviews

One of the best things you can do to prepare for interviews is to conduct practice or mock interviews. Interviews can be stressful, and practicing reduces that anxiety, boosts confidence, and leads to better performance. Prepare for all interviews thoroughly. Do not treat the first real interview as your "practice interview." It's entirely possible you could get into that interview, realize the position is more intriguing than you thought, be unprepared, and regret your performance.

To conduct a practice interview, ask a professional in your career placement office for assistance (or any other professional contact you know). Provide this person with the job description (or one very similar) and seven or eight questions you believe may be asked. In addition, ask your mock interviewer to come up with four or five questions on their own. This will make you think on your feet and be good preparation.

When conducting the mock interview, try to stay "in character" as much as possible. You can come out of character as you need to discuss responses, but just remember the more realistic you make it, the better prepared you will be.

Evaluate your performance and responses with your mock interviewer. Be open-minded to their critique and suggestions. Make necessary adjustments. Having more than one practice interview (instituting any changes in approach and responses) is encouraged.

What the Coaches Say:

Would you recommend practice (mock) interviews? If so, what would you recommend to graduates so they can get the most from the practice interview?

It is great if you can practice interviewing skills with a career counselor or people who interview candidates as part of their job. If you cannot do that, pair up with another student who is preparing for the job search. Here are some of the strategies I recommend:

• Think like an employer. Use job descriptions for positions in your field to identify the skills and experience employers are seeking. For each of these requirements, ask the question, "Tell me about a time when you (insert skill/experience)." In addition to these questions, use the following generic questions as part of your interview preparation.

• What would you like me to know about you?

• What are your strengths? What are your weaknesses?

• What do you know about our company/organization?

• Why are you interested in this position/what are your career goals?

• When are you available to start?

• Do you have any questions for me?

At the end of the mock interview, give honest feedback on these key points. Were the responses to the "tell me about a time" questions well organized? Were all of the answers given clear and easy to understand? Did the person being interviewed smile, seem enthusiastic, make eye contact, seem relaxed, and ask questions?

Lorraine Beaman, MA, CEIC, ACRW, CARW, NCRW, MCD

Answering Traditional Interview Questions: The UPAC Method ™

As you can well imagine, you will be asked many questions in the interviewing process. The UPAC Method is a very intuitive approach to answer these questions. Its effectiveness comes from the accomplishment component. When asked a substantive question, try to mention an accomplishment that supports your answer. Here's the methodology:

U   **Understand** the question, (ask for clarification if necessary).

P   **Provide** the employer with your (concise) answer.

A   Add an **Accomplishment** that supports your answer. This can be a success story or a mini-story of your skills and character traits in action.

C   **Confirm** that you answered the hiring executive's question satisfactorily, redirecting the question if needed.

Here is an example of this technique:

Question: "As you know, we are in the car rental business. We are looking for an entry-level management trainee to work with our current branch managers. Why do you believe you would be qualified and effective in that role?"

U   You understand the question and what the employer is asking. Proceed with a response.

P   *Over the last three summers, I worked full-time at Waterspray Gas & Wash. There are several locations around town. If you've seen them, you know each location is "quite an operation."*

A   *I started there as a car attendant, wiping down cars, cleaning and vacuuming. I was promoted to sales consultant where I greeted customers at the gas pumps and informed them about our services and special pricing. I was the #1 sales consultant several times. I was later asked to be an assistant manager and fill in when the actual managers went on vacations. In these positions at Waterspray, I demonstrated my work ethic. I was in constant motion to insure our customers were satisfied. I used my sales ability as reflected by my sales achievement as well as leadership and managerial skills by being asked to be the interim manager when others were on vacation.*

C   *Did I answer your question?* [You can bypass this if you are confident your answer is responsive to the question]

By pre-writing your success stories you will have accomplishments at the ready when you use this methodology in answering interview questions.

Telephone Interview

Some screening interviews are conducted over the phone. In this format, you must rely on verbal communication only. Slow your rate of speech and enunciate.

The advantage of a phone interview is the employer can focus on the substance of your answers without distractions. You can have information in front of you to refer to as needed. Taking notes is very useful during the interview and for follow-up communications. Here are some tips to improve your odds of a superior performance during a telephone interview:

Prior to the Call

1. **Prepare.** Research the company and position with the same due diligence as you would for a face-to-face interview. This preparation will shine through, especially if you're asked, "What do you know about our company?"

2. **Phone Zone.** Create the identical quiet place just as you did when you made your proactive marketing calls. Remove unnecessary paperwork and items from your work space and keep your resume, company information, job description (if you have one), success stories, questions to ask based on your research, water, pen, paper, and other necessary materials nearby.

As a matter of human practicality, go to the bathroom before the call. Some telephone interviews are reasonably short (twenty to thirty minutes) while others can last over an hour.

Use a landline or make sure your cell phone is fully charged and you take the call in a place where you know you have good reception.

Strategy During the Call

You have done your homework for the call and created your Phone Zone. Here are some strategic suggestions that will prove helpful during the call:

1. **After exchanging pleasantries, ask the employer what he or she is looking for**. This is the same strategy for opening an interview previously discussed.

2. **Smile and stand up.** Doing both of these things will have a positive impact on your tone of voice and portray a positive attitude. Standing will improve energy during a longer call.

3. **Dress the part.** Consider dressing for the telephone interview as you would a face-to-face interview. This will put you in an interviewing frame of mind.

4. **Remember your questions.** Use the ones you created during your interview preparation. Questions from you are a sign of interest. The quality of your questions is often evaluated as a part of the interviewing process.

5. **Be careful not to over-answer.** Most telephone interviews are screening calls. The employer is frequently seeking information about qualifications. Answer questions completely, but don't get mired in minutia unless asked for more information.

6. **Listen.** Don't formulate what to say while you should be listening to the employer. Be active and engaged. Take notes but do not worry about complete thoughts. Fill in the details after the call is complete.

7. **Ask about the next steps.** Do this at the end of the call. Indicate interest in proceeding to the next step. Consider asking whether you will be advancing in the interviewing process, which appeals to the persuasion principle of consistency and commitment (provided you've had a successful interview thus far).

8. **Follow up.** You must send a follow-up thank-you communication. The most time-efficient way is through email. Refer to the Cover Letters and Other Written Communications portion of this book.

The Unannounced Telephone Interview

There will be rare occasions when a call will come unannounced. Usually the un-announced call is a result of a scheduling mix-up. If this happens, simply tell the employer that you are in the middle of something. You can reschedule the call or simply delay it by fifteen minutes. Give yourself time to gather your thoughts to make the call productive. It is recommended not to proceed with an unannounced telephone interview.

Webcam or Skype Interview

Many employers use these to help speed up the interview process. In fact, it has been referenced that as many as six out of ten companies use webcam or video interviews in their hiring process.[157]

---

157 OfficeTeam. "Survey: Six in 10 Companies Conduct Video Job Interviews." news release. August 30, 2012. http://officeteam.rhi.mediaroom.com/videointerviews (accessed June 5, 2015).

Here are key strategies to help you succeed during a Skype interview:

1. **Get comfortable with the technology.** Be sure it's set up correctly on your computer. Adjust the webcam to pick up your face, shoulders, and maybe down to the middle of your torso. Practice with the webcam and chat with friends or family prior to your interview. Make sure everything looks good. When the time comes to answer interview questions, look into the webcam's lens to give the impression of eye contact. Good posture is also important here. Do your best to remain still (on camera, movement can be delayed and therefore distracting). Be natural, and relax.[158] Technical issues may still come up. Take them in stride.

2. **Control the scene.** Similar in concept to the Phone Zone, set up a clean, professional background for the interview. Be aware of what is behind you.[159]

3. **Wear professional attire.** Dress like this is a face-to-face interview. There are a few special considerations. Don't wear clothes with busy patterns, as they tend to distract others. And dress completely, not just from the waist up.[160]

4. **Have the hiring executive's telephone number.** If the technology simply fails, you'll want to schedule a telephone interview as a fallback.

Screening Interview Conducted by a Talent Acquisition Professional

Part of your job search strategy is reaching out to and having interviews with talent acquisition professionals. However, there is an inherit hazard with these interviews. More often than not, the talent acquisition professional likely has little or no influence on the ultimate decision to hire you (unless you are pursuing a position in HR), but has the power to eliminate you as a candidate for the job. Your goal for this interview is to survive it and move forward in the process.

Understand that talent acquisition professionals who conduct screening interviews are frequently evaluated based on the number and quality of candidates they pass along to the hiring executive. The last thing they want to hear from the hiring executive is, "This candidate is weak." Or, worse yet, "What in heaven's name were you thinking?" So, study the job description and match your qualifications to it. Work to put the talent acquisition professionals at ease that you are qualified and will make them look good.

---

158 Bricker, Eric. "How to Ace Your Video Interview." *On Careers Blog. U.S. News & World Report.* July 11, 2013. http://money.usnews.com/money/careers/articles/2013/07/11/how-to-ace-your-video-interview (accessed December 1, 2015).

159 Ibid.

160 Ibid.

Most times these interviews can be a bit scripted. The talent acquisition professional frequently has a set number of questions or topics to cover with each candidate. The key, and the tricky part, is to provide the correct or acceptable answer. Too often, the talent acquisition professional looks for elimination factors rather than the totality of your collegiate qualifications.

With some exceptions, the questions you will likely encounter will be the general kinds of interviewing questions or statements:

- Tell me about yourself.
- Why do you believe you are qualified for this position?
- What are your strengths?
- What are your weaknesses?
- Why are you interested in this position?
- What do you know about our company?
- Why are you interested in our company?
- A general evaluation of your qualifications and character traits.

These are questions that you should script responses. You will encounter them (repeatedly). If you need examples to spark your thinking when scripting your responses, a quick Internet search of these questions should give you an ample number of examples to get you started.

What the Coaches Say:

In your experience, what are common interview questions a college graduate must prepare in advance to answer?

Tell me about yourself.
What have you done that makes you qualified for this position?
What are your strengths?
What are your weaknesses?

What is your greatest accomplishment and why are you proud of it?

Where do you see yourself in 5 years?

Why should we hire you?

What are your salary expectations?

How do you like to be managed / supervised?

When are you available to start work?

What do you know about our company (organization)?

Give us an example of when you (refers to skills / experience required for the job).

Do you have any questions for us?

Lorraine Beaman, MA, CEIC, ACRW, CARW, NCRW, MCD

Toward the end of the interview, you will undoubtedly hear, "Do you have any questions?" Ask a few questions, especially ones you come up with based on your company research. Here are a few:

- What do you like about the company?

- What has made the company successful?

- What are the company's future goals and vision?

Close the interview professionally. *See* Closing the Interview topic later in this chapter.

Remember to be respectful, polite, and friendly. Endear yourself. The reality is that the talent acquisition professional holds the future of your candidacy in their hands.

Meal Interview

This interview could be the most difficult type—it can happen at any step in the interviewing process, with any meal (breakfast, lunch, or dinner), and can trip up even the most confident of tenured job seekers. Making this type of interview successful involves navigating a host of variables.

There are several reasons why employers conduct meal interviews:

1. **Convenience.** The hiring executive can multitask by conducting an interview during a meal.

2. **Information gathering**. This includes your collegiate background and qualifications, just in a social setting.

3. **Evaluation of personal factors.** These would include social skills (useful for gauging how you would conduct yourself with clients, vendors, suppliers, key business partners, co-workers, and so on), and your table manners. If you are the leading candidate, an added bonus of a meal interview could be to impress you.

The reasons for a meal interview don't really matter. What does is that hiring executives believe they can tell a lot about you by the way you eat, your table manners, and how you interact in a social setting. Occasionally, these interviews can go longer than traditional in-office interviews. Part of the key to success during a meal interview is not to be lulled into a sense of casualness. Make no mistake—this is an interview—you are being evaluated. It's not friends getting together just to catch up.

A meal interview is typically more conversational than a traditional face-to-face interview. It is fine if the conversation veers into personal topics. Remember, personal chemistry plays a significant role (up to 60 percent) in who the employer hires.[161] Follow the employer's lead. However, listen closely for when the conversation turns into questions or dialogue regarding your qualifications.

Here are some helpful things to remember about meal interviews:

1. Research the restaurant. Get the GPS out and know how to get there. Review the menu. Get some ideas on what to order.

2. Do not order messy foods like barbecue, pasta with lots of sauce, or any food that you would need to eat with your hands.

3. Order food that can be easily eaten with a fork and that can be cut into smaller pieces (that will help if you need to answer a question after taking a bite). Consciously cut your food into smaller bites.

4. Avoid speaking with your mouth full. Pause, indicate you are chewing, and then answer.

5. Do not order expensive entrees. Stay within the restaurant's mid-price range (you could make price part of your restaurant research).

---

161 DiResta, interview by Canters, "How to Blitz."

6. Turn off your cell phone. Give the hiring executive your complete, undivided attention.

7. Be polite. Use "please" and "thank you." Be courteous to the servers.

8. Do not order alcohol, even if the hiring executive does. Being under the influence of alcohol during an interview shows poor judgment, impacts your answers, and takes you off your game.

9. Brush up on your etiquette and table manners! Know how, which, and when to use the utensils. Good table manners will give you an edge over other collegiate job seekers.

10. Allow the hiring executive to lead the conversation. The interview questions may not occur until the meal is finished.

11. After the meal, show your appreciation to the hiring executive. Remember, the restaurant was likely chosen because he/she likes it. Compliment the choice of restaurants.

After the meal, do not worry about the check. The hiring executive will pay the tab. Make sure to ask about next steps. Write a thank-you note and send it within twenty-four hours of the meal interview. (Note: You should write a thank-you for every interview and especially meal interviews. The hiring executive did pay the bill.)

If you handle it professionally, a meal interview can give you a distinct advantage over other college graduates. It is an opportunity to build personal chemistry, display your social skills and table manners, and convey your abilities and accomplishments in a social setting.

Behavioral Interview

Behavioral interviewing is a very effective interviewing technique. The rationale for this interviewing technique is based on the premise that past behavior is a predictor of future performance. Although you have not been in a professional level position from which you can describe past experiences using on-the-job skills, you must still be prepared to answer these kinds of questions for more generic experiences and for your professional character traits. Being prepared for behavioral interview questions will impress the interviewer and make you stand out compared to others.

Behavioral interviewing questions require you to describe situations or past experiences where you have demonstrated certain skills, character traits, or behaviors. These questions are designed so you have to describe a situation, what you did, and the results of your actions. How did you use your skills and character traits to achieve success in your past?

Most behavioral interviewing questions begin with "Tell me about a time when . . . " or "Describe a situation where . . . " Theoretically, behavior-based questions help hiring executives avoid making hiring decisions based on emotions or gut feelings. Instead, the hiring executive is able to gather objective information that assesses your job aptitude, abilities, character traits, and so on.

These questions can be unnerving. They require you to quickly think of specific situations in your past where you used specific skills or traits. We generally don't remember things in this way . . . we just handle the situation. It is due to the unpredictable nature of these questions along with the nervousness associated with an interview that can stump any job seeker.

Although there is a myriad of topics or competencies an employer can inquire about, some of the most common are:

- Technical ability
- Analytical thinking
- Communication skills
- Time management, prioritizing
- Leadership
- Problem solving, innovation
- Collaboration
- Ability to learn, adapt

Notice that many of these competencies are the sought-after skills, transferable skills, and professional traits previously listed in this book.

Preparing for and Answering Behavioral Interview Questions

The first thing to do in preparation for these questions is to review (or write) your success stories. You should have five or six success stories describing your use of different skills and character traits (*See* the list above plus those listed in the topic on Professional Qualities and Character Traits). Reviewing or writing these success stories gets your mind thinking in terms of telling stories. It tends to awaken your memory about situations when you have used your various skills and character traits during your internship(s), part-time jobs, campus activities, and so on. As you remember situations or use of a character trait, write a success story.

The next thing you can do to prepare for these questions is to "sit on the other side of the desk." Put yourself in the shoes of the hiring executive and think about behavior-based questions you might ask if you were hiring for the position you are pursuing (A quick review of the topics on Understanding the Employer's Mindset and Knowing What an Employer Wants in an Open Position is a good starting point as you prepare.). One technique that occasionally helps is to actually think or speak the beginning of a behavior-based question. That is, "Tell me about a time when . . . [then you finish the question]." This will occasionally make you think of questions that you had not previously thought of and you can now prepare for.

Read the job description which has the important skills or character traits being sought. Those are often the areas that behavior-based questions will be directed toward.

Answering behavioral interview questions successfully involves being able to describe an experience directly related to the competency being asked about. Here's the framework on how to answer effectively:

1. **Understand the question.** Listen very carefully and be sure you understand what is being asked. If you do not, ask the hiring executive for clarification. It is permissible for you to reframe the question and repeat it back to the employer.

2. **Determine the professional competency being asked about.** Then think of a situation in your collegiate experience, activities, summer jobs or internships that illustrates the competency being addressed. Thinking in terms of identifying the competency makes it easier to recall a situation in response to the question. Take a moment. Don't panic if something doesn't come to mind right away. Ask the executive for more time if you need it. (Hopefully you will have prepared a success story that answers the question or is close enough to qualify as responsive to the question.)

3. **Tell a brief success story that describes a situation illustrating your skill, competency or character trait.** Highlight how your skill and character traits influenced the end result.

4. **Confirm that your response answers the question (if necessary).** Responses such as "Does that answer your question?" or "Does that example give you the information you were asking about?" work well.

Remember this shorthand, five-prong formula for answering behavioral interview questions:

Understand

Determine the competency

Think

Tell a story

Confirm

If the behavior-based question happens to be an experience you have dealt with, terrific! Tell your success story.

If the behavior-based question is not something you have dealt with directly, but you have an analogous situation, tell the hiring executive that you have not handled that situation directly, but you have handled a similar situation and tell your success story.

If the behavior-based question is not something you have dealt with directly and you do not have a similar situation, has a friend or summer job colleague handled that situation or one like it? If so, indicate to the hiring executive that you have not handled that situation but a friend or colleague has. Tell the story, and then indicate whether you agreed or disagreed with the way your friend or colleague handled the situation. If you disagreed with the way it was handled, explain how you would have done things differently.

Finally, if the behavior-based question is not something you have dealt with directly, you do not have a similar situation, and you are unaware of whether a colleague has handled the situation, then indicate that you have not handled the situation described and offer to answer it in the hypothetical—describe what you would do. This form of an answer is not ideal, since the hiring executive believes it's an important question, but it is better than no answer at all.

It is hard to predict whether you will encounter behavior-based interview questions as a recent college graduate. However, it is best to be prepared. And, by being prepared you will perform better *in all interviews* because you will be ready to tell stories about your abilities and character traits.

Your Interview Wardrobe

As a newly minted professional, one word sums up your attire for an interview: Conservative. Wearing traditional, professional business attire instantly communicates to the employer that you are confident. It also gives you an advantage over other college graduate job seekers, using the persuasion principle of authority.

Looking sharp also has the added advantage of making you feel in control and sets the stage for a superior interviewing performance (especially when you are well-prepared). As a result, the hiring executive and others will respond to your image of professionalism in a positive way.

When it comes to the specific do's and don'ts on what to wear, if you find yourself questioning whether or not to wear something to an interview . . . don't. Use conservative judgment and always err on the side of traditional, conservative corporate attire.

What the Coaches Say:

What advice would you give about a graduate's wardrobe for interviews?

There is a lot of psychology behind determining what to wear to an interview. Hiring managers tend to hire people who dress like they do. The best advice I can offer is to dress like a supervisor in the company with which you are interviewing. If your network cannot offer advice on what that looks like, it is okay to ask the person who is scheduling your interview about the appropriate attire for job applicants. If you are not able to gain insights into what to wear, the default is to wear a blue suit, white/pastel shirt/blouse, complimentary tie/scarf, black socks/nylons, and black shoes. Also carry a portfolio.

Lorraine Beaman, MA, CEIC, ACRW, CARW, NCRW, MCD

Lack of money can have an impact on wardrobe. Now is not the time to skimp. Reach out for help if needed. You can find inexpensive yet professional looking clothes in every community. You want to be neat, clean, and unwrinkled . . . .you want to show you made every effort because you want the job!

Ellen Steverson, NCRW, GCDF, CEIC

Closing the Interview

Closing an interview persuasively can be amongst the most important moments in an interview. It can differentiate you from other recent graduates. If done well, you can advance in the interviewing process and move closer to a job offer.

Provide a Summary Statement of your Qualifications.

Analogous to the closing argument of an attorney to a judge or jury, try to close the interview with a brief summary of how your college background, experience, and character traits match the position and how being hired will benefit the company. Here's a script on how to close an interview with a summation of your qualifications:

> *"Ms. Burke, I want to thank you for meeting with me today. As we have discussed, you are looking for a junior analyst to [re-state general responsibilities of the position]. Someone successful in the role will need to have a [state job qualifications and character traits]. I can fulfill and be successful in this role based on my [match your collegiate background and character traits to the position]."*

Ask to Proceed or Ask for the Job.

If you have a sincere and earnest interest in the position and the company, make sure to express your interest in the proceeding in the interviewing process.

Should your interview be the final step in the process, and you want the job, ask for the job! Doing so removes the mystery for the hiring executive and could be exactly what he or she wants to hear. Don't be coy. If you want the job, say so!

Ask about Timing

Make sure you get some commitment on the timing of a decision (Persuasion Principle of Consistency and Commitment). This could be a decision for the next step or the final hiring decision. Then, to control your own expectations, add one week. Discussions like these just seem to take longer than anticipated.

General Interviewing Tips

Some general suggestions to remember about interviews:[162]

- Arrive ten to fifteen minutes early. Being late is never excusable. If you are going to be late, call the employer.

- Smile. Maintain good eye contact with the hiring executive. If you don't, the hiring executive may draw a conclusion that you are being dishonest, have something to hide, or lack confidence.

- Get the hiring executive to describe on-the-job responsibilities early so you're able to match your education, achievements, character traits, and collegiate experiences to those requirements. This is an effective interview tactic.

- Try to avoid answering questions with a simple yes or no. Whenever possible, mention a success story when asked a substantive question regarding the position.

- Take extra copies of your resume. You may meet with others you did not know about. Don't be caught unprepared.

- Do not exaggerate (or lie). Answer questions truthfully.

- Do not over-answer or give long-winded responses. Give appropriate and responsive answers, but keep them on-point. There is anecdotal evidence that more job seekers advance in the interview process and receive more offers when the hiring executive talks more in the interview than the job seeker.[163] Answer questions, but be sure to listen.

- Do not ask about "perks" (paid time off, compensation, performance increases, and so on) in any first interview(s) unless the hiring executive does first.

- Ask questions throughout the interview—without interrupting the hiring executive—not just when the hiring executive is finished. An interview should be a mutual exchange of information, not a one-sided conversation. Frequently, you will be evaluated based on the quality of questions you ask.

- If you feel the interview is going badly or realize you've been passed over, do not let your discouragement show.

---

162 Portions adapted from Claycomb and Dinse, *Career Pathways*, Part 8.

163 "Understanding the Employer's Perspective." *Internships.com.* http://www.internships.com/student/resources/interview/prep/getting-ready/understand-employer (accessed July 10, 2015).

Debrief Yourself

After every interview, take a few minutes to reflect upon how it went. This self-debriefing is designed to help you collect your thoughts on what *you* liked or disliked about the company, opportunity, people, office environment, products, services, and so on. It is also an opportunity for you to reflect upon your interview performance and make necessary changes.

Ask yourself these questions:

1. *How long did the interview last?* As a general rule, the longer an interview lasts, the better. Remember that approximately 60 percent of all successful hires are based on personal chemistry.[164] The longer the interview, the more rapport is built.

2. *What things did I do well?* Praise yourself for those things you did well in the interview(s). Write them down.

3. *Was I unprepared for any questions?* Write them down and craft an answer. There's always the chance you'll be asked that question (or one similar) again.

4. *What important issues were mentioned in the interview?* You may use these issues as part of your thank-you letter.

5. *What did I learn during my research and interview that appeals to me?* List the positive things about the company, opportunity, people, and so on.

6. *Identify any concerns and negatives.* This is different from identifying unanswered questions. Items that go here are red flag areas (e.g., the company is about to file for bankruptcy).

7. *Rate the opportunity on a scale of one to ten.* This is an emotional, gut feeling. How do you *feel* about it? You are looking for an opportunity that not only seems right, but feels right, too.

8. *Was compensation discussed?* You will not bring up the topic of compensation, especially during initial interviews. However, if the hiring executive broaches the topic, it could be a sign of interest. Write down what was said.

9. *How was it left?* Were the parting comments simply a description of the interview process or was there a definite indication that you would be asked back for more interviews? Obviously, you want an expression of continued interest.

---

164 DiResta, interview by Canters, "How to Blitz."

10. *How do I rank this opportunity against others I am pursuing?* Keep track of the opportunities and how they compare to each other. If an opportunity is not for you, notify the company and release yourself from the interview process.

11. *Was there anything I could have done better or differently?* Honestly assess your performance. Make note of those things you would do differently or better.

Write a Thank-You Letter

You need to thank the hiring executive for their time. *See Cover Letters and Other Written Communications.*

- Immediately following the interview, debrief yourself. Think of the qualifications and character traits the employer is looking for and match your background and strengths to those.

- Send the letter (email or US mail, either is acceptable) no later than twenty-four hours following the interview.

- If there's no communication in one week's time, call and let the employer know you are still interested and want to move forward in the process.

Second and Home Office Interview Strategies

Second interviews (as well as home-office interviews) are conducted to clarify information. Questions tend to dig more deeply into your background, skills, and collegiate experience, secure additional input from others, and ensure you are a fit with company culture and personality. Planning and preparation are keys to a successful second interview.

The following tactics will help you achieve success at a second interview—hopefully leading to a job offer:

1. **Get an agenda that identifies your interviewer(s).** Once you have it, research their backgrounds, tenure with the company, promotions, previous employers, schools, and so on.[165] Look for something you share in common with them, and before the interview mention that you've read about them. Most executives will be impressed you took the time to research them (especially if you offer a sincere compliment). All of this taps into the persuasion principle of liking and personal chemistry.

165 Hansen, Katharine. PhD. "Do's and Don'ts for Second (and Subsequent) Job Interviews." *Quintessential Careers.* http://www.quintcareers.com/second-interviewing-dos-donts/ (accessed February 16, 2016).

2. **Review your notes from the first interview.** Try to decipher what about your collegiate experience and character traits scored enough points to earn you a second interview. Also, determine where you might be weak. Emphasize your strengths, and compensate with assets to offset weaknesses.[166]

3. **Prepare questions.** Focus on the company, position, and each of the hiring executives you will meet. Make sure your questions are focused on their area of responsibility. A good general question is, "What is the number one issue or challenge you are facing in the (Name of Department)?"

   There is a high probability that hiring you will not solve the issue or challenge facing this department (if it is a department that you will not be working). However, a good response could sound something like this:

   "Hiring me may or may not have a direct effect on the challenge you are facing, but having another set of hands-on-deck helping where I can, might."

4. **Be ready for in-depth conversations.** Fully engage every hiring executive in deep discussions about your education, activities, traits, etc. Remember the UPAC formula for answering general interviewing questions.

5. **Close (and, when appropriate, ask for the job).** As the second round of interviews winds down, close by telling the hiring executives how you can benefit the company and that you *want the job, and ask for an offer*. This is especially true if this is a final interview.

6. **One final thought: Get a good night's sleep.** Second or home-office interviews can be long, especially if your day is comprised of a series of interviews.[167]

Common Interviewing Mistakes

There are a plethora of mistakes that can be made during an interview. Many are common sense, such as don't chew gum in an interview. However, lesser known are verbal and nonverbal mistakes. This is a big deal. Research indicates that over 98 percent of hiring

---

166 Ibid.

167 Ibid.

executives base much of their hiring decisions on both verbal and nonverbal communication skills.[168] Below is a list of the most notable verbal and nonverbal communication mistakes:

- Not listening.[169] This includes interrupting the hiring executive.

- Not making eye contact.[170]

- Poor posture. Slouching.

- Being careless about appearance and hygiene. Wearing unprofessional attire (including accessories). Wearing too much perfume or cologne. Having bad breath.

- Failure to provide a coherent and organized response to the question asked.[171] Failing to articulate.

- Giving rambling responses. Providing needless information. Boring the hiring executive. Not staying on topic.[172] Being long-winded.

- Lacking enthusiasm about the position or company.

Not Getting the Job: Handling the Disappointment

Accept this fact: You will be rejected. For some, this can be one of the most emotionally difficult things to endure is the disappointment after progressing through the interviewing process for a job. It can come verbally, by email, or by written letter. It can be disheartening . . . all of your time and effort for nothing. Well, not exactly. Take some time to review and analyze the interviewing experience with this employer. After you receive the news, decompress for a while, process your feelings, and then evaluate the entire interviewing process with that employer. Think through it step by step. What did you do well that got you into the process? What did you do well during the process? What did you learn about the interviewing process? Now, what could you have done better? Take it apart and perhaps write it down. Reinforce in yourself what you do well and keep doing that. Learn from any possible mistakes and make adjustments. You don't want to make the same mistake

---

168 Peterson, Marshalita Sims. "Personnel Interviewers' Perceptions of the Importance and Adequacy of Applicants' Communication Skills." *Communication Education.* 46, no. 4 (1997): 287–291. Quoted in Kurtzberg and Naquin, *Essentials*, p. 31.

169 Kurtzberg and Naquin, *Essentials*, p. 31.

170 Ibid.

171 Ibid.

172 Ibid.

again. Call and ask the hiring executive (or someone in the process) for candid feedback. Many employers resist doing this for fear of possible litigation—some even have company policies prohibiting the giving of feedback. If you get feedback, learn from it.

Finally, after sending a thank-you letter, move on. Your future (for now) is not with that company, but some other employer. It's up to you to persevere and move forward. Your next career position is out there waiting for you![173]

What the Coaches Say:

Rejection is an inescapable fact of a job search. What advice would you give graduates to handle job search rejection?

It is never easy to hear you will not get an offer for a job after you put time and effort into writing a resume and cover letter, preparing for an interview, and sending a thank you note. There are a few ways to lessen the blow, though. Never stop applying for jobs until you have accepted an offer. If you get a rejection the same week you have two interviews scheduled, you will be less devastated than if you had no other job prospects.

A truth that you discover after you complete your job search, though it is often hard to believe it when you are in the middle of it, many employers do you a favor when they do not offer you a job. They are the experts on knowing who will be a good fit for their organization and who will not.

Lorraine Beaman, MA, CEIC, ACRW, CARW, NCRW, MCD

Understand that there are so many factors that go into NOT receiving the job that you are unaware of, so understand it's not a personal attack and keep applying . . . You will land a job!

Ellen Steverson, NCRW, GCDF, CEIC

---

173 Simpson, Cheryl. "10 Healthy Ways to Cope with Job Search Rejection." *LinkedIn*. March 27, 2017 https://www.linkedin.com/pulse/10-healthy-ways-cope-job-search-rejection-chery. (accessed March 29, 2017).

Life can hit hard at times. Author JK Rowling (Harry Potter) was rejected 12 times by publishers, and never gave up. Michael Jordan was cut from his high school basketball team sophomore year, pushed forward and never gave up. Rejection is like a GPS unit simply redirecting you to go another way. Have a moment, sit in the rejection, but don't unpack and live there. Refocus and move on—often rejection is a blessing in disguise.

Dr. Cheryl Minnick, NCRW, CCMC, CHJMC, CAA

Chapter 11

References

The key to your universe is that you can choose.

— Carl Frederick[174]

References could play an important role in your job search as a recent college graduate. Since you likely do not have much direct work experience, employers use references to learn more about you as a person (for cultural fit), as well as a potential employee, from someone who has interacted with you. They can have a significant influence on the hiring decision since they appeal to the persuasion principles of social proof. Put into a business context, references are your client testimonials.

Who to Ask to be a Reference

Get your references lined up early in your job search. You don't want to be asked for references, have none, then need to scramble to get some. Ask for references while your relationship is current and their thoughts and opinions of you are fresh.

Generally, you want to offer two types of references: academic and work (internship) related.

---

174 "Carl Frederick Quotes." *World of Quotes.* http://www.worldofquotes.com/author/Carl+Frederick/1/index.html (accessed June 10, 2015).

Academic. Choose one or two professors that you have developed a relationship. Professors are frequently asked to be references and your request is not unusual. Always ask permission to use them as a reference. After they have agreed to be a reference, sit down with the professor(s) and discuss their opinion of you and the positive character traits they can attest to. By doing so you know what will be said and you could possibly coach the professor on certain topics.

Work (internship) related. This is someone (or two) that you worked with during summer jobs or an internship. Obviously, select someone who will speak highly of you. And, like you did with the professor(s), discuss what could be said about you including character traits. Coach your reference on what would be helpful, if needed.

Occasionally touch base with your references regarding your job search, and notify them when you know (or have reason to believe) references will be checked. Prepare them with key information (details of the position, what the employer is looking for, etc.), so your reference can showcase you to the employer.

At the end of your job search, take the time to thank your references for supporting you. Even if a reference was not called upon by the employer, express your gratitude for their willingness to speak on your behalf.

What the Coaches Say:

What insight and advice would you offer graduates when it comes to references?

Create your "Circle of Champions" – a group of people who will support you by serving as your reference. Control their narrative about you by remaining in touch to share your career goals, resume, and the status of your job hunt with them.

Active management of your references can help or hurt a career. CareerBuilder reported 80% of the time references are checked by employers, and of those times, 29% found misleading/false references on resumes, 62% heard unflattering comments, and 69% of employers changed their mind after the reference check.

Dr. Cheryl Minnick, NCRW, CCMC, CHJMC, CAA

Your references are an important part of your job search strategy. Select references who think highly of you personally and can vouch for your ability to get things done, your integrity, how you will fit into a team environment, and how well you can work on your own.

People are honored when you ask them to be a reference, but may not know what to write or say. Give them some help. Tell them the name of the company and the job position for which you are interviewing, share a copy of your resume, and tell them why you are qualified for the job. Let them know when you are going to an interview, so they can be prepared for a call.

Don't forget to thank your references, and let them know when you get a job.

Lorraine Beaman, MA, CEIC, ACRW, CARW, NCRW, MCD

★ The Unsolicited Third-Party Affirmation

This technique, if properly used, can be extremely persuasive. It can be used any time during the interviewing process but can be most persuasive when a final hiring decision is about to be made. Here is how it works:

Ask one of your references to call the hiring executive, unannounced (it must be a phone call, not an email). The purpose is to speak with the hiring executive and provide persuasive information about you and your fit for the job (attempting to capitalize on the persuasion principle of social proof).

Imagine the scenario: The hiring executive is at his desk. Hiring for that entry-level position is on his mind. His receptionist pages him and says there is a person on the line who would like to speak with him about you. That's curious. If he has a moment, he will take the call. Then, out of the blue comes this glowing recommendation. Calls like this do not happen every day. That call and the contents of the conversation will linger in the mind of the hiring executive and differentiate you, which is the desired effect. You may or may not get the job, but you can feel good that you gave one last shot at persuading the hiring executive in your favor.

References can play a vital role in getting a job, especially if the decision to hire comes down to two or three candidates. The recommendation from a solid reference can move the decision in your favor.

PART IV

Job Offers and Other Important Information

Chapter 12

Negotiating a Job Offer

By fighting you never get enough, but by yielding you get more than you expected.

— Dale Carnegie[175]

Receiving a job offer is the positive result of your hard work. Congratulations! The employer has determined that you can satisfactorily do the job, stay motivated, and make a contribution to the company, and fit into the company culture. In addition, the employer has decided how much they will offer in salary and compensation.

Receiving the Offer

Offers can be extended over the phone, by email, or face to face. Always express your appreciation and interest, but ask the hiring executive for some time to evaluate the offer. It is not uncommon for an offer to have a deadline. However, most companies will give you at least forty-eight hours to one week, and perhaps more, in some cases.

---

175 Carnegie, Dale. *How to Win Friends and Influence People*. New York: Simon and Schuster, 2010. p. 134.

Your Negotiating Leverage

Negotiating your first salary as a recent college graduate can be tricky and unnerving. Since you likely do not have a lot of previous experience, accept the fact that you do not have a lot of negotiation leverage. But that does not mean you do not have any bargaining power. You do, though you must use it correctly.

Research Salaries

If you have not done so already, start doing as much salary research as you can for the position you are pursuing. There are several websites that provide information on compensation for a variety of positions within an industry (www.salary.com, www.rileyguide.com). LinkedIn also provides salary information through its Salary Insight tool (www.linkedin.com/salary). This tool allows you to search by title and location. It also allows you to compare salaries based on education, experience, and company size, among others.

Be mindful that salary and compensation information can be dated and is not always an accurate reflection of current compensation. However, the published information will give you some benchmarks to guide your thinking.

Take into account the size of your employer and location. A smaller employer in the Midwest will not offer as much as a larger employer on the west coast.

Once you have thoroughly researched salary, you can provide your research findings to the employer if the offer is lower than the research indicates. Occasionally, the employer will be unaware that their salary range is not competitive and make an upward adjustment. We'll discuss how to present your salary findings in negotiations in just a moment.

Get Benefits Information

Ask for employee benefits information that you will be eligible (health insurance, 401(k), vacation policy, and so on). If possible, have a call with a company HR representative for an explanation of benefits. This will give you a better understanding of the overall value of the offer. This will also "buy you some time" if you have other offers forthcoming.

Having Another Offer

You do have some negotiating leverage if you have another offer. That offer must be real and the salary and benefits are more than what this employer is offering. With this other offer in hand, you can nudge the employer to improve the offer to be more competitive. However, only do this if the employer is your number one choice.

Negotiating Other Things

There are other things you can negotiate other than salary. For example, parking costs should your job be located in a downtown area. You can also inquire whether you can have a paid vacation for a pre-planned (and perhaps already paid for) vacation. Frequently, the employer will have policies in place to deal with these situations, but it can be worth asking to see if there is room for an exception or partial exception (e.g. paid parking for the first four months of employment).

★ Negotiations: Establish a Tone of Cooperation and Justify Your Requests

Establish a Tone of Cooperation. Call the hiring executive and express your interest and enthusiasm about the opportunity. This next point is important: Hopefully you have established good rapport with the hiring executive or HR contact. Set the tone for the negotiations by indicating that you are interested in the job, and by working together you should be able to reach an agreement that will benefit the company, the hiring executive, and you. This step is important because it establishes a tone of cooperation. Inform the hiring executive that there are a few topics that need to be discussed, and once they are resolved, you would be in a better position to accept the offer.

Justify Your Requests. Employers do not mind negotiating job-offer terms with recent college graduates as long as the requests are reasonable and the negotiating process is done quickly. One of the most powerful negotiating techniques is providing logical and reasonable justification for a request. Research indicates that people have a deep sense of fairness. Justification appeals to the hiring executive's sense of fairness. It does not always work, but it can help.

Silence Is Golden

One of the most difficult things to learn in negotiations is silence. Silence in negotiations is not a bad thing; in fact it can be golden (literally).

For some, enduring silence can be hard, especially when you really want the job. You don't want to make the hiring executive uncomfortable or risk having the executive pull the offer altogether. That is very unlikely to happen. Just make your request, justify it, and resist any urge you have to speak—bite your lip if you have to; it'll heal. The employer has the ball in their court. Do not interpret any silence as a rejection from the hiring executive. Give the hiring executive the time necessary to process your request. If you speak and break the silence, there is a high probability that you will not get your request (at least in the form you requested). The end result is you may have just negotiated against yourself!

Close Negotiations and Reach an Agreement

Sometimes during negotiations a new or better term may be offered and other considerations come into play. That's normally good news! But when negotiations are near a point of agreement, you need to close the negotiations by telling the hiring executive that if she/he can meet the points of negotiation, you will:

- Accept
- Discontinue discussion with other companies
- Start on an agreed-upon date

These are closing statements that finalize the negotiations. If the hiring executive accepts your requests, there are no more negotiations and you must follow through and accept.

Sample Negotiation Script

Mr. Burris, I was excited to receive your email yesterday offering me the management trainee position with XYZ Company! Thank you!

This is a position I am very interested in and if we can come to an agreement on just a few things, I believe I would be able to accept the offer.

[Salary increase based on research] I've done some market research from a variety of sources and the average compensation for a position of this type in the industry appears to be $45,000. Your offer is $38,000. Is it possible for you to match the industry average (or

move your offer closer to the industry average)? If so, I think I would be in a better position to accept, discontinue my discussions with others and start on an agreed upon date.

[Salary increase based on a competing offer] *I have another offer with a salary of $45,000. However, I would like to come to work for you. Your offer is $38,000. Can you match the other company's offer? If so, I would accept, discontinue my discussions with the other company and start on an agreed upon date.*

[Salary increase for parking expense] *As you know, I will need to use a parking garage as a part of my employment. I've looked into the monthly rates and the most inexpensive rate is $65 month. That monthly cost is an out of pocket expense for me. Is it possible for you to pay for or offset some of that parking cost? It would really be helpful.*

Accepting the Offer: Be Timely

Accept an offer immediately (or as timely as possible), especially if the terms have been negotiated and mutually agreed on. Doing so starts the employment relationship on the right foot, with optimism. Your excitement about the company and opportunity will also be communicated to the employer.

Get Final Offer in Writing

Ask for the final offer in writing and establish a start date. Start dates are generally negotiable if you have special circumstances that prevent you from starting when the hiring executive wants.

What the Coaches Say:

Due to the (frequent) negotiating advantage most employers have when hiring recent college graduates, what advice would you give when negotiating a job offer?

Always try to negotiate more; if you don't start trying to negotiate, you never will. Prepare a budget so you know what you need to make. Be respectful and have reasons to ask for a little more. Don't be unrealistic either on your salary request, do your best to research salaries, and make sure you know the salaries in the local area. Salaries vary greatly from the south to the north, which is why research will help.

Ellen Steverson, NCRW, GCDF, CEIC

Before you begin a negotiation, know the following:

The salary you need to earn.

The salary range for this type of position.

What the employer is willing to offer.

The salary and benefits the employer is offering.

When you negotiate:

- Stay calm and do not take offense; in the throes of a negotiation, an employer can ask questions that can sound critical but really are just an attempt to find common ground and judge your commitment to the company.

- Avoid, ignore, or downplay ultimatums of any kind; they are often used to end negotiations before a candidate has the opportunity to ask for changes.

- Allow an employer time to respond to a counteroffer; some requests may need to be reviewed by others in the company before a response can be provided.

- Negotiate all aspects of the offer at one time; each part has value and you may be willing to take less in one area if you are offered more in another.

- If you do not get everything you want during the negotiation of a job offer, ask if unresolved issues can be revisited in 6 months.

Lorraine Beaman, MA, CEIC, ACRW, CARW, NCRW, MCD

Declining an Offer of Employment

The key to declining an offer is to do so professionally and gracefully. The employer has put in hours of time and effort and concluded that you can add value to the company. However, for any one of a hundred reasons, the job is just not right for you.

Your decision to turn down the offer must be prompt and professionally done. The employer has a position to fill, and your decision allows them to move forward with their process. Delaying your decision and notification is not fair to the employer.

It is always best to verbally tell the employer of your decision. It's the mature and professional way to handle the situation. Also, follow up your call and conversation with a brief email declining the offer.

In your communications, always show your appreciation for the hiring executive's time and interest. Pay a sincere compliment to the hiring executive, the company, its future, and so on. If you are not already connected to the hiring executive on LinkedIn, extend a customized invitation. This creates a line of communication for future employment opportunities.

Below is a letter that contains the important points mentioned above, which can function as an outline for your call to the hiring executive as well:

Thank you so much for the offer of the manager trainee position. I am flattered to be chosen. I do appreciate your time and consideration. ABC Company is a dynamic organization with innovative products and services. Its future is bright!

However, after careful consideration, I have decided to pursue another opportunity that I believe is a better fit for me.

It has been a true pleasure getting to know you and the other members of your team!

Sincerely,
Your Name

Although the hiring executive will likely be disappointed, you want the hiring executive to come away from the engagement with good feelings about you, as a professional.

Chapter 13

Starting Your New Job

You miss one hundred percent of the shots you don't take.
— Wayne Gretzky[176]

How to Make a Great First Impression When Starting Your New Job

First impressions on the job are important. Your boss and new co-workers make initial judgments that can form long term perceptions of you as a professional. Below are ten ways to make that positive first impression when starting your new job.

Routinely arrive early and stay late

Arguably, this tip could be the most influential in creating a solid first impression. By coming in early it shows enthusiasm, interest, work ethic and a host of other positive character traits. You will endear yourself to others who also come to work early.

Try to work beyond the required hours for the job. As a matter of strategy, stay at work after your immediate supervisor leaves. With a little luck, you could be viewed by your supervisor as "ever present" if you arrive before he or she does and is there after he or she leaves. You will be viewed as a dedicated hard worker.

---

176 "Wayne Gretzky Quotable Quote." *Goodreads.* http://www.goodreads.com/quotes/4798-you-miss-one-hundred-percent-of-the-shots-you-don-t (accessed July 13, 2015).

Dress/Appearance

All companies have a dress code (formal or office custom). Become aware of what is acceptable. How you physically appear in office attire forms a lasting impression especially when you dress consistently professional. Dress the part by always looking professional and crisp. This could mean a trip to the clothing store after you receive your first paycheck (or two).

Learn the job and watch others

When you start your job, you will be trained. Start learning the functions of the job, the software, read and study all training materials. Excel at the training. Then, watch others. See what they do well and emulate those positive behaviors.

Ask questions

It's a good strategy to tell your boss that you will ask questions and some of those questions may be elementary. But, also tell him or her that the sooner you can put all of the building blocks in place, the sooner you can contribute.

Be helpful

Look for opportunities to help. Offer to go beyond what is expected of the job, even in small measures. But, be aware of your time so you don't over-commit. Being eager to help others shows you are committed to the company and creates good relationships with your boss and co-workers.

Socialize

Work hard, but find the time to get to know your co-workers. It is important to fit in culturally. Visit with others. Go to lunch. Just remember the demands of your job trumps socializing.

Positive Attitude

Show optimism about your work. It may not be the most exciting work, but show a positive attitude. Better and more interesting work will follow, especially for those who show a positive outlook and on-the-job performance.

Do your job well

Excel at every project given to you. Go beyond what is expected. Create the impression through your work that you are a high achiever. Become someone the company can look to for superior performance.

Request an early evaluation

Approach your supervisor about your job performance two to six weeks into the job. Ask how you are doing and seek feedback. Find out what you are doing well and areas where there may be deficiencies. This early evaluation allows you to correct course and prevent future issues.

Warning! Avoid gossip, office politics, and all controversial topics

The previous nine tips were "to do's." This one is a "do not." You are the newbie and you do not know any of the history of the internal relationships within the company. Stay away (even if you need to diplomatically excuse yourself from a conversation) from all discussions that are gossip or political maneuvering. Getting involved can have significantly negative ramifications.

Avoid all discussions of controversial topics, most notably politics, race relations, and religion. This includes discussion of these topics at the company water cooler, drinks after work, as well as off-premises company functions.

Following these nine "do's" and the one "do not" sets you up for creating a positive first impression in the beginning days and weeks of your new job. Establishing a positive good impression gets you off on the right foot and positions you for a good job experience.

What the Coaches Say:

What advice would you offer graduates so they start their new job on the right foot?

Understand your first 30, 60, 90 days goals with your boss and strive to achieve (and exceed) them. Stay away from any negative employees. Arrive early, prepared to start, and stay a tad longer, when necessary.

Ellen Steverson, NCRW, GCDF, CEIC

Your goal is to begin developing positive working relationships and learn as much as you can about your new responsibilities when you start a new job. Some first steps to achieving this goal are:

- Turn off your personal cell phone and check it only during breaks.

- Smile as you meet and greet your new coworkers; you are making that all-important first impression.

- Take notes and ask questions during orientation and project meetings.

- Stay busy. Sitting around doing nothing, or saying you have nothing to do is not the way to impress your boss or coworkers. Finding and reading manuals, the company website, or old files are ways to use extra time wisely.

- Be sensitive to the fact you may be replacing a beloved coworker who retired, was fired, or died. Do not make disparaging remarks about the status of projects you have inherited.

- The team you are joining has found ways to complete projects and meet deadlines. Discover what works for them. Ask questions before you start making or suggesting changes.

Lorraine Beaman, MA, CEIC, ACRW, CARW, NCRW, MCD

What You Want to Achieve in Your First Job

As you start your first job, there are a number of goals you ideally want to achieve. Realizing your first job will not be your last, achieving as many of these goals as possible will put you in a position to leverage your experience for a better job (or promotion) in the future.

Learn skills. You will be trained to perform the functions of your new job. Every company does business differently. Learn everything you can. Master the duties and responsibilities of your job as best you can. Understand how things are done as well as why they are done the way the company does them.

Learn how to work in a company environment. You will likely be a part of a team, a group or department within your employer. Learn how to successfully work in a teamwork environment. Get along. This includes using social and networking skills. The relationships you develop with your boss and colleagues may benefit you in significant career or personal ways.

Tenure. Stay in your first job for the right amount of time. Try to build some tenure, at least a couple of years, if you can. Being able to show employment stability in your first job is viewed favorably by your next employer.

Develop a track record of success. Keep track of what you do and look to measure your success. You want accomplishments, success stories, recommendations, and anything else that indicates that you were successful in the position. You need these accomplishments to differentiate you from other job seekers when you choose to change jobs (or compete for promotions).

What the Coaches Say:

In your opinion, what should a graduate strive to accomplish (or learn) from his or her first job?

Continue to learn and develop skills. The transition from college to career does not signal the end of learning. During the first 30 days on your new job, set learning objectives; ask yourself what you should learn to improve your skills and the best way to gain the knowledge. Plan to take advantage of the training your employer provides.

Grow your network. Start with the people you work with; get to know them, what they do, and how you can help them accomplish their goals. Continue to connect with individuals in your field, participate in discussions. Consider joining a local service organization or becoming a volunteer for a favorite charity.

Prepare to take on leadership roles. Watch how your team lead/manager handles projects. As you observe how he/she manages people and projects, determine what works and what does not work. Ask for advice on how to improve, and act on the advice you are given. When it is your turn to lead a project, you will have a blueprint for success and be recognized as an outstanding employee.

Understand your industry. Learn as much as you can about what is happening in your industry: trends, innovations, regulations, and opportunities. Being part of a professional organization is a great way to nurture this habit. You will be prepared both to contribute to your organization's strategic plan and interview questions asking you about your industry knowledge.

Lorraine Beaman, MA, CEIC, ACRW, CARW, NCRW, MCD

Everything you can! Really understand how tasks/projects impact the larger picture. Ask good questions, be curious (not annoying though), and absorb as much as you can to keep advancing your skills.

Ellen Steverson, NCRW, GCDF, CEIC

Chapter 14

Required Job Search Skills for Long-Term Career Employment

Life Rewards Action!
— Chris Widener[177]

Statistically, professionals entering the job market today could have ten to fifteen jobs during their career. Sound like a lot? Let's do some math.

On average, most professionals stay in their current employment between four and five years,[178] then change jobs (or positions), either by choice or otherwise. Employment trends indicate that people are working longer before retiring, either by choice or necessity.[179] This employment "life span" can now last forty to fifty years. If the statistics hold true, more than ten jobs (or positions) during a career is quite possible.[180]

177 Widener, Chris. "Life Rewards Action." http://chriswidener.com/life-rewards-action/ (accessed May 27, 2015).

178 Bureau of Labor Statistics. "Employee Tenure Summary." News release. September 18, 2014. http://www.bls.gov/news.release/tenure.nr0.htm (accessed May 29, 2015).

179 Woods, "Working Longer." http://cached.newslookup.com/cached.php?ref_id=105&siteid=2098&id=10359558&t=1419339600.

180 Bureau of Labor Statistics. "Number of Jobs Held, Labor Market Activity, and Earnings Growth Among the Youngest Baby Boomers: Results from a Longitudinal Survey." News release. March 31, 2015. http://www.bls.gov/news.release/pdf/nlsoy.pdf (accessed May 29, 2015).

Consequently, and as a result of these statistics, it is now *imperative* that you learn job search skills to ensure long-term career employment. Mastering these skills is not hard but it is necessary.

The Seven Job Search Skills You Must Know

Broadly speaking, today's professional must understand the following job search skills:

1. **Knowing the necessary components that comprise an effective job search.** This includes the use of branding, success stories, employer mentality, elevator speech, use of professional qualities and character traits, among others.

2. **How to effectively execute a job search strategy.** Knowing how to start a job search from a dead stop and moving it forward to create a job leads that turn into job offers.

3. **How to compose a professional resume.** You don't need to know the mechanics of how to actually write a persuasive resume (font use, graphic design, etc.), just understand how to present the contents of the various components.

4. **How to create and maintain an online professional profile.** This is optimizing your LinkedIn profile to be discovered by hiring executives and then impressing them with your background and achievements.

5. **How to write persuasive and professional job search communications**. This includes emails, letters, thank-you notes, follow-ups, business cards, and so on.

6. **How to create, nurture, and leverage personal and, perhaps more importantly, professional networks.** Being connected and in touch with those that can help you or hire you in a job search.

7. **How to match/relate your background to the needs of the employer and sell yourself through the use of accomplishments.** This is the understanding of how to interview to get a job offer.

Are these job search skills that important? Think of it this way: Job search skills are those skills that allow you to market your professional abilities so you can get a job, earn an income, and have a fulfilling career experience. You decide.

Your Career . . . Your Responsibility

What is a career? Setting aside the dictionary definition, a career is a series of experiences in your professional working life, which could last forty to fifty years. This career longevity is especially true as our population grows older and we choose to work longer.[181] It is your responsibility to make your career as fulfilling as possible.

Sadly, too many people set out on a career path just to have the wind blow them in directions they really did not want to go, or perhaps had no choice but to go. They had the best of intentions, only to have circumstances dictate their career direction, leading to a disappointing and unfulfilling career experience.

As you move forward, here are some perspectives to consider adopting. They will add clarity and understanding that will benefit you now and throughout your entire career. Adopt the following:

1. **I am solely responsible for my career success.** You took the initiative and put in the hard work to get the necessary education that qualifies you for your chosen career. Own that career by guiding and directing your job-search pursuits.[182]

2. **It is my responsibility to enhance my value proposition.** All industries and all functions within industries evolve, advance, and change. Falling out of touch can have serious and negative career ramifications. It is your responsibility to your career to stay up-to-date and enhance your skills.

3. **I must deliver an ROI (Return on Investment).** Staying in a job where you do not deliver value is not fair to your employer, you, or your career. It puts you at risk of demotions, pay decreases, job termination, and employment stagnation. It can also be a sign that your career is stalling. It is your responsibility to bring value to your employer.

4. **I am responsible for my work-life balance.** Your work-life balance will likely change. For many, there is intense focus early in a career to get established (Where you are today). Then, at some point, as marriage, children, aging parents, and a host of other life dynamics come along, the intensity can shift for a period. It is common for career

---

181 Woods, Jennifer. "Working Longer—Whether You Want to or Not." *CNBC.com.* December 23, 2014, http://www.cnbc.com/id/102264601 (accessed June 9, 2015).

182 "Proactive Career Planning at Any Age." *Aequus Wealth Management Resources.* http://www.aequuswealth.com/newsletter/article/proactive_career_planning_at_any_age (accessed July 10, 2015).

intensity to resume, for example, after kids are out of the house. But regardless, you control where you place your priorities.

5. **It is my responsibility to stay informed about the financial health and well-being of my employer and the industry in which I work.** Be informed and be aware of how your employer is doing. Look around. Is your employer investing in the company, technology, people, and other resources? Are people leaving? Is there expansion and hiring? Is the industry contracting or expanding? Are there new competitors (a possible sign of a healthy industry)? How are other competitors doing? Read about your company (for publicly traded companies, take a look at the annual report). Ask a stockbroker to assess your company or industry. Do your best to stay ahead of possible negative career events.

6. **Change is inevitable in my career. How I respond to change is completely within my control.** Unforeseen things will happen in your career—Mergers. Acquisitions. Reorganization. Layoffs. Loss of funding. Downsizing. Promotions! Change often creates opportunities that can be capitalized upon if given perspective, knowledge, a positive attitude, and focused effort. Change often comes with a natural level of discomfort, uncertainty, and a dose of anxiety. But change frequently accompanies growth, which is the gift of change.

Conducting a professional job search is also a responsibility to your career. This includes job search preparation, your resume, LinkedIn, to interviewing and professionally negotiating an offer. It's all within your control.

Chapter 15

My Personal Letter to You about Career Management

A bold heart is half the battle.

— Dwight D. Eisenhower[183]

I wanted to write the final chapter of this book differently from the others. For this last chapter, I want to offer you some career management advice. This advice is based on my 25+ years as an executive recruiter interacting with thousands of job seekers.

Some of the advice you should use immediately while some is written out-into-the-future. Regardless, I hope you take this advice seriously. It could save you a lot of heartache later in your career.

Create a rainy day fund

To some, this first point doesn't seem like it has much to do with career management at all. But it does. Future job searches can take four to six months, sometimes longer. Save your money to cover living expenses for at least six months.

With this strategy, if you lose your job unexpectedly, you won't panic. You can engage in a self-motivated job search with purpose and strategy and find the right career opportunity, not just a job to pay the bills.

---

183 Maxwell, John C. *The Maxwell Daily Reader: 365 Days of Insight to Develop the Leader Within You and Influence Those Around You*. Nashville, TN: Thomas Nelson, 2011. p. 227.

The rainy day fund also gives you resources to invest in job search tools and services. This could include a resume writing service, business cards, wardrobe necessities, a career coach, or other services. The rainy day fund has emotional benefits as well, allowing you to pay the bills, prevent feelings of desperation, and keep fear at bay.

Keep your resume current

As you progress through your career, it is easy to let your resume grow stale. That's understandable—you are busy doing your job. But you're not managing your career. It takes precious little time to keep your resume up-to-date. Whenever something positive happens in your career or at least once a year—use your annual job performance as a reminder—update your resume. Or, at minimum, put an update at the end of the resume and handle it later. The point is to jot it down, with a date, so you don't lose track.

Keep your LinkedIn profile current, too

The same line of thinking applies to your LinkedIn profile (and any other professional online profiles). Keep it as vibrant as possible. As you know, your LinkedIn profile is pivotal to a job search and equally important for career management. Your LinkedIn profile is how opportunities will often find you. It is imperative that your online presence is up-to-date.

Stay informed about your employer, industry, and the value of your job

There is a lot to talk about here. When I speak with candidates that have lost their jobs, a sizable number noticed warning signs of trouble. Either they ignored the red flags and hoped they would be saved from any layoffs or thought the situation would blow over. As you should now know, you are personally responsible for your career. There are few times when a candidate loses their job without any warning. People do get blindsided, but frequently there are warning signs.

Be aware of how your employer is doing financially. Is there talk about mergers, acquisitions, or IPOs? Significant governmental or regulatory threats? Ask yourself, How does this information positively or negatively affect my career? Evaluate the information, assess the situation, do research, communicate with others, make a determination, and judge timing. Use your business knowledge, common sense, and trust your instincts. Then act if needed.

The same kind of analysis applies to your industry as well. It is important to be knowledgeable and aware of its overall health. Industry shrinkage by market forces or governmental intervention should cause a moment of pause and evaluation. It is always better to move away from an industry in decline to one that is growing and expanding, if in fact your transferrable job skills permit.

Finally, stay acutely aware of the value of your role in a company. Do you, in your job and function, make or save the company money? Does your role further the organization's mission? If the value of your job is fading, seriously consider making a career move.

Plan your career path

In my opinion, you must allow yourself to dream and explore what you want to do and where you want to take your career. This could be anything from climbing the corporate ladder to starting your own business. What do *you* want to do?

For any plan to be effective, you must write it down. It is remarkable how writing something down solidifies a plan and creates a sense of self-accountability. Start with one, three, and five-year plans. In my experience, going much further is not realistic. Too many things can change . . . interests, opportunities, setbacks. In other words, life happens.

Write down the specific actions and steps to move you forward. Add timelines. It's been said that "a goal is a dream with a deadline."[184]

Networking

Network actively. Build contacts within and outside your company or organization. Review the Networking chapter and focus on strategies most impactful to you. Ask yourself this question: If I lost my job today, do I have enough inner circle contacts that I could reach out to that would help me?

The power that professional networking can have on your career is remarkable. Remember that in networking, those who give, get.[185] When the time is right, networking can propel your career to heights and a level of professional satisfaction that you might not have thought possible.

---

184 "Napoleon Hill Quotable Quote." *Goodreads.* http://www.goodreads.com/quotes/244859-a-goal-is-a-dream-with-a-deadline (accessed June 11, 2015).

185 Vlooten, "The Seven Laws."

> ### What the Coaches Say:
>
> **Informal interviews and career management can be a great part of an over-all job search success plan, and are an excellent part of ongoing career management. The benefits to informal interviews are most commonly believed to include the opportunity to network and the chance to meet with a potential employer before a position is posted.**
>
> ---
>
> However, additional very powerful long term benefits include the skills you learn from informally interviewing with people, and the network you develop in the process. Successful career management includes ongoing informal interviews throughout your career. Whether it's a simple coffee conversation or a longer meet-up, the ability to continually meet with and learn from people relevant to your career development is essential to your overall career health. Conducting informal interviews as soon as you can in college gives you a head start to developing the skills that will last a lifetime.
>
> Bryan Lubic, M.A., J.D., CCMC, CJSS

Stay sharp and develop new skills

One of the keys to long-term employment and career management is to become indispensable. I don't think this can be completely achieved in most organizations, but you want to get as close to it as you can. At a minimum, you want your employer to perceive you in such a way that it will "hurt" if they should ever lose you.

To me, this is achieved by enhancing your current skillset and developing new skills. Even though you have just graduated college, attend workshops, seminars, and conventions, stay informed about emerging trends and technology or products.

I highly recommend that you earn an industry designation. I fully realize that the thought of additional "schooling" is not exactly what you want to hear having just completed college. However, as the next few years pass, it is a very good idea. An industry designation adds credibility to your name and your brand (more on that in a moment). It will differentiate you from your peers. Getting a "certificate of completion" from a one-day seminar is not what I am talking about. Rather, pursue those industry designations that take effort and have substantive meaning both in content and with your peers. It may take time and effort, but the knowledge and differentiation you gain with your current employer and for future employment opportunities makes it well worth it.

Many job seekers have told me over the course of time that pursuing an industry designation rejuvenated them. New learning opens the mind and can keep you creative and sharp, growing and vibrant.

What the Coaches Say:

Skills and career management.

Having a career means you have to manage it. Sadly, most people lack career management skills. A career needs to be nurtured and it will be a journey. Having plans, reviewing your skills, improving your skills over the years, and having goals will help you move your career forward.

Ellen Steverson, NCRW, GCDF, CEIC

Nurture your brand

Good career management encompasses brand management. Even though you have just started your career, you are creating a brand (or a professional reputation) for yourself. Review this book's Branding section. Stay aware of your value proposition, ROI, and differentiation factors. These and other factors create your brand, which must be nurtured and guarded.

To nurture your brand, ask yourself a two-part question: What am I known for (or, what do I want to be known for)? And is that getting communicated to those that matter? Assess, evaluate, and make adjustments as needed.

Ensure your visibility at work and in your industry

Closely tied to branding is the concept of visibility. Work to get known within your company, organization, and your industry, in ways that support your brand. It could be as simple as some internal networking—but don't become a politician. You can be subtle to get your work noticed. I suggest finding a professional association that piques your interest. Find a way to get involved. Your involvement does not have to be time-consuming. The point is to contribute and become known. It will enhance your networking efforts and career opportunities.

Be aware of opportunities in the market

It is incumbent upon you to be aware of new opportunities that can enhance your lifetime career experience. LinkedIn has ways for you to be alerted about opportunities that would interest you or be your next progressive step in your career. Use it when the time is right.

Return calls and emails from recruiters and others; listen to opportunities they present. The bottom line is this: whether you stay with your current position or pursue a new opportunity, ultimately, it is your choice. You are proactively managing your career. What a great position to be in!

Consider getting a mentor or career coach

I want to draw a distinction between a mentor and a career coach, though both can serve similar purposes regarding your career management. A mentor, as I am using the word, is normally a person in your field that you know and respect. You want to emulate this person. It is someone with whom you have established a good relationship.

A career coach, on the other hand, is a paid professional who coaches and advises others on career matters.

A mentor will be guiding you based largely on personal experience. For most mentors, this is an opportunity to share relevant past experiences, insights, and hard-earned wisdom. Many mentors feel they are passing along a piece of their legacy as a result of the relationship. They give, but they also receive good feelings from the relationship.

A career coach is paid. Evaluate a coach to ensure they have the insight necessary to benefit and guide you. While a mentor will give advice based largely on past experience, an experienced career coach can draw from the experiences of scores of professionals that the coach has worked with. Also know that a mentor will "tell" in guiding you, while a true coaching professional will ask more questions to explore potential answers. It will be a different kind of communication and relationship.

Whether you choose a mentor or coach, it is important to define and mutually agree on what is expected from both to make the relationship work. Notably, the frequency of communication should be discussed, even if it is on an as-needed basis.

The most important thing for you to remember about a mentor or coaching relationship is to engage in conversation but also be able to listen and learn. Frequently, you will receive not only valuable insight and knowledge, but also wisdom. This information can have a profound impact on your career.

It's a matter of attitude, introspection, and perspective

Over the course of my career, I have reviewed the career paths of thousands of people. One frequent theme is common to most: Your career will be an unpredictable journey.

Regardless of your intentions and plans, there will be twists and turns. I highly encourage you to always maintain a positive outlook and attitude. Consider it an invaluable career management strategy. Want proof? "Nearly 88 percent of the 3,785 senior-level executives surveyed by ExecuNet said they would rather enhance their team with that individual who possesses a good attitude, even if he or she does not perform to the highest level or have top qualifications."[186] This statistic directly applies to internal promotions as well as external job opportunities. Having a positive attitude will enhance your career opportunities.

Another related career management concept is introspection. I have spoken to professionals who have developed in their careers and wake up one morning regretting the ways their career reshaped them. I remember one candidate shared he had become irritable, impatient, and overly consumed with thoughts about money, among other things. He wanted a change from the demands of his current job so he could return to a less stressful career existence and back to the person he truly was.

Career management means remaining true to who you are, and being comfortable with the fit between you and the demands of your job. When they do not match close enough, you—and your family—will likely experience outward signs of the internal friction (irritability, reclusiveness, impatience, and so on). Good career management requires times of introspection to examine you for who you are (or are becoming) as a result of your career. The outcome of that introspection may be motivation for a career move.

Tied to introspection is the concept of perspective. Introspection is an internal evaluation while perspective is an external evaluation. Perspective, as I am using the word, frequently comes to the surface with tenured career professionals. They begin to ask themselves these kinds of questions:

"What is the purpose of what I do?"

"Am I helping anyone?"

"Do I provide any value?"

---

186 ExecuNet. "Senior-Level Business Leaders Say Positive Attitude is the Key to Getting the Job." News release. March 25, 2013. http://www.execunet.com/m_releases_content.cfm?id=4812 (accessed June 11, 2015).

Or, in a grander sense . . .

"Why am I on this earth?"

These are deep questions and ones that are perfectly normal to ask. From my experience, the key is to discover and name at least one, and hopefully more, redeeming values that your work brings, directly or in conjunction with coworkers or others.

The naming process identifies and solidifies the value of your work in your mind (intellectually) and your heart (emotionally). What your heart and mind hold onto will bring feelings of professional worth. It's a great feeling that your heart and mind know your work matters.

Let's tie this all together: attitude, introspection, and perspective. Working backward: When you genuinely feel your work matters, you have professional self-worth. When your job is consistent with who you are as a person, there is internal peace and a match with you and your career. Both affect your attitude in a very significant and positive way. Having a positive attitude is a career strategy and leads to more or better career opportunities, which is a component of proactive career management. I love it when it all comes together!

I hope these pieces of advice, based on my experience and the experience of others, impart valuable insight on proactively managing your young career. It is my heartfelt and sincerest hope that you experience the most successful and emotionally fulfilling career you possibly can!

Best Wishes Always,

Brian E. Howard

Chapter 16

More Job Search Insights
and Stories of Inspiration from Jered Lish

Throughout the book you have seen and read advice on a variety of job search topics from Jered Lish. He is truly an insightful career coaching professional.

Some of Jered's responses were too detailed for the instructional part of this book. They include experiences, job-search insight, and stories of inspiration. It would be unfair to you not to include his stories and experiences. So, in this chapter you are given the opportunity to read more of Jered's responses to the job search questions. His stories should inspire you and perhaps humor you along the way.

Job Search Methods

In your experience, what are the most effective job search methods for recent college graduates (e.g. on-campus career fairs, networking, job boards, etc.)?

Strategizing with students on how to generate employment opportunities is one of my favorite conversations. The process is multifaceted and requires a strong understanding of oneself, requires creativity, and most importantly requires resiliency and grit. When I engage my students in the conversation I like to speak from a 60/30/10 hypothetical breakdown of their time.

The 60 represents statistically the breakdown of people who find employment from networking, or through their networks. Engaging students in the question of "who do you know? Who do those people know? Who are your parents? What do your siblings do? And have you shared your career goal with your network so they can help you in your journey?" are questions I dissect with recent graduates. Most the time, recent graduates I've worked with aren't in a place of strategic thinking determining who within their network can advance them, whether in knowledge of industry or employment opportunity. Career fairs, young professional groups, LinkedIn, are a few of a multitude of ways to advance a network, and I encourage students to focus the majority of their time sharing their pitch and career objective with anyone who will listen (of course done in a humble, engaging, and thoughtful way).

Next, the 30 number represents the amount of people from our university who tend to find jobs through an application process online. Throughout my own career I have secured all of my jobs through an online portal process and fall into this category. I have come to realize however as I grow in my professional career that networking is a "work smarter, not harder" approach because it enables the job seeker to learn about positions that a job description won't fully capture and helps to identify potential fit in the process.

Lastly, the 10 number represents your marketing and branding documents. If a recent graduate lacks the understanding of how to brand and tailor a resume to the needs of their desired company of choice, they won't advance through the process. I jokingly will tell students and recent graduates that their marketing documents need to look like their dating profile in the sense that it needs to be aesthetically pleasing and attractive to the eye (because humans love to judge ugly resumes), and more importantly it needs to tell the graduate's success story of relevant competencies and experiences they can bring to the company that will advance them. When a resume is placed next to a job description, it needs to scream "this is the perfect match!" In general, I believe recent graduates appreciate strategies around how they can work smarter, and not harder in their job search, and knowing statistically speaking, what processes yield faster outcomes can allow the recent graduate to decide how best and deliberately to utilize their valuable time.

Social Media

What is your advice about cleaning up social media sites before starting a job search?

I was once in an appointment with a student who was talking about the importance of googling their name to see what popped up in preparation for job searching, in order to ensure all outward facing social media was in alignment with the image they wanted to portray professionally. The student shared, "I haven't checked that in a long time, let's see what my name generates." I agreed and we Googled their name. In the process of searching the search engine, a Youtube video popped up of the student, and they immediately turned red in the face. They then proceeded to tell me not to click on the icon, and I, of course, laughed with the student because it was a case and point of the importance of knowing what exists out there, and to "clean up" anything that could be deemed questionable by a future employer. Long story short, I encourage students and recent graduates to reflect on how they desire to present themselves professionally through social media, and remembering whatever they put out to social media is a representation of their values, identities, belief systems, and that ultimately, they don't get to control how a person interprets what they see. It is better to be conservative and "clean up" their social media in order to present a polished and professional, outward facing image.

Importance of G.P.A.

What is your opinion regarding the importance of a G.P.A. and its influence on a graduate's job search?

Depending on your career goals, a strong GPA can be helpful to opening doors and statistically speaking, there is a strong statistical tie to faster job placement with a strong GPA. There isn't, however, a strong tie to GPA after a person seeks out their second professional position. One could argue it's only really helpful for your immediate post-graduation job search.

On the flip side, a low GPA doesn't necessarily equate to reduced opportunities upon graduation. Certain opportunities might be limited due to a GPA requirement, especially in such areas as engineering or if applying to medical school, for example. A GPA, however, isn't the end-all-be-all to obtaining the dream career because at the end of the day, a GPA is a like a standardized test score, it only tells part of the story.

If I could put a greater emphasis on job placement influencers, it would be associated with how a recent graduate lived out their passions, strengths, talents, values, and curiosities towards experiential learning. Whether this is in the form of an internship, externship, service/volunteering, research, shadowing/informational interviews and the list goes on, these experiences ultimately will generate new skill sets that can be strategically marketed and packaged towards particular employers as either direct or transferable skills.

One of my favorite coaching stories was an engineering student who had a low GPA and his dream was to either work at Space X or NASA. Every job posting he perused from those particular companies had a high GPA requirement, and he felt deflated in his job search process because he didn't think he could achieve his dream. The student, however, had a very impressive background of experiences both in the classroom and outside of it. He engaged in a multitude of experiential learning projects that were both self-generated and self-taught. He built small toy rockets for fun, drafted blueprints of the designs, and took pictures of the entire process start-to-finish. He was very active in student organizations related to his field and designed a couple of projects with his group which won a few design competitions both locally and nationally. He also had a cue of very impressive classroom projects that highlighted and captured his innovative, creative, and entrepreneurial spirit and it was that combination of traits which prepped his next steps of applying to Space X and NASA.

While he knew his GPA wouldn't allow him to pass the online screenings, he began to brainstorm other ways to seek out interviewing opportunities. He utilized a social media e-portfolio online tool called Portfolium.com to help him tell his success story. He uploaded all of his previous designs, projects, accomplishments, and more and began to use that tool to help paint the type of future employee he could be for an organization. Long story short, he sent his Portfolium e-portfolio to recruiters at Space X, NASA, and a few other companies of interests and not only did he generate interviews at Space X and NASA, but he had landed interview after interview, and job offer after job because he took a different approach to his job search.

At the end of the day while his GPA appeared to close some doors, this student figured out how to open those same doors using a different key. The moral of this story is to not let traditional and direct pathways to certain careers limit how you seek out opportunities in those areas. Be creative, be diligent, and be an advocate for your dreams because you never know what you can achieve until you wholeheartedly try.

What are your thoughts regarding the importance of a G.P.A. and the overall success of a college graduate's career?

If possible, it is important for a college student to obtain as good of grades as they possibly can. A higher GPA can result in more open doors to different career options. However, for the career coaching community, we understand not every student's journey through college is equal as it pertains to access, opportunity, and resources. We know some students will work 2-4 jobs in order to pay for school on top of a full course load, some are sending money back to family to help support their communities, and that can be difficult to manage at a high achieving academic capacity. We do also know that students who do get involved with something outside of the classroom, perform better in their classes, have higher GPA's, and this is theorized to be the case because it is tied to better time management skills. In short, know that a low GPA isn't indicative of the overall career success of a college graduate, but rather how a student engages in the learning process throughout college both in and outside of the classroom. It is not a precursor to the success a graduate will experience.

What are employers looking for?

In your experience, what are employers looking for when hiring a recent college graduate?

From my experience employers report looking for innovative, team oriented, strong communicators, and solutions based thinkers, who can thrive in the complexities of the unknowns and the unexplored. In short, companies want to hire creative, smart, fun, engaging critically thinking, and hard-working graduates who also have a high emotional intelligence.

Now how does a recent graduate articulate all of that to them? I was speaking with a recruiter from Google and was asking them if they could give any piece of advice to students pursing software engineering positions at their company, what they would recommend. I was surprised to learn they will often score a resume higher if they saw tutoring in a recent graduate's documents. This insight was particularly interesting to me because it validated the importance of soft skills such as communication and coaching, and it was apparent as a value of Google to find good critical thinkers who have great soft skills.

I was speaking with a CEO out in San Diego who owns a staffing company, and he shared he often scored resumes higher if he saw a student was an athlete. His company has a high performing sales team and he attributes the recruitment of athletes being tied to them being team oriented, competitive, and disciplined, and those are attributes he seeks when hiring recent graduates.

With these two examples in mind, employers seek out candidates who they theorize will be strong contributors to their teams, and it's through impressive experiences, competencies gained and soft skills demonstrated, do most candidates advance when those attributes are presented.

First Job

How important is the first job out of college?

I would say the first job out of college isn't as important as your first boss out of college. I encourage recent graduates to not only search for a job around interest areas, values and strengths but to also be diligent in seeking a supervisor who can serve as a facilitator of professional growth in your first position post college. This is particularly important for the *post college millennial job* seeker to find a boss who can serve as a mentor and facilitator of their growth. With this being said, while interviewing for any position, I encourage my recent graduates to be inquisitive around the work values of the supervisor, along with learn their philosophy of professional development. Any insights gained in those areas can be an indicator of what their first job will mean for them, and it can make all the difference in how they grow and thrive in their first position.

Common Job Search Mistakes of Recent College Graduates

In your experience, what are the common job search mistakes that recent college graduates make?

The most common mistake I've seen is a lack of reflection around how a recent graduate could leverage their personal networks to advance opportunities available to them. I feel many recent graduates feel they're having to "sell" themselves to people which either feels unnatural or manipulative, and so I work with recent graduates to help practice reframing and telling their story of successes in a way that leverages interest and curiosities from their networks to learn if they can help and how they can help.

Humans like to help humans and when a person hears a goal or a challenge a person is facing in seeking employment, it is natural for them to want to assist and provide direction. For recent graduates, your network wants to help you. Share your goals, share your thoughts, be inquisitive, and be intentional in planning next steps with your network as they'll help shape your strategies in a way that yields the outcomes you seek for employment.

Criminal Record

What is your advice for college graduates who have a criminal record?

Depending on the depth and severity of the criminal record, there are definitely ways in which opportunities can be generated. This topic can be incredibly complex and every individuals situation is different. In general, it can be advantageous for the recent graduate to target locations that may not be as popular and desirable for job placement; for instance, in smaller cities, colder cities, and more rural communities. Essentially the strategy I'm recommending is the "go where the employers are who will hire you" approach, and this can be an effective job search strategy as long as the recent graduate isn't overly picky or bound to a particular geographical location.

If a recent graduate has any specialty skill sets they can leverage, becoming an independent contractor can be a great way to continue to build skills while generating income. Entrepreneurial initiatives based on previous skills can be an approach to take. And, quite honestly, who wouldn't want to be their own boss? Lastly, if you're struggling to find something, don't forget to check out either your alma mater's resources for navigating the job search, or sign up with job placement organizations. Within the career center where I work, we have a PhD level career coach who specializes in helping alumni navigate both their criminal record and job search. Her clients yield successful outcomes in their efforts for landing employment. In short, if a recent graduate has a criminal record, I encourage them to do their research on the job market in both desirable and less ideal locations. To practice both verbally, and in writing, how to disclose that information in an application or interview if prompted. To utilize the resources they have access to at their alma mater, and remember to keep pushing forward. The resiliency they've developed in life will serve them well in their job search.

Getting off to a Successful Start with a Job Search

What would you recommend that would get a recent college graduate off to a successful start to their job search?

I would encourage a recent graduate to set a goal to have coffee/tea/drink of choice, with as many connections per month whether known or unknown as possible in an informational interview capacity. I had an international student who was determined to land a job in the USA, and he had specific and targeted cities he wanted to live in which included: San Francisco, NYC, Miami and LA. He set up nearly 50 coffee/connect sessions within a 2.5-week period. He jokingly told me he had the jitters for weeks after those interviews because of the amount of coffee he had drank. He flew from coast to coast for these meetings, and through his intentional informational interviewing he was able to meet a high-level executive who connected him to one of his colleagues who eventually ended up helping him land a great job in NYC. His inquisitive and go-getter spirit resonated with the decision maker and because of his intentionality, great 30 second pitch, and resilient process, did this student land a great opportunity. The famous phrase goes, it's not what you know but who you know and through informational interviews you meet a lot of people and gain a lot of insightful information which can generate opportunity.

Elevator Speech

What is your advice for recent college graduates in creating an "elevator speech?"

Elevator speeches might be one of the most important things to develop, practice, and have prepared at all times, because you never know when you're going to use it and/or need it.

To share a personal story, I'm a musician, play six instruments, love to write music and always had the dream of writing music for television or films. When I was deciding on career paths, as a first year student at Colorado State University, I didn't know if I'd be able to make it in that industry because it's so competitive. As a result of that uncertainty, I decided I'd likely never pursue it formally and picked a "safe career". Fast forward ten years later, I'm at a gym in Miami, Florida and there was a guy there who needed assistance on a heavy bench lift, so I naturally offered to spot him in the process. I helped him out with the lift and I noticed he had a particular band on his cut off t-shirt that I liked and small talk began. After a few minutes of talking music he asked me about my story. I shared with him I was a career counselor at a university in the area and that I was also a musician with a background and passion for writing strings arrangements. As luck would have it, he disclosed he was an award-winning music producer for cinema, television, and commercial work and that he was recently looking for someone to help do studio musician work, specifically with strings. That interaction led to studio musician work for myself, which eventually led to me become a published commercial recorder for television commercials for HGTV, Travel Channel, Food Network and a few other networks. This story is important because the 30 second pitch isn't just for career fairs, or a networking event. The 30 second pitch is also for the little moments in life, and for me, it enabled me to pursue a lifelong dream of writing music for television.

The great thing about the 30 second pitch is you can, and should, use it anywhere anytime; at the gym, at a wedding, at a holiday party and especially, when you're out there and your uncle asks you "what are you going to do with a degree in X", those are those moments for you to share and practice your pitch.

On-Campus Career Fairs

What preparation would you recommend prior to attending an on-campus career fair? What strategies would you recommend to recent college graduates to get the most from attending an on-campus career fair?

Generally speaking, the majority of attendees at a career fair aren't going to walk away with or land a job from that process. So, is it a wasted effort? Absolutely not! Attending career fairs is the perfect and safe place to practice a 30 second pitch, to physiologically feel how your body responds to nerves when speaking with a company of interest, and attending an on-campus career fair can enable you to learn about a multitude of companies in a short amount of time. So how does one prepare for an on-campus career fair? Well, a variety of things can be done:

1. Prepare your resume and do your research on a few companies that will be in attendance and make sure your documents speak to your targeted companies.

2. Utilize social media platforms such as Linkedin and Portfolium to help paint and tell your success stories and utilize those links in marketing documents.

3. Practice your pitch with friends, family, and mentors. Understanding how to tie your strengths, interests, goals, and areas of growth, all into an engaging conversation with a recruiter will be an important practice to get exposure to before the career fair.

4. With your list of companies, identify a few companies you can practice your pitch with before you go and speak with the dream company. If you start with your dream company, that can feel overwhelming so a warm up session is recommended.

5. Dress to the culture of your dream company. If you're going into tech and they have a lax dress code, dress to their culture. If you're unsure of the dress code, it's recommended to dress business casual.

Alumni Associations

What is your advice about using an alumni association as a part of a graduate's job search?

If a university has a strong alumni connection platform, I've seen many students land internships and jobs from just outreaching through the university's alumni data system. I had a student in California who greatly desired to work at the San Diego Zoo and after perusing the alumni database, she found an alumna who worked there. The story is short and sweet in that she set up an informational interview with the alumna, and after her time spent with her, she landed an opportunity to interview formally, and then eventually started her dream job. It truly can be that simple. I encourage students to connect with alumni with intentions of learning pathways of success, seeing patterns within the stories they can use to strategize for their own journey, and to ultimately, practice, practice, practice managing and maintaining valuable connections with people who they find inspiring. Also showing gratitude for people's time in the form of hand written or electronic notes is another thing to practice. On a quick tip note, if a recent graduate is on LinkedIn, and their university doesn't have an alumni connection option they should:

1. Search the university they attended on LinkedIn

2. Click the "See Alumni" button

3. Type in companies they may want to work at

4. Read profiles and skills of current alumni, who are currently/former employees

5. If they want to reach out to those alumni they are interested in, write a personalized message highlighting what intrigued them about their profile, and request an opportunity to conduct an informational interview over the phone or in-person over coffee to discuss their professional journey

6. Thank the alum/na for their time and ask if it would be okay to stay connected with professionally after your chat.

Interviewing - Common Interview Questions

In your experience, what are common interview questions a college graduate must prepare in advance to answer?

I have seen students and recent graduates stumble through a variety of different questions in an interview setting, and I'll highlight a few that at first glance look easy but actually require some thought.

The first question, what are your areas of weakness/improvement? These types of questions are somewhat of a trap. The employer is trying to see if they can get you to disclose information that can be used against you in determining why you wouldn't be a good fit for their company. Strategies for answering could include talking about knowledge gaps. For instance, if a specific computer system is required for the job, highlight how you've never used that but then highlight a strength of how you're a quick learner. By not actually disclosing a character or behavior weakness but rather a knowledge based weakness, you successfully navigate that question.

Another strategy can be strengths flipping. Essentially, disguise strengths as weaknesses and then flip it back to a positive. For example, if your strength was making things, ideas or processes, good, better, great, you could say: "I'm a maximizer of people, product, and processes, however sometimes this can show up in the form of me being a perfectionist, and I can often find myself drowning in the details of the little things. If excellence isn't at the core of what I'm producing, I can be unpleasant to work with. As I've become more self-aware I have successfully managed this by . . . " and go on to provide some tangible examples of ways you improved your "weakness".

Another popular question is, how do you manage conflict? This question is a soft skills question. I recommend using the STAR method (situation, task, action, result) to answer this and at the end of the day, have some examples of how you navigated people successfully in a way that yielded a positive outcome.

Lastly, this question "What role do you like to play on a team?" is one that traditionally people fall into the common answers trap which either includes I'm a leader, follower or it depends on everyone else on the team. I coach students on this question to be creative in how they articulate their presence or how they show up within a team or organization. I encourage students to take the strengthsquest.com and learn about their top strengths and practice how they would infuse their answers into this question. For example, if a person was high in ideation, if they were to be asked their role on a team, they could state: "The role I love to play on the team is the brainstorm extraordinaire! I am a person of ideas and I enjoy the complexities surrounding how we creatively solve this problem using a method we haven't tried before. I get the idea rolling with the team which ultimately helps facilitate new and innovative approaches. An example of that happening in my previous role includes . . ." I utilize the Strengths Finder in order to help provide the language needed to navigate nearly all behavioral based interviews.

Interview Wardrobe

What advice would you give about a graduate's wardrobe for interviews?

This section of advice is both simple and complicated all at the same time. The reason for that is there's been an increase in the diversity of the types of work cultures that exist, and each culture has its own rules. In general, a recent graduate will want to do their research on wardrobe rules for particular companies and organizations and gain an understanding of whether that culture is actually a good fit. Formal wear, casual dress, and self-expression are all things to note when navigating the cultural norms of an organization's a recent graduate is considering. I keep advice simple in this area:

1. If self-expression is important to you in what you wear, find a company where you can self-express comfortably and without judgement.

2. If you don't appreciate a structured work atmosphere, avoid overly formal work cultures.

3. If you appreciate the aesthetics of business formal and the status quo of a standard of dress, find a great tailor and your power suit!

4. And most importantly, dress at the level of position you seek and that's to be interpreted entirely off of your work norms and culture you seek to be a part of.

Handling Rejection

Rejection is an inescapable fact of a job search. What advice would you give graduates to handle job search rejection?

Remember these five things when applying for a position:

1. They may have internal candidates. You could be the best candidate in the world and if they have an internal candidate, you unfortunately may just be a formality for them having to interview you. Those are unfortunate situations, but they happen. It isn't you, it's them.

2. If you send out a bunch of resumes and don't hear back, your resume format may be dated/in need of tweaks or maybe, it isn't passing scanning software (jobscan.co if you aren't sure how your resume scans). REMEMBER: sending out a resume is like fishing. You put bait on a hook and hope something bites. If the fish (employers) don't bite, change the bait (format/language of the resume) and try again.

3. Apply and forget (kind of): Take a moment right before you press "send" on an application, and think "did I tailor everything and does this reflect the brand I want to put out to the world?" If yes, press send, and remember there's a lot of other people likely applying for this position. Celebrate that you sent it, make note of it, and move on to the next application.

4. If you receive a "we didn't select you" email, remember that everyone has faced rejection, EVERYONE, and that you're waiting for the RIGHT yes, that matters. Remember things happen for a reason, to trust the process, and keep moving until the right yes comes your way. Resiliency and grit is an important life skill to develop, and how you bounce back and try again is a muscle you want and need to build.

5. Lastly learn from the rejection, and move forward with confidence in your new

developed strategy. Try new things, be creative, put yourself out there, and develop your own best practices. Repeat.

References

What insight and advice would you offer graduates when it comes to references?

You're only as strong as your weakest reference. Make sure when requesting a reference that if you're able to do so, request if the person would be willing to serve as a GREAT reference on your behalf and make sure the caliber of reference is consistent across all of your recommenders. The person who provides the weakest reference will be listened to the most by the hiring authority. Consistency in a recommendation process is key. Unfortunately, I have seen too many pre-medical students apply to medical school and they ask a faculty member who didn't know them well, and they receive a mediocre evaluation from the faculty which results in a lost opportunity.

Job Offer Negotiation

Due to the (frequent) negotiating advantage most employers have when hiring recent college graduates, what advice would you give when negotiating a job offer?

I encourage creativity when negotiating with employers especially for recent college graduates. Often, salaries may not be negotiable however, if a person is a Mac user and the company uses PCs, that can be easily negotiable. If a company has a wellness policy, getting the company to pay for a gym membership or fitness membership can be provided.

I once had a student negotiate for a treadmill work station because she integrated her values of health and wellness into her interview and shared that would be critical to her success in the position. She got it. Negotiating for specialty computer programs like memberships to Adobe Suite or other specialty programs can be easy negotiables. Think "what would make my life/job better/easier & more fun?"

Starting a New Job

What advice would you offer graduates so they start their new job on the right foot?

First and foremost, build rapport, build trust, and build relationships with your colleagues. Even if you don't identify as a people person, or an overly relational person, in order to advance professionally or even advance an idea, the people you work with have to trust you and believe in you. Relationships should be your number one priority when starting a new job.

What to Achieve in Your First Job

In your opinion, what should a graduate strive to accomplish (or learn) from his or her first job?

My top 7 recommendations for things to accomplish in your first job:

1. Be curious: Explore your profession and learn everything you can about it.

2. Be observant: Watch your leadership. Learn best practices from them and things you would want to change. Pay attention to how people motivate and inspire others, and mimic their practices.

3. Find a mentor in your field: Identify potential mentors who can help you navigate hard obstacles or challenges. Identify someone who can serve as a sounding board to your thoughts so you make good, strategic decisions.

4. Ask good questions: Be inquisitive. The more you ask the more you'll learn.

5. Be relational: Build rapport and trust with your colleagues once you start. It will go a long way for you professionally.

6. Reflect often: Dissect what you're learning and how you can apply it for the success of yourself and the company.

7. Grow: Remember your first position will come with massive growth personally and professionally. Enjoy the process during the highs and the lows as it'll prepare you for that next professional step you take whenever opportunity comes knocking.

For your first job, you'll experience a lot, you'll see a lot, you'll see success, you'll see areas of growth, and be patient with yourself in the process. Know your life will feel like it's in transition especially if you move away from a support system. Give yourself the breathing room to try new things, to fail quickly, to learn from those moments, and ultimately, you'll eventually see the success you always dreamt of.

Jered Lish

PART V

Resume Samples and Other Written Communications

Chapter 17

Resume Samples and Other Written Communications Provided by Your Coaches

Dr. Cheryl Minnick, M.Ed., Ed.D, CCMC, NCRW

Ellen Steverson, NCRW, GCDF, CEIC

Lorraine Beaman, MA, ACRW, CARW, NCRW, CEIC, MCD

Mary Jo King, NCRW

Paula Christensen, CPRW, CJSS, CCMC

Tina Kashlak Nicolai, PHR, CPBA, CARW

Resumes Provided By

Cheryl Minnick , M.Ed., Ed.D, CCMC, NCRW
University of Montana – Academic Enrichment

(406) 243-4614
cminnick@mso.umt.edu

AMY GRANDE

San Francisco, California – 509.123.4567 – AmyGrande@gmail.com

SCHOOL COUNSELOR ... *helping children become academically, socially, vocationally, and personally successful.*

Group Counseling	• Provide comprehensive school counseling programs that address academic, vocational, personal, and social development.
Behavioral Contracts	
Community Resourcing	• Offer students developmental, preventative, remedial, and responsive services in individual and small group sessions and in the classroom.
Diagnostic Interpretation	• Employ leadership, advocacy, and collaboration to promote student success by responding to identified student, school, and system goals.
Psychoeducational Groups	
Cross-Cultural Effectiveness	• Interpret student behavior and collaborate with administration, parents and teachers to offer appropriately structured services and support.
Multidisciplinary Conferences	
Family & Teacher Consultation	• Utilize accepted theories and effective techniques in adherence to laws, policies, procedures, and ethical standards of the counseling profession.

M.S., Counseling Psychology, University of San Francisco, San Francisco, California, May 2017
Sexual Assault & Recovery Peer Counselor ~ Academic Peer Counselor

■ ■ ■

B.S., Child Development, Washington State University, Pullman, Washington, 2015
Athletic Advisory Council ~ Athletic All Academic Team ~ NCAA Division I Volleyball

PROFESSIONAL EXPERIENCE

JEFFERSON ELEMENTARY SCHOOL, Counseling Intern, San Francisco, California, January 2017–May 2017

School of 360 students with an active parent community, it is called a Rainbow School due to a culturally-diverse student body. A 2010 recipient of a Great Schools Rating of 9:10 and API base score of 871, each FTE teacher instructs 19 students.

- Interpreted standardized tests and other assessment data to guide students in individual goal setting and planning, and to provide services to students with mental health, behavior disorders, or learning disabilities.
- Created and facilitated groups with special and regular education students to teach goal-setting, interpersonal effectiveness, decision-making, communication, problem-solving skills, and responsible behavior.
- Collaborated with multidisciplinary team members to promote understanding of student development, individual behavior, the student's environment, and human relationships.
- Prepared social development histories and individualized education plans (IEP) and provided professional expertise to advocate for individual students.

SUNNYSIDE PRESCHOOL & CHILDCARE, Pre-School Teacher, Pullman, Washington, 2009–2011

Large childcare center for children 1 month to 12 years offering opportunity for socialization, learning, and a head-start on academics. A staff of 5 teachers educating 50 students year-round.

- Promoted literacy and language development through encouraging interactions, thematic curriculum, and age-appropriate story hours to stimulate children's emotional, intellectual, and social growth.
- In a child-centered environment, helped children explore interests, develop talents and independence, build self-esteem, and learn to interact in a socially acceptable manner. Prepared and served nutritious meals.

WORK EXPERIENCE ... *balanced part-time work with full-time academics to self-finance graduate school.*

BRICK CAFE, Server, San Francisco, California, 2015–present
SEPHORA, Cosmetic Sales Associate (seasonal), San Francisco, California, 2015–present

COLLIN FOOTE

Philadelphia, Pennsylvania | (123) 456-7890 | collin.foote@gmail.com

Career Goal:
FINANCIAL ANALYST

Dynamic college graduate with a one-team mentality and eagerness to provide financial, operational and technical research talents to support accounting, management and external reporting. Goal-driven professional with disciplined work ethic and willingness to learn. Innovative problem solver offering experience manipulating large data sets and advanced technical skills in Excel, VBA programming, macros and SQL. Key competencies:

Data Management & Analysis | Influence Management | Financial Research & Analysis
Technical Troubleshooting | Database and Data Manipulation | Data Entry and Data Mining
SQL | C++ | Python | Java | Visual Basic Application | Microsoft Office Suite

EDUCATION

The Wharton School of Business, University of Pennsylvania, Philadelphia, Pennsylvania, December 2017
Bachelor of Science in Finance – Bachelor of Science in Computer Science

• • • •

Capstone: Researched and analyzed the operational structure and practices of Topgolf, the global sports entertainment community; documented and presented recommendations for effective globalization of operations.

M&A Analysis: Analyzed Wrigley's equity vs debt and resultant merger transaction into a subsidiary of Mars, Inc.

Bankruptcy Analysis: Analyzed financial distress, bankruptcy, and rebirth of Coleco.

IPO Review: Researched history, legal, financial, and reputational results of FaceBook's IPO— a forced move that resulted in $104B peak market capitalization.

Related Coursework: Corporate Managerial Finance; Micro/Macroeconomics; Financial Analysis and Working Capital; International Finance; Business Ethics; Investments; Managing, Organizing and Leading; Database Systems.

PROFESSIONAL EXPERIENCE

FINANCIAL ANALYST INTERN, Northwestern Mutual, Philadelphia, Pennsylvania, June 2017–Present

- Assisted 4 financial advisors with research to offer innovative solutions for lifetime financial needs of individuals and businesses in retirement solutions, insurance and investment services, estate analysis, business needs analysis, education funding and employee benefits.
- Established standard processes and procedures using MS Excel to manage clients' accounts; analyzed trends to produce, direct, validate and deliver accurate, presentation-quality ad hoc reports.

TECHNOLOGY SUPPORT INTERN, The Wharton School of Business, University of Pennsylvania, 2015–2016

- Aided faculty with MS Office application use and setup; installed technical software, hard drives and computer hardware; set-up monitors, projectors and educational enhancements; problem-solved technical issues.

SERVER, Capital Grille, Philadelphia, Pennsylvania, 2013–2017

- Conducted front-of-house functions for a busy restaurant next to City Hall. Increased average sales via up-sales and showcase of excellent service. Gifted a dozen exceptional experience cards from diners. Worked part-time evenings, full-time weekends and summers to self-finance college tuition.

FRANK WUNG

Relocating to Seattle ▪ 406-123-4567 ▪ frankwung@gmail.com

STAFF ACCOUNTANT – ACCOUNTING MANAGER
Supporting Successful Decision-Making through Accurate, Timely Financial Reportings

Team Relations | Financial Management | Business Strategy | Compliance Oversight

CORE VALUE AND CONTRIBUTIONS

> Establish internal controls, policies and procedures adhering to regulatory compliance to lead accounting processes as a self-driven team member. Deliver honesty, integrity and unsullied professionalism in highly controlled industries.

> Orchestrate daily accounting operations for pioneering and traditional industries to drive long-term value dedicating experience in investment management, international banking and luxury property development.

> Hold H1B work visa valid 2016-2021 with permitted extension to 2022. Fluent in Chinese, French and English.

Audit and Attestation
General Ledger & Financial Statements
Accounts Payable/Accounts Receivable
Financial Systems and Reporting
IFRS / GAAP Principles and Practices
Tax Preparation and Filing
Internal Controls and Compliance
Month-End Reconciliations & Close
Budget Preparation & Control
Travel Expense Report/Reimbursement

PROFESSIONAL EXPERIENCE

ACCOUNTING MANAGER
Luxury Property Development, Phoenix, Arizona, June 2016–present

Bringing communities high-quality, concept-to-completion luxury living developments

- Oversee process establishment and implementation to ensure accurate, timely reporting of assets and liabilities captured in financial statements and monthly reporting. Conduct budget forecasting.

- Ensure processes are fully documented and comply with internal, external and regulatory requirements; design operational efficiencies, optimized processes and cost structure controls for multiple LLCs.

- Prepare audited financial statements for project-based companies coordinating with internal audit; assist with audit schedules and tax packages, and auditor's internal/external questionnaires.

- Display detail-organization in preparation of sales tax reports, personal and corporate tax documents.

- In concert with construction manager, execute construction draw requests utilizing approved schedule of values to establish proper outlined budgeting system per individual LLC development project.

- Confer with third-party consultant to resolve accounting questions, issues and discrepancies to deliver accurate, timely financial guidance to management addressing strategic and regulatory challenges.

- Conduct new employee onboarding: create individual HR files, prepare payroll-related tax documents 1099s and employee benefits.

FRANK WUNG • 406-123-4567

ACCOUNTING INTERN
ABC Companies, Scottsdale, Arizona, September 2015–May 2016

Conducted accounting practices for a regulated medical marijuana leader in Arizona and Nevada

- Maintained accurately reconciled and timely A/P, A/R and G/L accounting records and supporting files, cash receiving/expenditure posting, fixed assets and balance sheet reconciliations.
- Led transition from QuickBooks to Dynamic NAV (ERP system); managed the system providing counsel to managers and departments, and ensured procedures were correctly reflected and reported in ERP.
- Tracked, prepared and filed tax-related documents: modified business tax (MBT), sales tax, excise tax, personal tax, business license renewal and 1099s. Reviewed bank statements, accounts and ledgers.
- Created bi-monthly cash management and performance reports (cash status, cash flow, A/P and A/R), including on-demand monthly forecasts, performance reports and corporate reporting.
- Assisted with internal/external periodic audits via preparation of timely, accurate supporting schedules showcasing strong interpersonal skills, positive communications and a cooperative team spirit.
- Analyzed financial data and created ad hoc reports for departments companywide consisting of 5 office directors and 150[+] employees distributed over 3 entities.
- As supporting accounting professional, provided guidance for continued company growth (increased staff to 256 from 10 in 1 year), mitigated risk of technical error and safeguard off assets.

STAFF ACCOUNTANT – INTERN
Investment Management Co., Hangzhou, China, summers 2014 & 2015

Supported accounting, payroll and tax processes and functions as temporary summer staff. Completed month-end closings and reconciliations for accounting areas, including Payroll and Tax; posted, reviewed and adjusted general ledger accounting transactions. Helped prepare internal financial reports for budgeting, and with financial oversight and controls, monthly financial close, bank reconciliations, A/R and A/P.

TECHNICAL PROFICIENCIES

Microsoft Office Suite: Word, Excel, Access, PowerPoint. **Accounting Software:** Zoho Books; QuickBooks; Dynamic NAV; Great Plains; SAP ERP. **Accounting Standards:** IFRS, International Financial Reporting Standards; GAAP, Generally Accepted Accounting Principles. **Travel and Expense Software:** Concur; Certify; Abacus. **Work Management Platform:** Smartsheet. **Programming Languages:** SQL, Python, JavaScript.

EDUCATION & CERTIFICATION

ARIZONA STATE UNIVERSITY, Tempe, Arizona
Master of Accountancy, *magna cum laude*, 2016
Bachelor of Science in Accounting – Computer Science minor, *summa cum laude*, 2015

• • •

Bank of China Accounting Intern: Input data and reviewed remittance and bill collection processes. Analyzed information and options by developing spreadsheet reports to verify complex data. *Summer 2014*

• • •

Certified Public Accountant Exam, *in process*
(AUD) Auditing and Attestation, 10/16 and (FAR) Financial Accounting and Reporting, 12/16

John Scrudge

www.linkedin.com/in/JScrudge
Miami, Florida ▪ 321-456-7890 ▪ JScrudge@gmail.com

Career Goal: Financial Analyst

Business Performance Analysis
Financial Reports – MS Excel
Decision Support Data Compilation
Market Expansion Research
Project Management Planning
Statistical Analysis
Risk and Compliance Assessment

Finance Major – Campus Leader – Community Volunteer

Senior finance major with Fortune 500 experience performing business performance analysis to identify growth opportunities and understand root cause. Draft reports for executive leadership team to support data-driven decision-making. Young professional dedicated to campus leadership and community service volunteering time in youth mentoring, event planning and nonprofit administration. Seeking career-start in financial analysis to use advanced skills in financial research, data mining and manipulation.

Professional Experience

FINANCE INTERN
Otis Elevator, Farmington, Connecticut, Florida, May–August 2017

Hand-selected by CFO & VP of Finance for the Fortune 500 global passenger mobility and transportation system innovator with 1,000 branch offices, 66,000 employees and $12B in sales for summer internship program.

- Reported directly to U.S. leadership team. Gathered data for monthly business performance analysis, cost calculation and margin analysis of New Equipment, Modernization, Service and Repair lines of business.
- Developed project plans, reviewed short- and long-term financial goals and monitored progress. Identified potential issues to alert key stakeholders, avoid risk, ensure compliance and trace costs back to activities.

REMOTE WRITER
NBADraft.net, San Francisco, California, 2014–2017

Men's 2014-2017 college basketball season writer for website that projected NBA drafts for 17 years specializing in top players on the NBA horizon, player profiles, scouting reports, rankings and prospective international recruits.

- Created content and wrote weekly blogs summarizing the Conference week and analyzing top athletes' career performance, projected performance and probable first-round draft picks.
- Researched and produced public data, articles, statistical analysis and scouting reports on top high school, college and international basketball prospects.

Education and Leadership

FLORIDA STATE UNIVERSITY
B.S. in Business Finance & B.A. in Communication (GPA 3.98), *expected May 2018*
Six-time Dean's List achievement – Honors College Academic Achievement Scholarship award-winner

Campus Leadership
Florida State Investment Association – President
Florida State Intramural Sports Club – Basketball, volleyball and soccer

Community Engagement
Mentor for Special Needs Youth, Special Olympics, Miami, Florida, 2014–present
Food Service, St. Peter Paul Homeless Shelter, Miami-Dade County, Florida, 2013–present

Resumes Provided By

Ellen Steverson, NCRW, GCDF, CEIC

(843) 832-4567
ellen@startingblockcs.com
www.linkedin.com/in/ellensteverson

LAURYN C. LANZA

City, ST ZipXX | XXX-XXX-XXXX | email.address@gmail.com | LinkedIn

POSITIONED FOR BUSINESS SUCCESS

College student with distinct combination of marketing and sales experience leveraged with dual degrees, international studies, and leadership activities. Sharp communication and interpersonal skills to work with diverse teams and independently to execute projects. Dedicated to strong work ethic to remain flexible and dependable to reach goals.

KNOWLEDGE & KEY QUALIFICATIONS

Marketing | Customer Service | Event Planning | Sales | Social Media | Blogs | WordPress | MS Office Suite

EDUCATION

Marist College, Poughkeepsie, NY; Dual Degree Program   Graduation: December 2017
Bachelor of Science in Business Administration
Bachelor of Science in Hospitality and Tourism Management
GPA: 3.5/4.0
Study Abroad Semester Program:
Barcelona University of the Arts, Barcelona, Spain (1/2017–5/2017)
* Studied tourism and hospitality; visited historic landmarks and gained insight on traditions that impact business.

Leadership:
Board of Directors, Founding Member (9/2015–Present) | VP of Programming (10/2015–12/2016) – Delta Kappa
* Played key role in establishing new organization on campus; recruited members and served on Executive Board to contribute to laying foundation and leading 120 new members.
* Organized, planned, and executed large events for 100+ attendees; managed volunteers and held 7 events to support educational and leadership development; managed calendar, speakers, and vendors.

Active Member (12/2015–Present) | Graduation Marshal (12/2015–5/2016) – Student Alumni Association
* Selected to serve as Marshal in December and May graduations based on high GPA; attend Marist College President hosted events to build relationships with alumni and volunteer at events to assist alumni program.

Content Contributor – Marist College, Fork University (9/2015–12/2015)
* Contributed recipe and original photos that The New York Post published; link: hyperlinked

PROFESSIONAL EXPERIENCE

Marketing Coordinator — Laura Nelson Photography, Cold Spring, NY   July 2016 –December 2016
Hired to implement and sustain marketing tools to drive growth of privately-owned business, increased brand awareness, and improved communications with clients. Utilized marketing strategies to increase foot traffic.
* Launched and wrote company blogs, updated company website, and maintained social media accounts.
* Exceeded expectations and extended 8-week paid internship to 6-month position; top-notch writing landed blog being published on highly-acclaimed Fairytale Weddings website.

Sales Associate | Store Key Holder — Lands' End Kids, Danbury, CT   May 2015–July 2016
Generated sales by building rapport with customers, recommending merchandise, and answering questions. Trusted with keys to open and close store, organized inventory, and handled processing payment transactions.
* Collaborated with management on organizing and running monthly events, used consultative approach and up-selling techniques to achieve sale goals, and photographed styled merchandise for mass email campaigns.

Exhibit Guide | Reptile Handler — New England Aquarium, Boston, MA   June 2014–July 2016
Created positive experiences, engaged guests, and held reptiles while interacting, educating, and answering questions.
* Honored to consistently receive positive feedback from guests and made-my-day moments per feedback.

Resume by Ellen Steverson — StartingBlock Career Services, LLC | www.startingblockcs.com — Resume Results: Although no financial experience, she landed interviews with global financial company and others to accept great offer.

LILLIAN P. BELLFRIED

Street Address | City, ST ZipXX | XXX-XXX-XXXX
email.address@gmail.com | Link to LinkedIn Profile

RETAIL & FASHION PROFESSIONAL

Highly motivated and creative retail professional with 3 years of experience in fashion, brand marketing, and fashion forecasting. Deliver outstanding customer service with confidence to build relationships at all levels to drive sales. Effective communication skills to provide fashion and accessory advice to customers that generate loyal, repeat customers, and brand awareness. Flexible schedule, able to travel, and willing to relocate.

Key Qualifications

Bachelor's Degree in Retail& Consumer Science: May 2016 | Merchandising | Retail Sales | Customer Service Excellence
Loss Prevention | Merchandising & Stocking | Microsoft Office Word, Excel, PowerPoint | JDA Software | SPSS Software

EDUCATION

Bachelor of Science in Retail and Consumer Science, Minor in Business Administration
University of Nebraska (UN), Lincoln, NE — Expected Graduation: May 2016

PROFESSIONAL EXPERIENCE

Ann Taylor Loft, Baton Rouge, LA |Lincoln, NE (February 2015–Present)
– American clothing and accessories retailer owned by LOFT, Inc. with 600+ national and international stores.
Sales Associate | Brand Ambassador | Stylist

Drive sales by developing rapport with customers on merchandise, fashion, styles, accessories, and customers' needs. Stock and restock merchandise, answer questions regarding brand and accessories, and watch/recognize security risks. Perform maintenance tasks, open and close store, and delight customers by handling sales transactions with speed while building rapport to ensure customer satisfaction.

- ▸ Increased sales inspired merchandising displays, implemented promotional strategies, and offered add-on products; foot traffic in store can hit 2K customers per day, during holiday season.
- ▸ Exceeded credit card promotion 40% during months historically slow with opening new credit card accounts.
- ▸ Engaged customers and boosted sales; requested by management to strategically oversee service in dressing room area due to ability to build rapport and add-on merchandise to hit sales and promotional goals.
  - — Shared passion for fashion, knowledge on style and fashion, and social media pictures to highlight celebrity and specific fashion styles, and delivered quality service by explaining to clients how to achieve same great style.
  - — Provided honest feedback to customers on style, fit, and options; used social media and company website to show customers how to pair outfits, layer multiple items, and incorporate accessories.
  - — Sought-out by regular customers, by name, for providing high-levels of customer service, expertise and ability to pair new items to previously purchased items to extend wardrobe options.

Advantage Solutions, Baton Rouge, LA (May 2015–August 2015)
– Contemporary multiline sales agency representing 15+ apparel and accessory brands, located in Baton Rouges' Retail Mart.
Fashion Marketing | Sales Internship

Earned desired internship and leveraged academic retail background with proactive, positive attitude to meet milestones, deliverables, and tight deadlines. Built relationships with international and domestic clients from department stores and independent, specialty stores/retailers. Greeted customers, worked with Sales Reps on strategic projects, updated account database, supported processes, worked with samples, and handled administrative projects.

- ▸ Selected by CEO to set up and work in showroom for fast-growing designer label from UK: Infinity Apparel.
  - — Provided insight to President/CEO of Advantage Solutions and Retail Mart Consultant on college apparel trends and dress codes at schools to guide buying and merchandising decision-making.
  - — Worked with Infinity Apparel's CFO on inventory samples, proper packaging, and shipments.

Fashion Marketing | Sales Internship – The Advantage Solutions (Continued)

▶ Increased purchase orders by designing showroom to influence buyers; completed display project ahead of schedule with complete accountability for creative ownership and received positive feedback with bonus for job well done.

▶ Promoted brand awareness and utilized Instagram to market events; worked and contributed to sales and marketing at 3 prominent trade shows and 4-day events.

Miami Fashion Week, Miami, FL (March 2015)
– Five-night celebration featuring 40+ runway shows, highlighting emerging designers and model talent.
Model Team Assistant

Managed multiple tasks during exciting and fast-paced, backstage environment; mastered art of laying out changes, tracked inventory, and kept things running smoothly.

▶ Remained calm to effectively handle several outfit changes and properly prepare models; conveyed instructions from designer and worked around hairstylists and makeup artists to complete touches.

Macy's, Inc., Miami, FL (December 2014–January 2015)
– One of the nation's largest privately owned department store with 270+ stores and sales over $3.0B.
Sales Associate | Holiday Season

Delivered prompt, courteous service to customers and efficiently processed transactions within fast-paced, retail environment. Worked full-time during season, operated cash register, scanner, and computers to collect payments, make change, and process credit cards.

▶ Increased sale by suggesting apparel, recommending accessories, and providing gift-giving ideas; pleased customers and team by displaying positive, helpful attitude.

Omaha Fashion Week, Omaha, NE (March 2014)
– Week-long event with goal of creating buzz and giving outlet to fashion houses and buyers while connecting consumers with fashion.
Clothing Designer Assistant | Fashion Show Dresser

Examined garments on models and assisted designer with modifying placement and accessories to achieve desired effects. Consulted with production staff to ensure smooth production and gained styling tips first-hand from designers.

▶ Praised for ensuring models walked the runway on time and with look designer intended.

▶ Selected to greet and walk VIP to seats; answered questions and shared enthusiasm for event and fashion.

RELEVANT PROJECTS | LEADERSHIP EXPERIENCE

Buyer Project — Traveled to NY City with Buyer from Macy's to collaborate and purchase for winter/holiday season.
▶ Assisted with product development, reviewing patterns, and meeting with vendors; visited Star/Leafinger Group to discuss and learn more on fashion forecasting and trends; received A on project.

Target Project — Researched, wrote, and presented to 4 Target managers on E-commerce and Back-to-College season.
▶ Praised for knowledge on retail industry, Target, and trends in retail industry: college students' trends with subscription boxes/shopping patterns; Target requested copy of presentation to send to corporate leaders; received A on project.

Entrepreneurship | Small Business Project — Created business plan and presented multiple times throughout course.
▶ Commended for presentation skills, communicating business concerns and accurate solutions, and ability to seek answers and incorporate into presentations and project; received A on project.

Active Member — National Retail Federation Student Association, NU, Lincoln, NE (January 2014–Present)
▶ Participate in programs that promote careers in retail and gain access to retail industry research.

Active Member, Philanthropy Event Planner/Chairperson — Sigma Alpha, NU, Lincoln, NE (November 2011–Present)
▶ Planned, organized, and executed 15 events with 3 large events in one year that raised $300K for charities.

Resume by Ellen Steverson — StartingBlock Career Services, LLC | www.startingblockcs.com
Resume Results — Although her college professor insisted she keep a 1-page resume for job fair trip to NY City with class, she had too much experience to simplify down to 1-page. She landed the most interviews out of 30+ students on trip and praise from many hiring managers at job fair for having a solid resume. Upon graduation, she relocated for target job in NY.

J. DYLAN LAURENCE

Street Address | City, ST ZipXX | XXX-XXX-XXXX | jdlemail@gmail.com

MULTI-DEGREED AND LICENSED AIRCRAFT MAINTENANCE PROFESSIONAL

Technically trained and highly motivated, college graduate with 3 years of hands-on experience working on aircraft projects independently and with teams. Leveraging solid educational foundation combined with strong work ethic and interpersonal skills to lead teams, meet goals, and adapt in fast-paced environments.

KNOWLEDGE & KEY QUALIFICATIONS

Aircraft Drawings | Electrical Systems | Aviation Materials & Processes | Ground Operations | Corrosion Control
Airframe Structures | Aircraft Covering & Finishes | Welding | Assembly & Rigging | Airframe Inspections
Landing Gear Systems | Hydraulic & Pneumatic Power Systems | Cabin Atmosphere Control & Instrument Systems
Engine Overhauls | Communication & Navigation Systems | Powerplant Systems | **Willing to Travel**

EDUCATION

Bachelor of Science (BS) in Business Administration
James Madison University, Harrisonburg, VA; Graduated: May 2014; GPA: 3.4/4.0

Associate in Applied Science (AAS), Aircraft Assembly Technology
Blue Ridge Community College (BRMCC), Weyer's Cave, VA; Graduation: July 2017; GPA: 3.7/4.0

Associate in Applied Science, (AAS), Aircraft Maintenance Technology
Blue Ridge Community College, Weyer's Cave, VA; Graduated: May 2015; GPA: 4.0/4.0

Aircraft Certificates, Blue Ridge Community College, Weyer's Cave, VA:

Certificate in Aircraft Maintenance Airframe| Certificate in Aircraft Maintenance General
Certificate in Aircraft Maintenance Technician: Powerplant

- Self-financed 100% of college expenses by working 30+hours weekly to graduate debt free.

FEDERAL AVIATION ADMINISTRATION LICENSES

Licensed FAA Airframe Mechanic and Licensed FAA Mechanic
Aviation Maintenance Technician: Powerplant: License Exam September 18, 2017

AIRCRAFT & PROJECT EXPERIENCE

Aircraft Mechanic— Dynamic Aviation Company, LLC, Bridgewater, VA (January 2017–May 2017)

- Inspected, repaired, modified, and performed maintenance on private aircraft; identified avionics systems malfunctions and determined correction action. Removed, installed, and aligned integrated avionics systems.

Jet Engine Overhaul Project | Powerplant Project, BRMCC:

- Met 8-hour deadline to disassemble jet engine and check for clearances, corrosion, and required maintenance needs; worked collaboratively with team of 3 and used numerous hand tools, including torque wrenches, wrenches, depth gauge, feeler gauge, and power drills.
- Referred to J-34 overhaul manual and rebuilt properly, running several tests including EGT and RPM engine percentages to check proper levels.

BRMCC– Airframe | Aircraft Inspection Project, BRMCC:

- Performed 100-hour inspection on Cessna Citation 500 Aircraft; used service manual and partnered with one student to complete airframe inspection.

Welding Project, BRMCC:

- Removed nose tire of aircraft and replaced with new tire in accordance with Cessna Service Manual, located 3 missing static wicks and replaced, and successfully passed Inspection Authorization (IA) approval process.
- Set up welding station using oxyacetylene welding technique and performed 8 different types of welds, including Gas Metal Arc Welding, Gas Tungsten Arc Welding, and Shielded Metal Arc Welding.
- Worked independently from selecting correct type of safety lens for oxyacetylene welding to correct tip size, welding torch, and gas/oxygen combination to get neutral flame to weld.
- Performed butt weld, tee weld, lap weld, corner weld, double butt weld, edge weld, cluster weld, and tack welds on steel metals and successfully passed Inspection Authorization (IA).

Carburetor Overhaul Project, BRMCC:

- Disassembled two types of carburetors: float type and pressure type; verbally described operations of each carburetor and direction of flow of the fuel and air, then reassembled carburetors.
- Utilized Bendix and Marvel Schebler service manuals and researched information on5 main systems: carburetor mixture control, main metering, idling, acceleration, and power enrichment; learned different components to identify and describe functions
- Measured carburetor at different points to check float level in correct position and used depth gauge to check. Used information about carburetors to inspect, remove, and replace carburetor on IO-470 reciprocating engine.

Composite Project, BRMCC:

- Gained knowledge on strength to weight ratio for aerodynamic importance with manufacturing technology; independently constructed aircraft structure using fabric, resin material, polyester foam, honeycomb material and hand tools. Passed initial IA inspection who then introduced defects, allowing project to expand into proper repairs being completed.

Sealant Project, BRMCC:

- Completed 4 different types of sealing applications using different sealing techniques: fay surface, encapsulating, injection seal, and fillet sealing to protect aircraft parts from corrosion and damage.

Additional BRMCC Projects:

- Accomplished passing numerous inspections on a broad range of projects, including sheet metal bending and rivet projects; aircraft electrical system projects; wood fabric, cover, and painting projects; welding projects; and checking blade angle and prop balancing projects.

PROFESSIONAL EXPERIENCE

Four Brothers Italian Restaurant, Harrisonburg, VA (January 2015–Present)
Front-Point Manager | Server

Lead, motivate, and coach 8-person, wait-staff team to drive sales and deliver customer service excellence in fast-paced, popular restaurant. Provide clear directions to foster environment of teamwork, positive energy, and flexibility for team to accurately serve 100+ customers during peak hours and generate loyal, repeat customers and positive reviews.

- Increased operation efficiencies by initiating reorganization of storage and work areas, installing racks for improved workflow, organizing /maintaining inventory for grab-and-go availability, and supporting safety goals.
- Decreased employees' tardiness by implementing section plans to promote being on time.
- Boosted service and reduced learning curve by implementing and managing 2-week, 6-shift comprehensive training program for new hires that included full cycle of services from greeting customers to running payments.

Resume by Ellen Steverson — StartingBlock Career Services, LLC | www.startingblockcs.com — Resume Results:
This client graduated with a BS and then went back to school to get technical AAS degrees and certifications to break into a field he loves. He received many offers and mentioned having such a strong resume really helped him discuss projects during interviews.

JOHN P. ROSEBERY

1 Mourning Dove Drive | Kings Park, SC 294XX| XXX-XXX-XXXX | jpr1email@ymail.com

TARGET POSITION — SOFTWARE ENGINEER

Leveraging strong education, advanced mathematical ability, and proven programming experience to perform technical and analytical duties to create systems and deliver results. Well-honed communication and interpersonal skills to work effectively with diverse groups across all levels. Knowledgeable in Agile/Scrum protocols, programming languages, and managing concurrent projects. **Willing to relocate.**

KNOWLEDGE & QUALIFICATIONS

Customer Service | Network & Technology Analysis | Systems Development | Presentations
Unity3D | Gaming & Interactive Content Creation | Game Development | C#/.NET Framework
Advance Microsoft: Word, Excel, and PowerPoint

TECHNICAL SKILLS | LANGUAGES

Proficient in C#, C++, and Java; Used in:

C# — CIG and Chroma Games | C++ — Algorithms Analyses, Design, and Data Structures
Java — Multiple Networking Projects

Practical Application Knowledge in LISP, Icon, SQL, and Xml; Used in:

LISP — Projects on Artificial Intelligence & Programming Languages | Icon — Completed Study Comparing Icon to C
SQL — Database Management Systems | Xml — Chroma Game and Information Systems

EDUCATION

Bachelor of Science in Computer and Information Science
University of South Carolina, Columbia, SC — Graduation: December 2017

Relevant Courses: Artificial Intelligence: LISP Project, Programming Language Courses, Data Structure: C++, Algorithm Analysis and Design, Discrete Structures, Software Engineering, Database Management Systems: SQL, Computer Networks: JAVA, Operating Systems, Technical Writing for Engineers, Mobile App Design/Implementation, Information Systems: MySQL, SQLite, SDLC, Xml

Bachelor of Science in Mathematics
University of Alabama, Tuscaloosa, AL — Graduation: May 2014

PROJECT EXPERIENCE

University of South Carolina, Columbia, SC (May 2016–Present)
Product Owner and Lead Software Engineer — Chroma Game

Apply math expertise and software design experience to design, develop, and implement 2D top-down, puzzle game. Push players in direction based on surrounding colors and used Unity 3D engine with C# language.

- Initiated Independent Study course to create iOS game called CID; met with professor throughout semester to review design and discuss engineering, troubleshooting, and programming challenges/solutions.
- Earned A on project; continue to develop game, have 2 prototypes completed, and received positive feedback from players during testing phases.

University of South Carolina, Columbia, SC (January2015–December 2016)
Senior Designer— Learn Agile Scrum Methodologies, Play CIG: http://linktoCIGgame

Designed, tested, and earned highest score on process improvement education tool/computer process improvement game. Served as Scrum Master; coached team of 3 and helped members with Scrum process to build product. Directed weekly meetings on gameplayfeatures, milestones, deadlines, and objectives. Diagnosed/solved performance and quality issues, tested and validated techniques, refined requirements to develop proof of concept applications, optimized usability for mobile platforms, and followed programming standards.

JOHN P. ROSEBERY

PROJECT EXPERIENCE CONTINUED

Senior Designer — CIG Project, University of South Carolina (Continued)

- Developed and inspired further creation of interactive game with product owner (PO)/customer; met multiple times throughout project to define requirements and received Client Letter of Acceptance ahead of schedule.
- Utilized knowledge of Agile/Scrum methodology to design program created for undergraduates to be introduced to Project Management, Scrum, and Agile methods using player's created sprints.
- Held training sessions using Unity 3D/game development platform; collaborated in code reviews with team members as each produced quality lines of code for finished build; introduced team to using Design Change, Time, Task, and Test Case Logs.
- Led in-depth presentation with team to 30+ attendees/students and client; reviewed overall project, including project plans, requirements, case documentation, design, software quality assurance (SQA), testing, and final demonstration of The Continuous Improvement Game (CIG).
- Maintained involvement in CIG pro-version software, mobile application, and emerging technology with client and reviewed costs/budget ofproduct.
- Co-authored research papers highlighted at conferences:
  —*Work in Progress: An Agile Software Engineering Improvement Game*, shared at IEEE Frontiers Conference.
  —*A Web-based Process Management Game* published for Meaningful Play 2016 Conference.

University of South Carolina, Columbia, SC (September 2016–December 2016)
Information Technology (IT) | Networking Project

Created design documentation and gained understandingof differences between Transmission Control Protocol (TCP) and User Datagram Protocol (UDP) while establishing/maintaining network conversations.

- Implemented and added upgrades to protocol messaging, including Peer-to-Peer (P2P) networking, messaging, and handshaking to set parameters of communications channels established between entities before normal communication over channel begins.
- Designed and implemented distance vector routing protocol using Bellman-Ford equation.

University of South Carolina, Columbia, SC (September 2015–December 2015)
Software Design Lead — Software Engineering National Scope Project

Served as Design Lead on team with 5 members. Created use case, gained experience with test case strategies, and used additional design documentation. Coded in C++; earned A on project. Gathered and followed instructions and guidelines to compete on national level against 6 other teams.

- Designed and implemented butterfly tracking system/software; managed components of project and met with team weekly; used data mining and analysis to determine butterflies locations to track.
- Managed project from conception to completion; tested software for month before competition.
- First team to successfully match all project requirements out of 6 teams and earned top ranking.

WORK EXPERIENCE

Waffle House, Irmo, SC (October 2013–August 2016)
Shift Leader | Supervisor

Greeted and served guests, prepared food, and maintained food safety standards. Delivered exceptional customer service by building rapport with customer and displaying positive customer service attitude. Remained flexible with schedule and dependable throughout tenure.

- Trained all employees on new point of sales (POS) system and new employees on policies, procedures, food preparation, and customer service techniques.
- Self-financed college expenses and attended college full time while working 20-30 hours week.

■■■■■

Resume by Ellen Steverson — StartingBlock Career Services, LLC | www.startingblockcs.com
Resume Results — This resume shows how projects can make a huge difference on a resume. This generated numerous interviews and he accepted job with leading Fortune 500 company.

Resumes Provided By

Lorraine Beaman, MA, ACRW, CARW, NCRW, CEIC, MCD

(866) 966-2665
Lorraine@interview2work.com
www.interview2work.com
www.linkedin.com/in/lorrainebeaman/
www.facebook.com/interview2work/
Twitter: @interview2work
Instagram: Interview2work

GEROME CLARK Bakersfield, CA | (715) 294–7194 | GClark@aol.com
PORTFOLIO: www.GeromeClark.com

May 29, 2018

Jacob Roberts
Human Resources Director
Virtual World Game Technology
937 Broadway
Los Angeles, CA 90001

Dear Mr. Roberts:

Are you searching for a young artist willing to take on any task that will let him learn the art of game development from the very best? Since I first discovered and started playing VWGT's "Search for the Stars," I have wanted to be part of the team that expands this virtual world into yet-to-be -discovered galaxies. When I read your announcement of job opportunity for an entry 3D artist posted on my college job board, I knew I had the talent, drive, and knowledge to be a top candidate for this positon.

I will complete the coursework to earn my Associate of Arts degree in Digital Media Arts, Animation, and 3D Modeling from Harper College, Fresno, CA, in June. If you ask any of my professors, they will tell you how enthusiastically I approach each technical and creative challenge. Not only did I want to deliver the most captivating project, but learn everything I could about the tools we used and design something users would find engaging.

My favorite project was the creation of a dancing numbers game that challenged the player to use arithmetic functions to move from tyro to professor. The assignment was to create a game for children. When we tested it, we found both children and their parents loved to play. Besides developing an engaging and fun game, this project was an opportunity to learn how to work as part of a creative team.

I look forward to discussing how I can become part of the VWGT team. I will call you next week to arrange a time to meet. If would like to speak before that, please contact me by email at GClark@aol.com or by phone at (715) 294-7194.

Sincerely,

3D Artist

Gerome Clark

Going where no artist has gone before; pushing the limits of technology.

GEROME CLARK Bakersfield, CA | (715) 294-7194 | GClark@aol.com
PORTFOLIO: www.GeromeClark.com

3D Artist

Innovative, self-directed artist prepared to merge a passion for development technology, understanding of industrial design principles, and knowledge of rigging processes to create story-enhancing models. Highly productive individual contributor and team member respected for ability to nurture collaborative efforts and ensure on-time completion of projects. Demonstrated aptitude to master and integrate technology to expand virtual worlds.

Model/Gaming Projects

Discover these and other examples of my work at: www.GeromeClark.com

2D hand-drawn stop-frame dialogue animated short film using Movie Maker and Adobe Audition.

New character for Mass Effect Andromeda using Maya. Model is a character rig with facial rigging system.

Story of kind-hearted palace guard easily distracted by the smell of flowers. Created and clothed 3rd rig character and used Morpheus Rig.

Antique lantern using Maya; unwrapped model for UV mapping, then tossed it into Mudbox for finer sculpting and painting.

Created soldier using Maya; extruded individual planes.

Technical Skills

White Boxing
PlayMaker
Illustrator
Mudbox
Lighting
3D Max
Unity
UDK
C#
Maya
Rigging
Audition
Premiere
Photoshop
After Effects
Unwrapping/Texturing
Dragonframe

WORK HISTORY

Sales Associate/Cashier	Best Buy	Bakersfield, CA	2017
Counselor	City of Bakersfield Recreation & Parks District	Bakersfield, CA	2015

EDUCATION

A.A., Digital Media Arts, Animation, and 3D Modeling, Harper College, Fresno, CA
Anticipated graduation: June 2018
Coursework included: Digital Design & Storytelling   Motion Graphics   Video Fundamentals
Animation & Game Design   Graphic Design

B.S., History, California State University, Fresno, Fresno, CA,   2016
Minor: Theatre

Going where no artist has gone before; pushing the limits of technology.

ROBERT JOHNSON
People Skills/Marketing Experience

Dixon, CA | 707-921-9601 | robert.johnson@gmail.com

SALES AND MARKETING ASSOCIATE

Outgoing, enthusiastic, self-motivated, soon to be college graduate with superior organizational, communication, and time management skills prepared to launch a career in sales and marketing. Consistently demonstrate outstanding work habits and business ethics. Excel in fast-paced, goal-driven environments. Quickly gain trust of prospective customers. Prepared to make significant contributions in the following areas:

Project Management	Presentations	Community Relations	Client Engagement
Lead Cultivation	Social Media	Research	Networking

EDUCATION

B.A., Business Administration, California State University, Sacramento, Sacramento, CA
Areas of Emphasis: Marketing, Accounting, Finance
Honors: Dean's List, Fall and Spring 2017, Fall 2017
Anticipated Graduation: May 2018

PROFESSIONAL EXPERIENCE

EDUCATIONAL SERVICES, Sacramento, CA   2017
Program Assistant/Intern

Selected for 6-month internship; assisted with the creation, production, and marketing of materials for 3-day course on teaching algebra.

- Edited copy, suggested graphics, and worked with curriculum team to assure materials met state teaching requirements.
- Assisted with the creation of a 30-second video on advantages of using instructor course; shadowed videographer during production and editing.
- Worked with printer to assure materials arrived in time for product launch at annual math teacher's conference.

ASSOCIATED STUDENTS OF CALIFORNIA STATE UNIVERSITY, SACRAMENTO, Sacramento, CA   2016
Volunteer: "Take Back the Night"

Created social media campaign to educate students on ending sexual, relationship, and domestic violence and encourage participation in campus rally.

- Liaised with national organization to secure relevant statistics and trends for college campuses.
- Met with campus administrators to determine campus-specific issues and concerns.
- Created Facebook page for rally; posted daily for the month before and after campus rally; responded to comments; and built a following of 3000+ students, faculty, and administrators.
- Secured onsite media coverage for rally; local television included coverage on the evening news, and local radio station broadcasted live from the rally.

WORK HISTORY

Part-time, school break, and temporary positions held during high school and college.

STARBUCKS, Sacramento, CA	Barista	2015–Present
DIXON UNIFIED SCHOOL DISTRICT, Dixon, CA	Custodian	Summer/Winter 2017
CITY OF DAVIS, Davis, CA	Youth Program Volunteer	2011-2013

TECHNICAL SKILLS

MS Word	Excel	Photoshop	Outlook
Instagram	Twitter	Internet Research	Facebook

ROBERT KLEIN

(916) 976-6701
robertklein@gmail.com

MANAGEMENT TRAINEE

Student Athlete/Sports Enthusiast/Business Major

Possess superior organizational, communication, and time management skills necessary to build community engagement and promote a professional sports team. Consistently demonstrate and inspire outstanding work habits and ethics on the field, in the classroom, and at work. Excel in fast-paced, goal-driven environments.

Fluent in English and Spanish.

EDUCATION

B.A., Business Administration, California State University, East Bay, Hayward, CA

Areas of Emphasis: Economics, Accounting, and Human Resources
International Study: England, Fall 2016
Affiliations: Member, Sigma Beta Delta
Activities: Planned and participated in annual faculty vs. student baseball game to raise funds for Make-a Wish-Foundation.

Anticipated graduation: May 2018

ATHLETICS

Baseball Team, CSUEB—2015–Present
Track & Field, CSUEB —2014–2016
Basketball Team, Clovis High School, Clovis, CA—2012–2014
Rugby Team, Clovis High School, Clovis, CA—2010–2012

RELEVANT EXPERIENCE

Project Assistant, Geography Project, University of California, Berkeley, Berkeley, CA   Summer 2017
- Supported onsite program for teachers from across the US; assisted with meeting logistics and creation of educational materials.
- Participated in project to meet new curriculum standard; identified resources for enhancing lesson plans.

Program Assistant, Off-Campus Study Program, CSUEB, Switzerland Campus, Location?   Fall 2016
- Contacted and interviewed diplomats, businessmen, and project directors to create a report on effective methods for increasing small business success.

Youth Program Volunteer, City of Clovis, Clovis, CA   2010-2014
- Assisted staff in delivering sports-based programs for youth ages 6 years to 12 years. Created safe, supportive environment where participants could learn new skills and be part of a team.

WORK HISTORY

Part-time, school break, and temporary positions held during high school and college.

Custodian	Clovis Joint Unified School District, Clovis, CA	Summer/Winter 2015
Cashier/Server	Black Bear Diner, Clovis, CA	2012–2013
Administrative Assistant	William and Associates, Clovis, CA	2012

TECH SKILLS

MS Word	Excel	Photoshop	Outlook
Instagram	Twitter	Internet Research	Facebook

Making Business a Contact Sport

ROBERT KLEIN

(916)-976-6701
robertklein@gmail.com

MANAGEMENT TRAINEE
Student Athlete/Sports Enthusiast/Business Major

PROFESSIONAL REFERENCES

Jack Johnson
Baseball Coach
CSUEB

Phone: (415) 976-7897
Email: jjackson@csueb.edu

Mr. Johnson was my baseball coach for 2 years.

Susan Larson
Manager
Black Bear Dinner
Clovis, CA

Phone: (719) 765-9782
Email: susanl@blackbear.com

Ms. Larson was my manager for 12 months. She hired and trained me for my position as a cashier/server.

Mike Miller
Youth Program Director
City Parks & Recreation
Los Angeles, CA

Phone: (415) 987-4567
Email: mmiller@lacpr.gov

Mike was my supervisor when I volunteered for the youth program in Clovis, CA

Peter Jessup
Sales Representative
Nike Sportswear

Phone: (707) 673-9872
Email: peterjessup@sbcglobal.net

Peter and I were teammates on the CSUEB Baseball Team for 2 years.

MARGARET JOHNSON   Chicago, IL | mjohnson@gmail.com | (815) 582-6483

Dedicated to helping all children discover and develop their potential

SPECIAL EDUCATION TEACHER

SYSTEMATIC INSTRUCTION| FUNCTIONAL/DAILY LIVING SKILLS | ACC DEVICES | IEP/BIP

Adaptive, innovative teacher with experience and skills to develop and implement educational strategies for students dealing with learning, emotional, and behavioral disabilities. Partner effectively with paraprofessionals to achieve student learning outcomes. Consult with parents, guardians, and staff to set attainable IEPs and BIPs.

EDUCATION

B.S., Education–Special Education, University of Chicago, Chicago, IL   2018

Endorsement: Learning Behavior Specialist 1 Pre-K – Age 21

GPA (major): 3.82 / 4.0

Honor: Dean's List, Spring 2016

Activity: Students Supporting Individuals with Disabilities Club

LICENSE

Professional Educator

STUDENT TEACHING/PRACTICUM EXPERIENCE

CENTRAL CHICAGO HIGH SCHOOL, Chicago, IL   January-May 2017
Student Teacher-9th–12th Grade Students with Emotional/Behavioral Disabilities

Completed five-month student teaching assignment in culturally and educationally diverse inner-city high school; 50% of students were classified as low-income, 18% were students with disabilities, 29% were members of underrepresented populations, and 3% were ELL. Observed and taught 9th, 10th, 11th, and 12th grade students with emotional and behavioral disabilities.

- Monitored students' progress toward IEP goals; collected data on classroom achievements and initiated alternative strategies when desired behavioral changes were not achieved.
- Planned daily lessons and taught English, math, social studies, and life skills—including money management and strategies—for becoming a contributing community member.
- Created positive learning environment; successfully managed classroom behavior using "take a break" strategies.
- Supported paraprofessional; offered creative suggestions for engaging students and achieving desirable academic and behavioral outcomes.

Professional Experience Continued...

GRANT JUNIOR HIGH SCHOOL, Chicago, IL   August–December 2017
Student Teacher-6th-8th Grade Adaptive Life Skills
Selected to teach in low-income, educationally diverse inner-city school; 54% of students were classified as low-income, 11% as students with disabilities, and 4% as EEL. Developed lesson plans for 7 paraprofessionals working with students; advised on learning approaches and adaptive teaching techniques.

- Collaborated with paraprofessionals, speech pathologist, and occupational therapist to maximize learning outcomes.

- Instructed students on life skills in classroom and community setting; taught personal grooming, social skills, money handling, ordering food, and navigating retail stores.

- Planned weekly lessons; presented units on English, math, and world study using scripted lessons and structured instruction to develop individualized and small-group lessons.

- Collected and analyzed data on achievement of students' IEP goals; implemented alternate strategies to achieve goals when student failed to show progress.

SOUTH SIDE ELEMENTARY SCHOOL, Chicago, IL   January–April 2017
Classroom Observer/Co-Teacher

Collaborated and co-taught reading and math with second and third grade teachers in economically and educationally challenged school; 55% of students were considered as low-income and 11% as disabled.

- Taught third grade math, second grade RTI reading, and third grade RTI reading; managed third grade high-level reading center.

- Utilized systematic phonics program to engage students in reading instruction and achieve learning goals.

- Assisted with weekly lesson planning, recording progress toward achievement of EIP goals and grading.

- Met with parents to secure information necessary to develop FBA and implement BIP.

Resumes Provided By

Mary Jo King, NCRW
Alliance Resume and Writing Service

(262).681.5682
MJ@alliancewritingservice.com

JOLIE JOLLY

8495 MARSDALE AVENUE • MILWAUKEE, WI 53202 • 262.555.1234 • JOLIEJOLLY@YMAIL.COM

ESSAY

APPLICANT FOR

Japanese Exchange Teaching Program (JET USA)

November 17, 2016

To Whom It May Concern:

This essay addresses my purpose, qualifications, and desire to participate in the JET Program, which I first became interested in while still in high school. Japan is a very interesting country and has an enriching culture that is very unlike America. I have had many experiences that have pushed me onto this path, which I think I am meant to take. I want to continue the personal growth I have achieved in learning about other cultures.

As a child, my family and I visited Ireland for a wedding. It was interesting for me to see how they lived their lives, and how different it was from the life I knew in America. My interest in Japan grew in high school, and I wanted to experience Japanese culture and see how different and similar it was from my own culture and experiences. In my first year of college at the University of Wisconsin-Milwaukee, I discovered that there was a chance for me to study abroad in Japan through our International Studies office. In the summer of 2013, I journeyed with a group of students to Japan and fell in love with the culture and history of the country. I changed my major from Business to International Relations because I realized that I had a strong interest in learning more about the people of different cultures. I also decided to achieve a minor in Anthropology because of its focus on studying other peoples and cultures.

After that trip, I gained experience in teaching English to children who did not speak English as a first language. A trip to China was advertised for the summer of 2016, and I decided I would join that group of students. It was a study abroad trip in July-August of 2016 with a mission of teaching middle school students. It helped me improve my skills of teaching English, and provided insight on the school system in China and how it differs from the school system in America. I lived with a host family while in China, and proved to be a source of inspiration and joy. Staying with this family was a wonderful way to feel connected to the people of another culture, and they taught me as much—if not more—than I taught them. Another study abroad trip to Thailand is planned for January, from the 8th to the 22nd. I expect it to be as enlightening and enriching as my other trips have been.

I have remained in contact with people that I have met during my experiences, including my host family in China, through webchats. One of the students from Hanon University is also still in contact with me through Facebook. These relationships help me to feel connected with Asian cultures, and inspired to share my experiences with others. After my tenure is over with the JET Program, I look forward to applying my knowledge of and experience with the program in whatever role in international relations may be in my future.

In conclusion, as my résumé demonstrates, I am ready to contribute my "genki" to the program. I believe I can be an asset to the organization, to the country of Japan, and to any school where I would be assigned to work. I look forward to this wonderful opportunity and will do my best to achieve the best possible results.

Sincere Regards,

Jolie Jolly

JOLIE JOLLY

8495 MARSDALE AVENUE • MILWAUKEE, WI 53202 • 262.555.1234 • JOLIEJOLLY@YMAIL.COM

PROFILE

APPLICANT FOR

Japanese Exchange Teaching Program (JET USA)

BA degree in International Studies and Anthropology, with additional emphasis in language studies and several study abroad programs. Patient, intrepid, energetic, and enthusiastic individual with a passion for learning about other cultures, conversing with diverse individuals, and teaching children. Special expertise in English spelling, English grammar, and public speaking. Strong teamwork and problem solving skills.

——— CORE COMPETENCIES ———

Interpersonal Communications | Teaching Practices and Processes | Team Building | Public Speaking

EDUCATION AND PROFESSIONAL DEVELOPMENT

UNIVERSITY OF WISCONSIN–MILWAUKEE   2014–PRESENT
Bachelor of Arts in International Studies, Anticipated Spring 2018
Minor in Anthropology
A boad, interdisciplinary program affording a wealth of real life experiences and resources about life outside the United States. Complementary coursework includes:

Intercultural Communication	International Relations	Cultural Anthropology
Globalization & Development	Peoples of Southeast Asia	Society & Environment
Comparative Cultures & Societies	Japan Since the Samurai Age	Social Science Research

Study Abroad: Taught English (ESL) to middle school students in China, four weeks in 2016. This group teaching effort involved three teachers, each with ten students learning by storytelling and song. Academic program planned for Thailand in January, 2017, with a focus on cultural studies and shadowing people in their work.

Student Trip: Two weeks of cultural studies and travel experiences in Japan, 2013.

SPRINGFIELD COLLEGE, MILWAUKEE, WI   2017
Completed a semester of Japanese language studies (course not offered at UW–Milwaukee).

✦ **Language Proficiency:** Level 5 skill in reading and speaking English; Level 1 skill in speaking Japanese.

✦ **Clubs and Activities:** Forensics Club: Most Valuable Speaker, 2011; Tennis Club, Chess Club, and Concert Choir.

✦ **Technology** proficient in Microsoft Office (Excel, Word, Outlook, PowerPoint) and social media.

EMPLOYMENT EXPERIENCE

OUTBACK STEAKHOUSE, MILWAUKEE, WI   2012–2017
Hostess
Greeted guests, resolved guest problems, and coordinated team to optimize service. Suggested menu items, issued gift certificates, assisted service team with their duties, and participated in training new hires.

- Awarded Employee of the Month 4X; recognized for exemplary service and outstanding attitude.

JANE P. JONES

7373 Fernwood Avenue • Chicago, IL 60290 • 920.345.6789 • JPJones@ymail.com

SUMMARY OF QUALIFICATIONS

GIS Data Analyst

GIS certificate; BA degree in geography and computer science; over 3 years of experience in environments requiring accuracy and detail orientation. Strong skill level in oral and written communication, critical thinking, organization, and problem solving. Effective in team or independent settings; experienced trainer.

- ✓ Proficient in field and statistical methods, data collection and processing, data analysis, mapping, reporting, database management, and design and management of geospatial data sets.

- ✓ Extensive knowledge of computer information systems and software, including MS Office Suite, ESRI technologies (ArcMap), and remote sensing (LiDAR). Capable programmer and web developer.

EDUCATION AND TECHNOLOGY

Degree	**Adler University, Chicago, IL** **Bachelor of Arts in Geography w/minor in Computer Science, 2014** **GIS Capstone Project:** Spatial Analysis of Radon Levels in Eau Claire County. Collaborated with county health department to identify radon concentrations. **Relevant Courses:** Advanced Geographic Information Systems (GIS III), Web GIS, Geocoding, Interpolation, Spatial Data Analysis, Hot Spot Analysis, Advanced Remote Sensing (LiDAR), Computer Mapping, Geospatial Data Management, Database Systems, Programming, Quantitative Methods, and Field Methods (GPS navigation and data collection; aerial photography; georeferencing and mosaicking images).
Certification	**Geospatial Certificate, GIS Emphasis, 2014**
Technology	Broad exposure to computer technologies, GIS database management, programming (Java, JavaScript, PHP, JSP, JSF), ERDAS, ESRI technologies (ArcGIS, ArcMap, ArcCatalog, ArcToolBox, AutoCAD Map), QGIS, Topology SPSS, Global Positioning Systems (GPS), and Trimble GPS Pathfinder Office. Proficient with Windows and UNIX OS, Microsoft Office Suite (Word, Excel, PowerPoint), and Adobe Creative Suite (Illustrator, Dreamweaver).

WORK EXPERIENCE

1/15–Present	**GK International Distribution Center, Chicago, IL** **Merchandise Handler** Quality assurance position, using a hand scanner to complete orders. Consistent performance above 100% for speed and accuracy, where 95% is target minimum.
6/13–9/13	**Adler University Faculty-Student Collaborative Research Project, Chicago, IL** **Research Fellow** Georeferenced aerial photographs; identified methodologies to mosaic them together.
3/12–11/14	**Midwest Motor Manufacturing, Waukegan, IL** **Trim Picker** Detail-oriented position, using a voice recognition system to pick and pack orders. Asked to train new employees because of quality performance.

Professional Portfolio

MARGARET MAYBERRY

1234 22nd Avenue #10 ● Madison, WI 53705 ● 608.555.3298 ● Mayberry.Margaret@ymail.com

SUMMARY OF QUALIFICATIONS

Staff Accountant → AR, AP, GL & Journal Proficient, IRS Certified
Delivering accuracy and detail-orientation to customer-focused performance

Accounting graduate with 3.82 GPA and volunteer experience in tax preparation; stable employment throughout high school and college. Versed in general accounting principles (GAAP), journal and general ledger entries, full cycle AP processing, AR, banking, and year-end adjustments.

Proven to surpass expectations in environments where detail-orientation, versatility, critical thinking, and self-motivation were key to success. Exemplary communication skills extend to customer service, client relationships, team coordination, and collaboration.

Able to prioritize tasks and solve problems to keep projects and work processes moving forward. Strong mathematical aptitude; fast learner; excellent organizational skills; experienced with office technologies, MS Office, and digital systems for CRM, accounting, and tax preparation.

——— CORE COMPETENCIES ———

Billing | Accounts Receivable & Accounts Payable | Journal & General Ledger Data Entry | Month-End Closing
Tax Filings | Customer Service | Quality Control | Banking & ACH Deposits | End-of-Year Adjustments | Reconciliations

Record of Producing Quality Results and Exceeding Performance Targets

EDUCATION AND PROFESSIONAL DEVELOPMENT

UNIVERSITY OF WISCONSIN-MADISON
Bachelor of Science in Accounting, 2017
GPA 3.82; studies in accounting theory and techniques in real world scenarios, including Sarbanes-Oxley (SOX) compliance and coursework in payroll, taxation, microeconomics, higher mathematics, business law, project management, leadership, organizational behavior, business communications, and information technology.

Internship, United Way (see experience below), 2017

Advanced Volunteer Training Certification, Internal Revenue Service
VITA/TCE Standards of Conduct training; certified to prepare taxes and perform quality reviews of returns.

Technology proficient in Microsoft Office (Excel, Word, PowerPoint, Outlook); familiar with Andar CRM software, QuickBooks, cloud computing, POS systems, and a range of office technologies.

EXPERIENCE

AMAZON FULFILLMENT CENTER, MADISON, WI   2015–PRESENT
Fulfillment Associate
Serve on Quality Control Team to drive progress on group performance objectives. Receive products, unload shipments, pick customer orders; move quantities of merchandise using hand trucks and other equipment.

- Exceeded personal production targets by 125–130%, meeting customer demands across numerous departments in high-volume, high-risk environment.

- Continued -

Darby Williams

3500 Polar Ice Lane ♪ Anchorage, AK 99456 ♪ 907.555.1234 ♪ Darby.Williams@ymail.com

Instrumental and General Music Teacher → Individual, Group, Band, Concert
Determined to deliver the opportunity to succeed that every student deserves

June 4, 2016

Sharon Barret
Human Resources Manager
Anchorage Public Schools
1234 Dimond Avenue
Anchorage, AK 99123

RE: Music Teacher Position #2342, Polaris K-12

ALASKA TEACHING LICENSE IN K-12 GENERAL (1515) AND INSTRUMENTAL MUSIC (1506)
BACHELOR OF ARTS, INSTRUCTIONAL MUSIC AND SECONDARY EDUCATION

Dear Ms. Barret:

Polaris K-12 is the teaching environment of my dreams. As a student teacher there in the last school year, I came to love the differentiated learning environment that Polaris provides because it allowed me to collaborate with students to help them meet individual goals. Please accept the attached résumé in consideration for the current music teaching opportunity, and allow me to highlight a few of the contributions I could make as a permanent member of the team.

As my résumé indicates, I have worked since the age of 16 in public-oriented roles where teaching and collaboration were part of every day. While student teaching at Polaris and Whaley Elementary, I excelled in classroom management and held students to a high standard. We used a blended learning approach, including the online technology of Quaver Music, to engage students in a fun, interactive educational experience. My teaching tools include instruments, movement, technology, and singing—in whole group and small group configurations that support student learning with differentiated instruction.

I believe that every student deserves a chance to succeed, and I am passionate about finding creative ways to inspire them. If you are looking for a dedicated teaching professional with patience, adaptability, a positive attitude, and high standards for education, I would appreciate a personal opportunity to discuss the ways I can contribute. Thank you for your consideration.

Sincerely,

Darby Williams

Darby Williams

3500 Polar Ice Lane ♪ Anchorage, AK 99456 ♪ 907.555.1234 ♪ Darby.Williams@ymail.com

PROFILE

Instrumental and General Music Teacher → Individual, Group, Band, Concert
Determined to deliver the opportunity to succeed that every student deserves

Licensed educator with instrumental and general music endorsements; experienced band director and instructor; BA degree in instructional music and secondary education. Familiar with curriculum development processes, data-driven instruction, and performance tracking. Employed since age 16, acquiring skills in team leadership, interpersonal communication, organization, process improvement, and record keeping. Flexible and creative problem solver; technology proficient.

——— KEY CONTRIBUTIONS ———

Conducted solo and ensemble groups to category wins

Streamlined processes, improved customer satisfaction, and delivered bottom line results

Developed creative recipes that increased sales while protecting an iconic local brand

EDUCATION AND CERTIFICATION

University of Alaska-Anchorage
Bachelor of Arts, Spring 2016
Major in Music (Instructional Music Education); Minor in Secondary Education
Comprehensive curriculum included business, mathematics, technology integration, and a range of topics in education:

Techniques and Strategies for K-12 Schools	General and Instrumental Music Methods
Educational Psychology and Assessment	Instrumental Conducting and Techniques
Characteristics of Exceptional Learners	Voice and Orchestration
Developmental and Content Reading	Woodwind and Brass Instrumental Techniques
Differentiated Instruction	String and Percussion Techniques
Diversity and Cultural Anthropology	Wind Orchestra, Concert Band, Jazz Band
Music Theory, History, and Literature	Piano and Keyboard Musicianship

Alaska Department of Public Instruction (DPI)
Educator License and Endorsements
Initial Educator 5-Year #100123456, 2016–2021
Instrumental Music 1506 and General Music 1515, Early Childhood-Adolescence

Certified in First Aid, CPR-AED and Blood Born Pathogen Isolation

- Continued -

Resumes Provided By

Paula Christensen, CPRW, CJSS, CCMC
Strategic Career Coaches

(920) 264-0806
strategiccareercoaches.com
paula@strategiccareercoaches.com
www.linkedin.com/in/paulachristensen1

980-444-4444 | jamiefitzpatrick@gmail.com | Madison, WI

Targeted Role: **Plastics Engineer**

Diligent and well-rounded Engineering student combining Mechanical Engineering Education with injection molding experience. Known for a strong work ethic and the ability to develop positive team relationships.

MINITAB	SOLIDWORKS	INJECTION MOLDING
PROENGINEER	EXTRUSION EQUIPMENT	ASSEMBLY & PACKAGING
TOOLING DESIGN	QUALITY PLANNING (APQP)	PROBLEM SOLVING

EDUCATION

UNIVERSITY OF IOWA | Mechanical Engineering/Computer Science | *Iowa City, IA*   5/2018
GPA: 3.6
Relevant Coursework:
- Design for Manufacturing & Assembly, Energy Systems Design, Thermodynamics, Engineering Mathematics V: Vector Calculus.

ENGINEERING EXPERIENCE

NORTH IOWA PLASTICS | Plastics Intern | *Fort Madison, IA*   5/2017-8/2017
Assisted engineer with new customer projects, facility improvements, injection molding equipment installations and maintenance. Gained exposure to tooling design and Solidworks program. Served the medical device, automotive and commercial electronics markets. Used Microsoft Word, Excel, Visio, and Access daily.

- Reduced tooling lead time on medical device project by three weeks.
- Increased speed to market by two months for Greenfield project. Used Fused Deposition Manufacturing (FDM) and cycle testing equipment to prove functionality and reliability when designing components.
- Improved sustainability and saved 8% in material costs by researching and testing new material options.

J.A.D. PLASTICS | Engineering Co-Op | *Des Moines, IA*   5/2016-12/2016
Designed, built, and sampled injection molds and gathered/analyzed data on new process implementations. Participated in tool design meetings and trials, project scheduling, and customer communications. Prepared customer presentation materials and handouts. Supported the company's quality system, learning principles of ISO 13485 certification.

- Part of team that helped minimize waste by using materials that contained 50% post-consumer recycled plastic.
- Commended for quickly learning Minitab to validate first order inspections on Rockwell Collins project.

JAMIE FITZPATRICK 980-444-4444 | jamiefitzpatrick@gmail.com| Madison, WI

WISCONSIN PLASTICS | **Production Technician** | *Madison, WI*   Summers 2014, 2015
Assembled plastic parts from injection molding machines, retrieved parts, packed and assembled products and reported production to Inventory Quality Management System (IQMS).

- Line leader, performed quality checks of parts and reviewed co-worker's parts.
- Saved money by tracking the amount of scrap throughout the shift and completing daily Production Shift Reports.

OTHER WORK EXPERIENCE

TCB LAWN CARE AND LIGHTING SERVICES | **Customer Outreach Specialist** | *Iowa City, IA*   9/2015-5/2016
Introduced company to potential customers by canvassing door to door offering homeowners lawn care and holiday lighting quotes. Represented TCB with honesty and integrity utilizing excellent verbal communication skills.

- Exceeded company sales goals by 27% – sold and scheduled service to 12 customers per week.
- Worked independently, setting schedule to coordinate with customer availability.

UNIVERSITY OF IOWA | **Campus Bus Driver** | *Iowa City, IA*   9/2014-5/2015
Operated a transit coach on fixed-routes and special event routes. Provided safe, reliable and friendly service to students. Maintained a Commercial Driver's License (CDL).

- Earned promotion – entrusted to operate a specialized demand-response service for persons with disabilities (Bionic Bus).
- Chosen as Trainer after only six months. Provided new driver training, driver evaluations, driver spot checks, driver re-training, and service observations.
- 100% accident-free throughout employment.
- Assisted Supervisor in accident investigations.

ACTIVITIES

UNIVERSITY OF IOWA | **Pi Tau Sigma**   *9/2014-5/2017*
Mechanical Engineering honors fraternity.
- Served as Vice President 9/2016-5/2017.
- Organized networking events, corporate speakers, and engineering panels.
- Chaired MathCounts fundraising event raising $3000.00 for foundation supporting middle school student math programs.

VOLUNTEER

UNIVERSITY OF IOWA | **OnIowa! Volunteer** | *Iowa City, IA*   9/2014-12/2016
Helped new University of Iowa students feel welcomed and acclimated. Served as a mentor for 25 new University of Iowa Engineering students. Facilitated small group activities and assisted with residence hall move-in.

- Mentored students with diverse personalities and backgrounds showing excellent communication and leadership skills.
- Collaborated with UI administrators, faculty, staff, and other student leaders on creating programs, challenges with students adapting, and scheduling issues.

Hannah Brown

San Jose, CA
408-333-8888
brownh213@outlook.com
linkedin.com/in/hannahbrown

Targeted Role: GRADUATE ASSISTANT
Focused, Committed and Hardworking Practitioner

Well-rounded leader with the confidence, critical thinking, and time management skills to provide excellent support in academic settings. An effective listener who thrives working with individuals as well as managing groups. Dedicated to providing therapeutic care and excited to help other students.

Achievements

Chancellor's Leadership Award Recipient – 2015. Awarded to less than 1% of students.
Honor Roll –5 Semesters
1st Team WIAC All-Sportsmanship Team – 2013, 2014
Total Team Player Award – 2013, 2014

Strengths

•Leadership • Initiative • Communication • Time Management • Research
• Compassion • Organization • Event Coordination • Creativity • Attention to Detail

EDUCATION

<u>Master of Science</u> • San Jose State University, *San Jose, CA*   **May 2018**
Major: **Health Science-THERAPEUTIC RECREATION**
<u>Bachelor of Science</u>• San Jose State University, *San Jose, CA*   **May 2015**
Major: **Health Science-OCCUPATIONAL THERAPY**
GPA (cumulative): 3.39
Chancellor's Leadership Award Recipient – 2015 for academic, community and volunteer achievements.

WORK/VOLUNTEER EXPERIENCE

EVERGREEN INC., *Santa Clara, CA*   September 2016-Present
<u>**COMMUNITY REHABILITATION ASSOCIATE:**</u> Provide individualized home and community based mentoring support for adolescents and adults with developmental disabilities.
- Assist 20 participants, increasing their well-being and independence through recreational activities.
- Completed over 40 hours of training courses including; Working With Youth, Diversity, Working With Individuals With Disabilities, and Crisis Intervention.
- Earned highest proficiency rating on yearly review.
- Hit the ground running, quickly learned new software program to document hours, therapies, and training.
- Entrusted to train another rehabilitation workers within first month on the job.

AMERICORPS - Montessori Charter School, *San Jose, CA*   May 2015-August 2016
<u>**INSTRUCTOR/MENTOR:**</u> Assisted Kindergarten and 1st Grade students in literacy and language development skills. Provided opportunities for student achievement and enrichment activities.
- Increased student reading scores through individualized instruction.
- Over 1700 support hours. Helped first year teacher by designing, researching, planning, and instructing lessons.
- Strengthened classroom, handled discipline issues to free up time for instruction.
- Boosted family literacy through events at San Jose area schools and libraries. Utilized certified therapy dogs and targeted reading activities to enhance literacy.

━━ **Hannah Brown** • San Jose, CA • 408-333-8888• brownh213@outlook.com ━━

PROACTIVE CHIROPRACTIC & WELLNESS, *San Mateo, CA*   May 2014-May 2015
LEGAL SECRETARY: Organized work setting, interpreted insurance forms and communicated with patients, doctors, claims and insurance adjusters. Proactively solved problems with patients' accounts, claims and insurance issues.
- Efficiently adapted to new software program to manage insurance claims, explanation of benefits, worker's compensation, scheduling, and billing.
- Increased revenue by examining patient list to recoup outlying charges. Saw 37% increase in bill repayment versus previous year.
- Made manager's job easier by staying late and shortening claims processing turnaround. Complimented for professionalism and organizational skills.
- Enlarged customer base by 5 new patients per week through excellent customer management, referrals, and increased community visibility. Complimented by customers on timeliness and efficiency.

LOVE YOUR MELON, *San Jose, CA*   November 2013-May 2014
CREW CAPTAIN: –Start Up Raised awareness for childhood cancer, represented the brand through promotions and sales events.
- Formed, implemented, and directed campus team of 20 volunteers.
- Created care packages for local children battling cancer and reached goal of donating over 100 hats to a local pediatric oncology department.

NATIONAL MULTIPLE SCLEROSIS FOUNDATION, *San Jose, CA*   April 2013- October 2013
SPONSORSHIP CHAIR: Recruited to create a network with local businesses and secure donations.
- Raised over $15,000 for research to find a cure for Multiple Sclerosis.
- Managed a volunteer group of 20, communicated with donors, prepared documents and assisted in event organization planning and conclusion.

SAN JOSE STATE UNIVERSITY, *San Jose, CA*   November 2011-April 2013
                    August 2012-April 2013
EQUIPMENT MANAGER, LAUNDRY ASSISTANT: Maintained a clean working environment, managed laundry for practices and games, and communicated with athletic teams.
- Took on additional job duties outside of job scope. Added office management and communication responsibilities.
                    November 2011- August 2012
VOLUNTEER COACH: Mentored and supervised groups of more than 70 girls, kindergarten through 12th grade. Taught skills to play volleyball, build friendships, and grow confidence. Hosted overnight camps supervising all ages, provided meals and safety, planned all daily activities and encouraged team collaboration.

ATHLETICS

San Jose State University, Varsity Volleyball   2011-2014
Team Captain – 2013, 2014
NCAA Final Four – 2013, 2014
Earned American Volleyball Coaches Association's (AVCA)Team Academic Award.

TESTIMONIAL

" Ms. Brown worked collaboratively with others in my courses while simultaneously demonstrating confidentiality, and dedication to quality practices by openly giving and receiving feedback for improving performance. A specific example involved reviewing and revising written work demonstrating using confidentiality, precision, and attention to detail. I have observed Ms. Brown's critical thinking, communication style and interpersonal skills first hand. She displays emotional intelligence by being compassionate and empathetic, an excellent listener."

Jody L. Sullivan, RDH, Ph.D, Associate Professor, San Jose State University

Ryan Hauser

rhauser@uwmadison.edu• Madison, WI
920.777.3333 • linkedin.com/in/ryan-hauser

Targeted Role: PHYSICAL THERAPIST

Combining strong communication skills with comprehensive training in a broad range of PT treatment options. Working hard to build rapport and execute treatment goals.

CORE COMPETENCIES

Orthopedic PT	Developing Treatment Plans	Hospital/ER/Outpatient Modalities
Neurological PT	Leadership/Team Building	Evaluating Outcomes

EDUCATION

UNIVERSITY OF WISCONSIN-MADISON | Madison, WI

Doctor of Physical Therapy   **May 2017**
Relevant Coursework: General Medicine I, II. Orthopedics I, II, III. Neurological Disorders I, II. Pediatrics I, II. Motor Learning I.

Pilot Study: Collaborated with Exercise Science Masters students developing combined treatment plans to provide efficient and comprehensive care.

B.S. Biology   **May 2015**
Relevant Coursework: Advanced Anatomy and Physiology. Exercise Physiology I, II. Introduction to Evidence Base Practice.

CLINICAL INTERNSHIP EXPERIENCE

SAINT MICHAEL'S HOSPITAL | Internship III, Session 2 | Madison, WI   **3/2017-Present**

Identify, evaluate, and treat patients in a clinic setting. Structure treatment plans and establish functional/measurable outcomes.
➢ Record clinical documentation according to regulatory and professional guidelines.
➢ Develop familiarity with advanced treatment options for athletes including; repair and reconstruction protocols and physical therapy standards of care.

ORTHOPEDIC AND SPINE INSTITUTE | Internship III, Session 1| Rockford, IL   **1/2017-3/2017**

Provided outpatient physical therapy services and maintained accurate documentation/billing. Designed and modified therapeutic interventions including; therapeutic exercises, functional trainings, manual therapies, and patient-related instructions.
➢ Enhanced patient movement through dry needling of trigger points throughout the body.
➢ Developed osteopathic techniques used for identifying and treating mechanical dysfunctions.

ROCKFORD HEALTH CARE | Internship II | Rockford, IL   **5/2016-8/2016**

Assisted therapists with administering modalities in hospital, ER and Outpatient Orthopedic Clinic. Treated pediatric, adolescent, adult, and geriatric patients.

➢ Improved function. Helped a stroke patient walk unassisted, implementing hip strategies for self-postural corrections (changing from hand/therapist assist) to strengthen core and improve balance.
➢ Customized and adapted conventional PT techniques to meet the unique needs of individual patients.
➢ Complemented by supervisor and patients for providing high-quality, compassionate care.

SPORT AND SPINE PHYSICAL WELLNESS | Internship I | Madison, WI   **10/2015-12/2015**
Administered outpatient physical therapy and rehabilitation services for orthopedic and sports injuries.
➢ Performed diagnostic and prognostic exams to evaluate muscle, nerve, joint, and functional abilities and provide interventions. Educated patients and families on aftercare.
➢ Documented progress, completed discharge summaries and prepared home treatment plans. Ensured all documentation was clear, concise, and accurate.

RYAN HAUSER   rhauser@uwmadison.edu * 920.777.3333 * Page 2 of 2

WORK EXPERIENCE

APPLETON NORTH HIGH SCHOOL | Strength and Conditioning Assistant | Appleton, WI   6/2014-8/2014

Designed and managed summer strength and conditioning program for 150+ high school students. Shared college-level knowledge with coaches.

- ➤ Strength and Conditioning Assistant position was created after approaching coach with program ideas and specific information on ability to impact the team.
- ➤ Created and implemented small group workout programs, leading students through planned rotations.

UNIVERSITY OF WISCONSIN-MADISON | Resident Assistant | Madison, WI   8/2013-5/2014

Supervised 200+ residents providing assistance, guidance, and support. Leadership training included: listening skills, conflict resolution, campus resources, and event planning.

- ➤ Maintained safety and fostered a community atmosphere. Chosen for difficult Freshman dorm fostering a safe, inclusive, and supportive environment.

EDGEWOOD SPRINGS GOLF COURSE | Professional Caddie | Edgewood, WI   6/2012-8/2012

Carried equipment and provided insight on course challenges/obstacles and best strategies. Knowledgeable of overall yardage, pin placements and club selection.

- ➤ Stand out first-year caddie earning ability to work double-loops, usually reserved for those with more experience.

HAUSER LAWN CARE | Co-founder | Appleton, WI   4/2010-6/2012

Provide landscaping and lawn care for 30+ clients.

- ➤ Increased clientele 250% over last three years by exceeding customers' needs, working hard, and efficiently scheduling services.
- ➤ Juggled multiple priorities, balancing business needs with school/football obligations. Scheduled and completed services, maintained equipment and delegated jobs when necessary.

LEADERSHIP EXPERIENCE AND AWARDS

UNIVERSITY OF WISCONSIN-MADISON FOOTBALL | University of Wisconsin-Madison | Madison, WI

Involvement with varsity athletics built an outstanding team based work ethic, effective communication skills and the persistence to face challenges. Leadership skills were honed and sharpened. Time management was essential, balancing 20-30+ hours of practice, travel, workouts, and film.

- ➤ **Male Athlete of the Year**   2014-2015
- ➤ **Captain**   2012-2014
- ➤ **1st Team All-American Selection – USA College Football**   2014
- ➤ **Defensive Skill MVP of Mid-West Conference**   2014
- ➤ **Academic All-Conference**   2012-2015

TESTIMONIAL

"Ryan is a fast learner and was able to easily adjust between the different settings. He treated a wide range of ages from geriatrics to adolescents as well as multiple patient diagnoses. During the clinical rotation he performed various evaluations, determined plans of care, reassessments, carried out treatment sessions and aided in discharge planning. Ryan demonstrated his skills with progressing treatment sessions and exercises appropriately to meet the patient's current level of status while also challenging the patient. He has good communication skills, which aided in his ability to communicate effectively with other healthcare professionals including PTAs, MD, RN, 2social work and respiratory therapy for good continuity of care and patient safety. Ryan will be a great asset to his future employer."

Marcus Breager, Instructor, PT, DPT, CI, Rockford Health Care

# **Tanner Hanson**

tannerh53@gmail.com ▪ Denver, CO
999-444-6666 ▪ www.linkedin.com/in/tannerhanson

SALES REPRESENTATIVE

Ambitious Sales Representative candidate with experience building client relationships and understanding customer needs to maximize results. Self-motivated seller dedicated to giving extra effort to successfully generate sales.

Key Achievements

 Earned Platinum Club Award as Intern, #3 seller out of 187.

 Waterways #1 Sales Consultant in city and region multiple times.

 Colorado University academic *and* athletic scholarship recipient.

EDUCATION

UNIVERSITY OF COLORADO - BOULDER | Major: Business | Boulder, CO   8/2013-present

Relevant Coursework: Sales Management, Strategic Marketing, Business Communication, Business Law/Contracts, Principles of Management, Advertising, Public Relations, Macro-economics and Ecommerce.

➢ **Academic Scholarship Recipient** – Eagle Scholarship
➢ **Athletic Scholarship Recipient** – Baseball, Varsity Letterman
  Varsity athletics built an outstanding work ethic, effective communication skills and the perseverance to face challenges. Leadership skills were honed and sharpened. Time management was essential, balancing 20-30+ hours of practice, travel and workouts with school demands.
➢ **United Methodist Church Student Grant Recipient**

GRAND VALLEY HIGH SCHOOL | Parachute, CO   8/2009–5/2013

Ranked as the #1 Academic High School in Colorado.

➢ **Dean's List**
➢ **President's Community Service Award (100+ Hours)** – 2012, 2013.
➢ **2012 State Championship Baseball Team** – Grand Valley North High School Varsity Baseball Team.

SALES EXPERIENCE

SUMMER INTERN | Enterprise Rent-A-Car | Denver, CO   Summer 2016

 *Enterprise Rent-A-Car is an internationally recognized brand in the car rental industry with more than 7,000 neighborhood and airport locations throughout the world.*

Exceeded both business and individual customer expectations through relationship building, listening, and making decisions on how to best impact service. Managed a fleet of vehicles.

➢ **Named a top summer Intern** – earning a $500 scholarship. Scholarships awarded for exceptional job performance and a top-tier presentation to management.
➢ **Platinum Club** – July 2016, as an Intern (#3 seller out of 187).
➢ Worked effectively in team-based, competitive environment.

Tanner Hanson

SALES CONSULTANT | Waterway Wash & Gas | Denver, CO   11/2011-7/2013

Waterway *Carwash*   *Waterway Wash & Gas is a national leader in the car wash industry operating 20 locations in 5 cities.*

Professionally greeted customers and sold additional services by identifying customer opportunities.

➢ #1 Sales Consultant in the Denver market multiple times.
➢ #1 Sales Consultant regionally (Kansas City, Denver, Cleveland & St Louis markets) multiple times.
➢ Promoted from line worker after 8 months.

OTHER WORK EXPERIENCE

ACTIVITIES LEADER – CAMP COUNSELOR | Keystone Ranch | Keystone, CO   Summer 2015
Faith-based summer camp.
Managed, facilitated and maintained activities in a Christian atmosphere.

➢ Over the course of the summer, responsible for safety and supervision of over 1000 kids (10-16 years old) on ropes activities.
➢ Engaged with different small groups emphasizing accountability, mentorship, and fellowship.

CAMP COUNSELOR | Timberline Camps | Fort Collins, CO   Summer 2014
Faith-based summer camp.
Instructed activities, coached sports and encouraged kids while teaching spiritual values and fostering a supportive environment.

➢ Maintained safety and supervision of six groups of 9 to 12 boys (ages 7 to 10).
➢ Directed campers in scheduled activities, creating a fun and exciting atmosphere.

OFFICE INTERN | The Hanson Group | Denver, CO   8/2009-8/2013
The Hanson Group is a nationally recognized and award winning executive search firm.   *Winter breaks*

➢ Performed database build-outs, updates using LinkedIn.
➢ Conducted Internet research on companies that the firm specialized.

SEASONAL LAWN CARE | Tanner's Lawn Care | Denver, CO   3/2006-8/2013
Started business while in middle school.

➢ Maintained 3-6 lawns per week.
➢ Juggled multiple priorities, balancing business needs with school/baseball obligations. Scheduled and completed services, maintained equipment and delegated jobs when necessary.

VOLUNTEERISM

PRESIDENT'S COMMUNITY SERVICE AWARD
100+ hours of community service – 2012, 2013

TIMBERLINE CAMPS - MISSION SERVICE WEEK
Christian summer camp – 2010, 2011, 2012, 2013

Matt J. Aria

matty.aria@gmail.com • Franklin, IN
333-666-2828 • linkedin.com/in/mattyaria

May 27, 2018

John Smith
HR Director
Acme Supply Company
1470 Franklin Street
Franklin, TN 55763

Re: Information Systems Technician

Dear Mr. Smith:

Jeff Roberts recommended I contact you regarding your Information Systems Technician role. Jeff and I interned together at Christensen National last spring. My internship experience helped me understand the importance of customer-facing positions, PC and systems troubleshooting, and server configurations. My hands-on IT classes and internship experience have afforded me a deep understanding of Information Systems.

Key areas where my experience matches your job requirements:

> **Hardware/Software Knowledge:** Citrix, VMware, MacOS and JD Edwards experience as well as knowledge of patch management in a Microsoft Windows operating systems environment.
> **Customer Service/Problem Resolution:** Helped team improve response rates by 15% and customer satisfaction scores by 20%.
> **Equipment Deployment:** Tested configuration templates, and installed hardware, software, and systems for 200 users last summer.

I would appreciate the opportunity to meet with you in person. Thank you in advance for your consideration. I will follow up early next week.

Sincerely,

Matt J. Aria

Resumes Provided By

Tina Kashlak Nicolai, PHR, CPBA,CARW

(407) 578-1697
tina@resumewritersink.com

Katy Karson
Retail Management
~luxury fashion stylist~

Studied

Parsons ~ The New School For Design, Paris, France
BFA Fashion Design
Graduated #1 in class of 2017

Differentiators

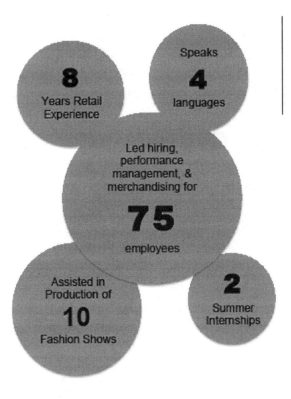

8
Years Retail Experience

Speaks **4** languages

Led hiring, performance management, & merchandising for **75** employees

Assisted in Production of **10** Fashion Shows

2 Summer Internships

Served teams & customers...

Le Chateau, Store Manager, Paris, 2 years
Maison de Paris, Visual Leader, Paris, 3 years
Fashion Walkway, Production Assistant, 3 years

"Katy skillfully led peers in her classroom projects as a result of her creative eye and natural leadership."
Professor Madeline Bordon

Leadership Style

Pragmatic Strategic Planner

Inclusive Innovative Inspirational

Contact Information
917-222-2222 | katykarsfashion@me.com

"Vickie"
Knoswik
Educator K-5
Hi! Teaching kids is my passion. We connect. The door unlocks and the journey to learn happens!

Education

University of Maryland
College Park, MD
Bachelor of Science

Expertise

- Early Childhood Development
- Early Childhood Special Education
- Child Psychology

Technical

- Microsoft
- PowerPoint
- Word Press
- e*Learning
- Web Teach

Languages

English | Creole | Spanish

"The world is one large text book. I believe all experiences help us learn. I have travelled to 6 countries and have enjoyed learning from children, which helps me pay-it-forward to my students. When we open our hearts, we open our minds, and learning takes place!" Vickie K.

Apprentice Learning & Practical Experience:

Middlebrook Elementary
Annapolis, MD
(Classroom Practicum)

George Washington Elementary
Baltimore, MD
(Classroom Practicum)

Byron George School
South Africa
(Apprentice)

E.G. Gonzalez Grade School
Puerto Rico
(Apprentice)

Other international school trips (Volunteer Studies):
Italy | Greece | Poland Germany

e-book published:
"The Unlock"
teaching w/heart & soul

Let's connect...

C: 310.222.2222
vickieteaches@me-now.com
linkedin.com/in/vickieteaches

1200 Students Learn Drive | College Park, MD

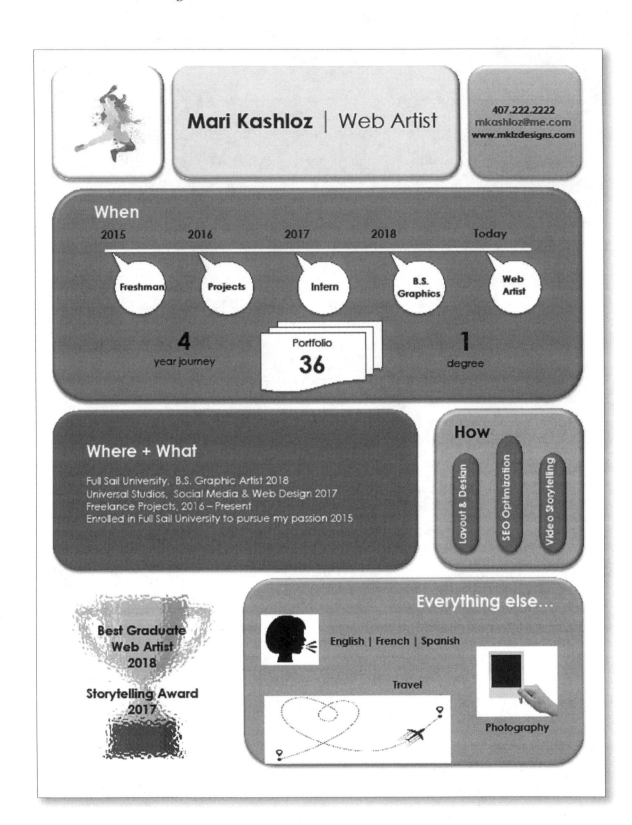

Tony Apolloti

813.222.2222 | tonyapolloti@my-me.com

Animal Behaviorist

Helping the world by helping the animals

Education

University of Central Florida Orlando, Florida
Expected Graduation – May 2018
B.S. Biology
Minor: Animal Sciences

Hi!

I've been working with animals since I adopted my first turtle and dog as a child. Since then, my interest in working with animals has been my passion and life.

I'll be graduating in May of 2018 from UCF.

For more information, please visit my website to see the animals that I've had the pleasure to work with over the years.

www.tonysfriends-splash.com

~Tony A.

Practicums

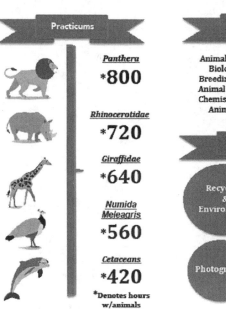

Panthera
*800

Rhinocerotidae
*720

Giraffidae
*640

Numida Meleagris
*560

Cetaceans
*420

*Denotes hours w/animals

Coursework

Animal Behavioral Management
Biology | Advanced Biology
Breeding & Social Responsibility
Animal (and Human) Psychology
Chemistry | Advanced Chemistry
Animal Behavioral Analysis
Animal Wellness

Interests

Recycling & Environment

Running & Cycling

Photography

Writing Short Stories

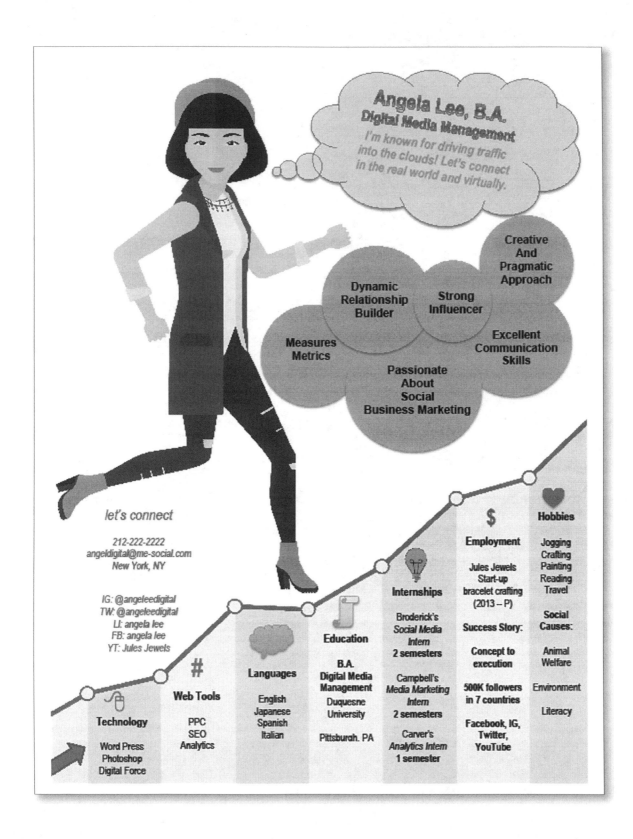

Bibliography

"10 Tips for the Perfect LinkedIn Profile." *LinkHumans, Slideshare.* Published July 1, 2014. http:// www.slideshare.net/linkedin/10-tips-for-the-perfect-linkedin-profile. (accessed November 11, 2015).

"10 Ways You're Building a Fantastic Brand." *Design Aglow.* February 3, 2015. http://designaglow. com/blogs/design-aglow/16728432-10-ways-youre-building-a-fantastic-brand (accessed May 28, 2015).

"2015 Candidate Behavior Study." *CareerBuilder.* http://careerbuildercommunications.com/ candidatebehavior/ (accessed February 15, 2016).

"2016 Recruiter Nation Report fka Social Recruiting Survey." *Jobvite.* http://www.jobvite.com/ wp-content/uploads/2016/09/RecruiterNation2016.pdf.

"About LinkedIn." *LinkedIn Newsroom.* https://press.linkedin.com/about-linkedin (accessed May 29, 2015).

Adams, Susan. "How to Ace Your Job Interview." *Forbes.* March 1, 2013, http://www.forbes.com/ sites/susanadams/2013/03/01/how-to-ace-your-job-interview-2/ (accessed June 15, 2015).

Arruda, William. "Is LinkedIn Poised To Be The Next Media Giant?" *Forbes.* March 8, 2015. http:// www.forbes.com/sites/williamarruda/2015/03/08/is-linkedin-poised-to-be-the-next-media-gi-ant/ (accessed June 5, 2015).

Ayele, Daniel. "Land Your Dream Job in 2015 with These Data-Proven LinkedIn Tips." *LinkedIn Blog.* January 29, 2015. http://blog.linkedin.com/2015/01/29/jobseeking-tips/ (accessed June 9, 2015).

Ayres, Leslie. "Why You Need a Resume Business Card." *Notes from the Job Search Guru: A Career Advice Blog.* March 16, 2009. http://www.thejobsearchguru.com/notesfrom/why-you-need-a-re-sume-business-card/ (accessed November 4, 2015).

"Ball at Impact." *Golfswing.com.* http://www.golfswing.com.au/139 (accessed February 15, 2016).

"Basic Privacy Settings & Tools." *Facebook Help Center.* https://www.facebook.com/help/3258 07937506242/?ref=contextual (Accessed 3/17/17).

Bell, Karissa. "LinkedIn will now help you secretly tell recruiters you want a new job." *Mashable,* October 6, 2016. http://mashable.com/2016/10/06/linkedin-tell-recruiters-you-want-a-new-job. amp (Accessed November 25, 2016).

Bergdahl, Michael. *What I Learned From Sam Walton: How to Compete and Thrive in a Wal-Mart World.* Hoboken, New Jersey: John Wiley & Sons, 2004.

"Bonus Programs and Practices." *WorldatWork.* June 2014. http://www.worldatwork.org/adim-Link?id=75444 (accessed June 1, 2015).

Bricker, Eric. "How to Ace Your Video Interview." *On Careers Blog. U.S. News & World Report.* July 11, 2013. http://money.usnews.com/money/careers/articles/2013/07/11/how-to-ace-your-video-interview (accessed December 1, 2015).

Bucknell Career Development Center. "Creating an Effective Resume." Bucknell University. http://www.bucknell.edu/documents/CDC/Creating_An_Effective_Resume.pdf (accessed February 19, 2016).

Bureau of Labor Statistics. "Employee Tenure Summary." News release. September 18, 2014. http://www.bls.gov/news.release/tenure.nr0.htm (accessed May 29, 2015).

Bureau of Labor Statistics. "Number of Jobs Held, Labor Market Activity, and Earnings Growth Among the Youngest Baby Boomers: Results from a Longitudinal Survey." News release. March 31, 2015. http://www.bls.gov/news.release/pdf/nlsoy.pdf (accessed May 29, 2015).

Byrne, Donn Erwin. *The Attraction Paradigm.* New York: Academic Press, 1971.

Carnegie, Dale. *How to Win Friends and Influence People.* New York: Simon and Schuster, 2010.

"Carl Frederick Quotes." *World of Quotes.* http://www.worldofquotes.com/author/Carl+Frederick/1/index.html (accessed June 10, 2015).

Cain, Aine. "Why you should still spend time perfecting your cover letter, even though most hiring managers won't read it." *Business Insider.* http://www.businessinsider.com/why-you-still-need-to-write-a-cover-letter-2016-10 (Accessed August 27, 2017).

"Character Limit and Changing your username." *Twitter Help Center.* https://support.twitter.com/articles/14609 (Accessed 3/14/17).

Cialdini, Robert. *Influence: Science and Practice*, 4th ed. Needham Heights, MA: Allyn & Bacon, 2001.

Claycomb, Heather, and Karl Dinse. *Career Pathways—Interactive Workbook.* (1995), Part 7.

"Cognitive scientists say it can take up to two hundred times the amount of information to undo a first impression as it takes to make one." Zack, Devora. "10 Tips for People Who Hate Networking." *Careerealism.* May 4, 2015. http://www.careerealism.com/hate-networking-tips/ (accessed July 17, 2015).

Collamer, Nancy. "The Perfect Elevator Pitch To Land A Job." *Forbes.* February 4, 2013. http://www.forbes.com/sites/nextavenue/2013/02/04/the-perfect-elevator-pitch-to-land-a-job/ (accessed May 28, 2015).

Cornerstone Coaching LLC. "What Winston Churchill Can Teach Us About Inevitable Success."

February 26, 2014. http://www.cornerstoneadvisoryservices.com/blog/what-winston-churchill-can-teach-us-about-inevitable-success (accessed May 28, 2015).

"David Ogilvy Quotable Quote." *Goodreads*, http://www.goodreads.com/quotes/262108-don-t-bunt-aim-out-of-the-ballpark-aim-for-the (accessed May 28, 2015).

Dexcreumaux, Geoff. "Top LinkedIn Facts and Stats [Infographic]." *We Are Social Media*. July 25, 2014. http://wersm.com/top-linkedin-facts-and-stats-infographic/ (accessed May 29, 2015).

DiResta, Diane. Interview by Christina Canters, "Episode 29—How to Blitz Your Job Interview—Secrets of Executive Speech Coach Diane Diresta." *DesignDrawSpeak*. Podcast audio, June 12, 2014. http://designdrawspeak.com/029/ (accessed June 19, 2015).

"Do Employers Expect a Job Interview Thank-You Card?" *CVTips*. http://www.cvtips.com/interview/do-employers-expect-a-job-interview-thank-you-card.html (accessed July 10, 2015).

"Doing What's Necessary, What's Possible, and What Seems to be Impossible." *The Recovery Ranch*. http://www.recoveryranch.com/articles/necessary-possible-impossible/ (accessed May 27, 2015).

Dougherty, Lisa. "16 Tips to Optimize Your LinkedIn Profile and Your Personal Brand." *LinkedIn Pulse*. July 8, 2014. https://www.linkedin.com/pulse/20140708162049-7239647-16-tips-to-optimize-your-linkedin-profile-and-enhance-your-personal-brand (accessed November 11, 2015).

ExecuNet. "Senior-Level Business Leaders Say Positive Attitude is the Key to Getting the Job." News release. March 25, 2013. http://www.execunet.com/m_releases_content.cfm?id=4812 (accessed June 11, 2015).

"Farewell to the Handwritten Thank-You Note? Survey Reveals Email, Phone Call Are Preferred Methods for Post-Interview Follow-Up." *Robert Half*. June 14, 2012. http://accountemps.rhi.mediaroom.com/thank-you (accessed July 9, 2015).

Foote, Andy. "Maximum LinkedIn Character Counts for 2016." December 10, 2016. https://www.linkedin.com/pulse/maximum-linkedin-character-counts-2016-andy-foote. (Accessed November 22, 2016).

Foote, Andy. "Why You Should Complete Your LinkedIn Profile." LinkedInsights.com. December 7, 2015. https://www.linkedinsights.com/why-you-should-complete-your-linkedin-profile/ (accessed November 22, 2016).

Franklin, Benjamin. "The Way to Wealth," *Poor Richard's Almanac*, July 7, 1757.

Frasco, Stephanie. "11 Tips To Help Optimize Your LinkedIn Profile For Maximum Exposure and Engagement." *Convert with Content*. https://www.convertwithcontent.com/11-tips-optimize-linkedin-profile-maximum-exposure-engagement/ (accessed June 10, 2015).

"General Limits for LinkedIn Groups." *LinkedIn*. https://www.linkedin.com/help/linkedin/answer/190/general-limits-for-linkedin-groups?lang=en (Accessed November 23, 2016).

"Give Thanks or Your Chance For That Job Could be Cooked." *TheLadders*. http://cdn.theladders.net/static/images/basicSite/PR/pdfs/TheLaddersGiveThanks.pdf (accessed June 5, 2015).

"Goodnight, Seattle: Part 2." *Frasier*. 13 May 2004 by NBC. Directed by David Lee and written by Christopher Lloyd and Joe Keenan.

Grant Tilus. "Top 10 Human Resources Job Skills Employers Want to See." *Rasmussen College*. July 29, 2013. http://www.rasmussen.edu/degrees/business/blog/human-resources-job-skills-employers-want-to-see/ (accessed July 10, 2015).

Hansen, Katharine. PhD. "Do's and Don'ts for Second (and Subsequent) Job Interviews." *Quintessential Careers*. http://www.quintcareers.com/second-interviewing-dos-donts/ (accessed February 16, 2016).

Hansen, Randall S., PhD. "Networking Business Cards: An Essential Job-Search Tool for Job-Seekers, Career Changers, and College Students When a Resume Just Won't Do." *Quintessential Careers*. http://www.quintcareers.com/networking-business-cards/ (accessed November 4, 2015).

Hansen, Randall S., PhD, and Katharine Hansen, PhD. "What Do Employers *Really* Want? Top Skills and Values Employers Seek from Job-Seekers." *Quintessential Careers*. http://www.quintcareers.com/job_skills_values.html (accessed May 27, 2015).

Helmrich, Brittney. "Thanks! 20 Job Interview Thank You Note Tips." *Business News Daily*. June 23, 2015, http://www.businessnewsdaily.com/7134-thank-you-note-tips.html (accessed July 9, 2015).

"Henry Samuel." *Brainy Quote*. https://www.brainyquote.com/authors/henry_samueli (accessed November 2, 2017).

Herman, Lily. "How to Clean Up Your Social Media During the Job Search." *The Muse*. https://www.themuse.com/advice/how-to-clean-up-your-social-media-during-the-job-search. (Accessed May 22, 2017).

Hill, Paul. *The Panic Free Job Search: Unleash the Power of the Web and Social Networking to Get Hired*. Pompton Plains, NJ: Career Press, 2012. p. 203.

Jamal, Nina, and Judith Lindenberger. "How to Make a Great First Impression." *Business Know-How*. http://www.businessknowhow.com/growth/dress-impression.htm (accessed June 2, 2015).

"Jarod Kintz Quotable Quote." *Goodreads*. http://www.goodreads.com/quotes/1234580-the-only-people-who-don-t-need-elevator-pitches-are-elevator (accessed May 28, 2015).

Jerome Knyszweski. "How to Use LinkedIn as a Student—And Nail That Dream Job." *LinkedIn Pulse*. April 28, 2015. https://www.linkedin.com/pulse/how-use-linkedin-student-nail-dream-job-jerome-knyszewski (accessed May 28, 2015).

"Jobvite Recruiter Nation Report." *Jobvite*. 2016. http://www.jobvite.com/wp-content/uploads/2016/09/RecruiterNation2016.pdf (Accessed March 15, 2017).

"Jobvite Social Recruiting Survey Finds Over 90% of Employers Will Use Social Recruiting in 2012." *Jobvite.* July 9, 2012. http://www.jobvite.com/press-releases/2012/jobvite-social-recruiting-survey-finds-90-employers-will-use-social-recruiting-2012/ (accessed November 10, 2015).

"Jose N. Harris Quotable Quote." *Goodreads.* http://www.goodreads.com/quotes/415120-to-get-something-you-never-had-you-have-to-do (accessed June 22, 2015).

Joyce, Susan P. "After the Interview, What is Taking Them SO Long?" *Work Coach Café.* September 17, 2012 http://www.workcoachcafe.com/2012/09/17/after-the-interview-what-is-taking-them-so-long/ (accessed February 15, 2016)

Lorenz, Mary. "New study shows job seekers what hiring managers really want." *CareerBuilder.* May 17, 2016, http://www.careerbuilder.com/advice/new-study-shows-job-seekers-what-hiring-managers-really-want (Accessed August 27, 2017).

LinkHumans. "10 Tips." See also, Craig Smith, DMR, "200+ Amazing LinkedIn Stats." Last Updated October 2016. http://expandedramblings.com/index.php/by-the-numbers-a-few-important-linkedin-stats/ (Downloaded November 28, 2016).

"Manage Your Career," *Experience,* https://www.experience.com/alumnus/article?article_id=article_1247505066959&channel_id=career_management&source_page=additional_articles.

Maxwell, John C. *The Maxwell Daily Reader: 365 Days of Insight to Develop the Leader Within You and Influence Those Around You.* Nashville, TN: Thomas Nelson, 2011.

McGregor, Jena. "Interviewing for a Job is Taking Longer Than Ever." *On Leadership. Washington Post.* June 18, 2015. http://www.washingtonpost.com/blogs/on-leadership/wp/2015/06/18/interviewing-for-a-job-is-taking-longer-than-ever/ (accessed February 15, 2016).

Moynihan et al. "A Longitudinal Study." Quoted in Kurtzberg and Naquin. *Essentials.*

"Napoleon Hill Quotable Quote." *Goodreads.* http://www.goodreads.com/quotes/244859-a-goal-is-a-dream-with-a-deadline (accessed June 11, 2015).

Nauen, Rachel. "Number of Employers Using Social Media to Screen Candidates at All-Time High, Finds Latest CareerBuilder Study." *CareerBuilder.* June 15, 2017, http://press.careerbuilder.com/2017-06-15-Number-of-Employers-Using-Social-Media-to-Screen-Candidates-at-All-Time-High-Finds-Latest-CareerBuilder-Study.

Networking 101 for New Grads." *U.S. News and World Report.* http://money.usnews.com/money/blogs/networking-101-for-new-grads.

"Networking." *BusinessDictionary.com.* http://www.businessdictionary.com/definition/networking.html (accessed November 12, 2015).

"New Research Study Breaks Down The Perfect Profile Photo. *PhotoFeeler.* May 13, 2014. https://blog.photofeeler.com/perfect-photo/ (accessed November 7, 2016).

Nsehe, Mfonobong. "19 Inspirational Quotes From Nelson Mandela." *Forbes.com*. December 6, 2013. http://www.forbes.com/sites/mfonobongnsehe/2013/12/06/20-inspirational-quotes-from-nelson-mandela/ (accessed May 27, 2015).

"Number of Employers Using Social Media to Screen Candidates Has Increased 500 Percent over the Last Decade." *CareerBuilder*. April 28, 2016. http://www.careerbuilder.com/share/aboutus/pressreleasesdetail.aspx?ed=12%2F31%2F2016&id=pr945&sd=4%2F28%2F2016 (Accessed March 16, 2017).

OfficeTeam. "Survey: Six in 10 Companies Conduct Video Job Interviews." news release. August 30, 2012. http://officeteam.rhi.mediaroom.com/videointerviews (accessed June 5, 2015).

Oswal, Shreva. "7 Smart Habits of Successful Job Seekers [INFOGRAPHIC]." *LinkedIn Blog*. March 19, 2014. http://blog.linkedin.com/2014/03/19/7-smart-habits-of-successful-job-seekers-infographic/ (accessed June 9, 2015).

"Pages." *Facebook*. https://www.facebook.com/help/282489752085908/?helpref=hc_fnav.

Pamela Skillings. "The Ultimate Infographic Resume Guide." *Big Interview*. June 18, 2013. http://biginterview.com/blog/2013/06/infographic-resumes.html (accessed February 17, 2016).

Pearcemarch, Kyle. "SEO for LinkedIn: How to Optimize Your LinkedIn Profile for Search." *DIYGenius*. March 19, 2015. https://www.diygenius.com/how-to-optimize-your-linkedin-profile-for-search/. (Accessed November 22, 2016).

Peterson, Marshalita Sims. "Personnel Interviewers' Perceptions of the Importance and Adequacy of Applicants' Communication Skills." *Communication Education*. 46, no. 4 (1997): 287–291.

Phillips, Simon. *The Complete Guide to Professional Networking: The Secrets of Online and Offline Success*. London: Kogan Page Limited. 2014.

Pine, Joslyn. Ed. *Book of African-American Quotations*. New York: Dover Publications, 2011.

Pollak, Lindsey. "How to Attract Employers' Attention on LinkedIn." *LinkedIn Blog*. December 2, 2010. http://blog.linkedin.com/2010/12/02/find-jobs-on-linkedin/ (accessed June 4, 2015).

"Proactive Career Planning at Any Age." *Aequus Wealth Management Resources*. http://www.aequuswealth.com/newsletter/article/proactive_career_planning_at_any_age (accessed July 10, 2015).

"Practices to Avoid When Optimizing Your Profile For LinkedIn Search." *LinkedIn*. https://www.linkedin.com/help/linkedin/answer/51499/practices-to-avoid-when-optimizing-your-profile-for-linkedin-search?lang=en. (Accessed November 23, 2016).

"Quotes on Perseverance." *The Samuel Johnson Sound Bite Page*. http://www.samueljohnson.com/persever.html.

"Ralph Waldo Emerson Quotable Quote." *Goodreads.* www.goodreads.com/quotes/60285-do-the-thing-you-fear-and-the-death-of-fear (accessed May 28, 2015).

"Rasselas: A Word of Caution." *The Samuel Johnson Sound Bite Page.* http://www.samueljohnson.com/rasselas.html (accessed June 2, 2015).

Regis University Career Services. "Interviewing Strategies for CPS Students and Alumni." *Regis University.* http://www.regis.edu/About-Regis-University/University-Offices-and-Services/Career-Services/Student-and-Alumni/Interviewing-Strategies.aspx (accessed June 19, 2015).

Reynolds, Marci. "How to Be Found More Easily in LinkedIn (LinkedIn SEO)." *Job-Hunt.org.* http://www.job-hunt.org/social-networking/be-found-on-linkedin.shtml (accessed June 4, 2015).

"The Role of Higher Education in Career Development: Employer Perceptions." *The Chronicle of Higher Education.* December 2012. http://www.chronicle.com/items/biz/pdf/Employers%20Survey.pdf.

Roosevelt, Theodore. *The Strenuous Life.* Speech. The Hamilton Club, Chicago, IL, April 10, 1899. http://www.bartleby.com/58/1.html (accessed May 28, 2015).

Torres, Brooke. "Job Seekers: Social Media is Even More Important Than You Thought." *The Muse.* https://www.themuse.com/advice/job-seekers-social-media-is-even-more-important-than-you-thought (Accessed November 4, 2015).

Safani Barbara. "Tell a Story Interviewers Can't Forget." *TheLadders.* http://www.theladders.com/career-advice/tell-story-interviewers-cant-forget (accessed May 29, 2015).

"Searching for Work in the Digital Era." *Pew Research Center.* November 19, 2015. http://www.pew-internet.org/files/2015/11/PI_2015-11-19-Internet-and-Job-Seeking_FINAL.pdf.

"Self-Limiting Beliefs." *Quotes from the Masters.* http://finsecurity.com/finsecurity/quotes/qm103.html (accessed May 28, 2015).

"Setting up and Customizing Your Profile." *Twitter Help Center.* https://support.twitter.com/articles/127871 (Accessed 3/14/17).

Simpson, Cheryl. "10 Healthy Ways to Cope with Job Search Rejection." *LinkedIn.* March 27, 2017 https://www.linkedin.com/pulse/10-healthy-ways-cope-job-search-rejection-chery.   (accessed March 29, 2017).

Smith, Craig. "133 Amazing LinkedIn Statistics." Last updated November 17, 2016. http://expandedramblings.com/index.php/by-the-numbers-a-few-important-linkedin-stats/.

Smith, Craig. DMR, "200+ Amazing LinkedIn Stats." Last Updated October 2016. http://expandedramblings.com/index.php/by-the-numbers-a-few-important-linkedin-stats/ (Downloaded November 28, 2016).

Smith, Jacquelyn. "7 Things You Probably Didn't Know About Your Job Search." *Forbes*. April 17, 2013. http://www.forbes.com/sites/jacquelynsmith/2013/04/17/7-things-you-probably-didnt-know-about-your-job-search/#71fe2c6e64e6 (accessed February 12, 2016).

Smith, Jacquelyn. "The Complete Guide To Crafting A Perfect LinkedIn Profile." *Business Insider*. January 21, 2015. http://www.businessinsider.com/guide-to-perfect-linkedin-profile-2015-1 (accessed June 4, 2015).

"Sundberg, Jorgen. "List of 140 Employers Posting Jobs on Twitter." *Undercover Recruiter*. http://theundercoverrecruiter.com/list-employers-posting-jobs-twitter/ (Accessed March 16, 2017).

Sutton, Robert I., PhD. *The No Asshole Rule: Building a Civilized Workplace and Surviving One That Isn't*. New York: Warner Business Books, 2007.

"Thank-You Note Etiquette." *CareerBuilder*. http://www.careerbuilder.com/JobPoster/Resources/page.aspx?pagever=ThankYouNoteEtiquette (accessed July 9, 2015).

Townsend, Maya. "The Introvert's Survival Guide to Networking." *Inc.com*.http://www.inc.com/maya-townsend/introvert-networking-guide.html (accessed November 4, 2015).

U.S. Department of Labor. "Soft Skill #2: Enthusiasm and Attitude." *Skills to Pay the Bills*. http://www.dol.gov/odep/topics/youth/softskills/Enthusiasm.pdf (accessed June 19, 2015).

"Understanding the Employer's Perspective." *Internships.com*. http://www.internships.com/student/resources/interview/prep/getting-ready/understand-employer (accessed July 10, 2015).

Uzialko, Adam. "LinkedIn's Open Candidates: How to Search for a New Job, Quietly." *Business News Daily*. October 6, 2016. http://www.businessnewsdaily.com/9468-linkedin-open-candidates.html (Accessed November 25, 2016).

Van Vlooten, Dick. "The Seven Laws of Networking: Those Who Give, Get." Science Mag. May 7, 2004. http://www.sciencemag.org/careers/2004/05/seven-laws-networking-those-who-give-get.

Vaughan, Pamela. "81% of LinkedIn Users Belong to a LinkedIn Group [Data]." *Hubspot Blogs*. August 11, 2011. http://blog.hubspot.com/blog/tabid/6307/bid/22364/81-of-LinkedIn-Users-Belong-to-a-LinkedIn-Group-Data.aspx (accessed June 8, 2015).

Victoria Andrew. "The Power of a Positive Attitude." *Kavaliro*. Kavaliro Employment Agency. May 23, 2013, http://www.kavaliro.com/the-power-of-a-positive-attitude.

"Wayne Gretzky Quotable Quote." *Goodreads*. http://www.goodreads.com/quotes/4798-you-miss-one-hundred-percent-of-the-shots-you-don-t (accessed July 13, 2015).

"What is Solution Selling?" *Sales Performance International*. http://solutionselling.learn.com/learn-center.asp?id=178455 (accessed June 8, 2015).

Whitcomb, Susan Britton. *Job Search Magic: Insider Secrets from America's Career and Life Coach*. Indianapolis, IN: JIST Works, 2006.

Widener, Chris. "Life Rewards Action." http://chriswidener.com/life-rewards-action/ (accessed May 27, 2015).

Williams,,Armstrong. "A Few Simple Steps to Building Wealth." *Townhall.* June 13, 2005. http://townhall.com/columnists/armstrongwilliams/2005/06/13/a_few_simple_steps_to_building_wealth/page/full (accessed May 28, 2015).

Woods, Jennifer. "Working Longer—Whether You Want to or Not." *CNBC.com.* December 23, 2014, http://cached.newslookup.com/cached.php?ref_id=105&siteid=2098&id=10359558&t=1419339600 (accessed June 9, 2015).

Yate, Martin. *Knock 'em Dead 2017: The Ultimate Job Search Guide.* New York: Adams Media, 2017.

Zolfagharifard, Ellie. "First Impressions Really DO Count: Employers Make Decisions About Job Applicants in Under Seven Minutes." *Daily Mail.* June 18, 2014. http://www.dailymail.co.uk/sciencetech/article-2661474/First-impressions-really-DO-count-Employers-make-decisions-job-applicants-seven-minutes.html (accessed June 5, 2015).